Always With'em
A Life to Remember

*Musings on publishing,
politics, and life
in a small town*

by
Donovan C. Witham

Editor: Joyce Newgard
Design and Layout: Phil Peterson
Cover Photo: David Samson
Special thanks to: Sue Cwikla and Bonnie Peterson

ISBN-10: 1463722923
ISBN-13: 978-1463722920

First edition – September 2011
Printed by CreateSpace.com
Printed in the United States of America

Contents:

Preface

DO YOU REALLY WANT TO KNOW?

Over the past few weeks I have cogitated about getting my columns and putting them into print and making a book of them. The reason for this is I might be able to leave something for people who are somewhat interested in them and also for my daughter to keep track of them after I've made my final trip.

I called Joyce Newgard, who had worked for the *West Fargo Pioneer* for 33 years, and she volunteered to start putting the columns together. We learned that the library in West Fargo has them on microfilm. So, Joyce is going to print them from that microfilm, and type them on computer so that they can be forwarded to Phil Peterson who will design and format for book form, and away we'll go.

I'm somewhat perplexed as to what I should say. Do I tell you where I was raised? Do I tell you that I served four years, one month and 11 days in the Navy? Do I tell you that I worked for Columbia Artists Management based in New York City for 20 years? Do I tell you about coming to West Fargo?

All this (the book idea) came about when I was talking to my doctor down at Essentia Medical. He said, "Who are you?" and "Where did you come from?" I told the doctor that for what I've been through, I should not even be here today.

I hope you will bear with me if I tell you that I was raised on a farm in South Dakota, graduated from high school, and had a snippet of college at South Dakota State. I ended up studying voice and music at McPhail's in St. Paul, Minn., and lived with the very wonderful Harry Benson family while there.

After a year and a half or so in St. Paul, I went home to Amherst, S.D., and went with Dad Witham to Aberdeen to join the Army. I might add here that I stopped into a Navy recruit office to ask where the Army office was and a big, heavyset guy there said, "Son, come on in."

Twenty minutes later I was in the Navy. That one bend in the road changed my life to this hour, from the people I came in contact with in my Navy life, through working for Columbia Artists Management, ending up in Windom, Minn., to learn just a dash of newspapering, and in March of 1967 landing in West Fargo.

I might mention here that I was visiting with Joyce about how much space my columns would take. She said, "Well, what do you think of a book that's over 12 inches thick?" Right away I knew we had trouble, so I said, "You pick what you think I should present and we'll go from there."

A young fellow interviewing me the other day asked, "How do you write a column?" I said, "I don't know. I walk down the street and there's a column just waiting to be written." For instance, living near the river in West Fargo, I walked out of the house one morning. Down the road on Center Street came a young guy on a bicycle and from each handlebar swung four or five fish. He'd been down to the river fishing. As he passed by me I looked again and in his left arm he had his dog. Now there was a column. But what did I do? I missed it because I didn't have my camera along. The next time I saw a column coming down the street as I was driving, I stopped the car, rolled down the window, leaned out and took a picture. Trundling down the sidewalk was a little fellow, maybe eighteen months old, buck naked. Behind him was his mother trying to catch up. I said to her, "Do you mind if I take a picture?" Her reply was "Absolutely I mind," and she grabbed him up and ran away. So you see there was always a column and I didn't get them all.

Don Witham

The 1960s

October 18, 1967

It has been my feeling for some time that someone should speak out in defense of our country. All I hear on radio, TV and read in the newspapers are the terrible mistakes we are making around the world. Doesn't any other country make a mistake? It seems to me these birds in Washington have plenty of complaints but when it comes to answering the problems they have to go check a poll or the calendar to see if it's an election year.

Of late, it seems the big deal is to burn one's draft card, go to jail for a spell, and become a hero. I'm beginning to wonder if there is something wrong with me... I still get a lump in my throat when I hear the *Star Spangled Banner* and watch our flag go by. However, I'm sure lots of people would call me a real square if they saw this and knew what was going on.

All I hear nowadays is "freedom." I wonder if all these people who want freedom know just what they want. What is freedom? I wish someone would tell me. Everyone wants it, but no one seems to have it. I think we could stand a bit of flag waving. I don't see the Russians or Chinese or Castro's Cubans parading for freedom. And I don't think they have found what everyone in the world is looking for.

The rest of the world is important, but how about a good cheer for a country that will fight for your right to say, "This is a darn poor place to live."

December 6, 1967

Last Thursday night a bit of America's real music lore passed in review at the new Moorhead State College concert hall. The place was almost full except for a seat here and there. I would say that 99 percent of the people in Fargo, Moorhead and West Fargo hardly knew that the opportunity to hear the last of the Giants of Jazz appeared in the area, and they went their way with hardly a ripple.

I have seen a lot of concert audiences come and go, but never an audience that gave two, and I repeat two, standing ovations. The reason for all this buildup is the Preservation Hall Jazz Band right from New Orleans. They played real jazz, not the loud, knock-you-out-of-your-seat kind we normally hear nowadays at the smoky night club. This was cool, smooth, sweet jazz played the way it should be played. It was played this way because these very people invented this first and real American music.

They were all over 70 years of age with the exception of the bass horn player. DeDe Pierce, who incidentally is blind, played the cornet like I have never heard before. No harsh, sharp notes from the music he plays. That is because he has a story to tell and it can't be told in loud, raucous sounds.

Billie, his wife, is one super gal on the piano. When the occasion moves her, she sings with all her heart those wonderful songs of the twenties. The voice has just a touch of gravel which, of course, makes it just that much more interesting.

All in all, it was one grand evening and my feet about jumped out of my shoes and my hands were sore from clapping.

February 7, 1968

Your Chamber of Commerce meets every second Friday morning at 7:30. These few people in your city give their time and efforts for you and themselves that things might be better for our city. Come to these meetings that we may make our town a better place to live.

Why have the people of this little city insisted on staying right here and fighting the battle? I am sure there are other places to live in this great big country of ours. I know darn well there are places that are warmer. It isn't far to the edge of town and I must say the wind blows twice as hard out there. But we all stay. I would like to ask, "Why?" Could it be the pioneer spirit that makes us fight to stay right here and go no place else? I'm sure those guys who traveled this country in the old days might have had the same feelings. They came, looked around and stayed, dug in and grew things to keep alive, and hung on no matter what.

In many ways I think the people of West Fargo have those very same intentions in mind. They have come here to make this a real town. Some day this is going to be a city. It will never be called FARGO. It will be WEST FARGO. We will have our fights. We won't like things the city commission does in many instances. We will say the school board is doing all the wrong things. We will say the middle school is in the wrong place. We will say the whole town is a disjointed, upside down place to live. But are we going to give up? NO, we are going to go ahead no matter what. We will make this a real alive town for everyone here to be proud of.

Some day they will call us a city, and I mean a city. The trees on the edge of town will no longer be country; there will be homes where now are open fields. There will be new businesses and new thinking people to help us become even stronger. This is a place where our children will say, "Do you remember when... ?"

We tend to look on things now as just a bit second class. We are not that in any sense of the word. We will be that way only if we ourselves say it.

Let's be active. Let's fight to make the right things happen. Let's go places. We are only as successful as we want to be and as attractive, I might add, as we ourselves want to make us.

March 23, 1968

Now that our first year anniversary issue is a thing of the past, I might add that we had wonderful help from unexpected sources.

After our paper is off the press in Hawley it is usually a race to get back to our West Fargo Post Office before they close the doors for the evening. In any case, on the special issue we forgot one very important thing. In that we were sending out 1,700 extra sample copies, they were all supposed to be stamped "Sample Copy." Dale Nesemeier, our postmaster, reminded me that they sure wouldn't go through without being stamped. This man didn't just inform me of this and then walk away. He pitched right in and helped with the problem and by seven in the evening the papers were ready for the eight o'clock truck to Fargo. Dale rates a well-deserved thank you from the *West Fargo Pioneer* for without his help we would have had troubles aplenty.

My story does not end here. At nine that same evening I received a call from Ernie Hoagen at the Fargo Post Office. He informed me there were 82 empty paper mailers in his mail. People would have missed the paper or received it very late had he not taken the time and trouble to look me up at nine o'clock at night. Somehow, in our haste, these empty mailers had slipped through without being filled with a paper. (This had never happened before, and I hope it doesn't happen again.) However, the point I want to make is that in two post offices in less than two hours the people who look after our mail went that extra mile to see that the mail arrived, and on time.

April 24, 1968

There comes a time in every town when young thieves seem to take pride in stealing whatever they can lay hands on. It's not that they need these things. No one is starving in West Fargo. This seems to be a special thrill to young people who don't realize or have common sense about what they are doing.

The worst part of all is the merchants in West Fargo cannot afford this kind of theft. If it isn't fishing tackle, it's candy and cigarettes. The merchant has to sell just that much more to make ends meet and there isn't that kind of money in our city. It means very little to those who took the articles, but plays real havoc with the merchant.

So parents, check your children. Where do they get the money to buy the things they bring home? Remember that discipline starts at home.

* * *

The people of West Fargo and West Fargo Industrial Park will be happy to know that safety first has been applied. Yes, the bridge in Industrial Park has gone the way of unsafe bridges. It was taken down last week by fellows right in the Park investing their time (with no pay, incidentally) so that no one's children would come to harm because of the bridge.

A special thank you should be extended to Tony Walz and Earl Larson who led the gang in its destruction of the span.

May 22, 1968

Folks might remember a picture and article last fall in the *Pioneer* on why the 13th Avenue bridge had to be closed.

I received a call from the highway department thanking me for informing the public about the situation. Seems that plenty of telephone calls had been received in regard to the bridge being closed.

Now I hear that the bridge is not to be opened this spring or maybe another spring or so... no money, they tell me.

Come on, West Fargo, just remember the squeaky wheel and all that jazz about the grease.

* * *

It has been my pleasure to watch and work with Glenn Whaley for the past few weeks in relation to the band's selling of *Pioneer* subscriptions.

I must say, this guy really works. He has been in and out of our office many, many times making arrangements for his subscription campaign. He didn't stop there, but went right on to organize his band members to cover West Fargo and surrounding area to see that everyone is contacted in relation to renewing their *West Fargo Pioneer* subscription.

Please keep in mind that the band has $4,000 to go for new uniforms, and a subscription to the *Pioneer* makes that $4,000 grow smaller.

June 18, 1968

The past two weeks businesses in the city of West Fargo and area have received letters from the West Fargo Chamber of Commerce in relation to membership for the coming year. It behooves me to say that each and every year is a crucial year for your Chamber. There is never any money for a backlog and every penny spent is discussed and rediscussed before it is spent.

The Chamber this past year spent its money well and wisely for the good of our city. The men on the Board worked long hours away from their businesses. If we are to remain a city and not just an area where people come to sleep we must do everything we can to make our city move forward.

We all can do this by supporting the West Fargo Chamber of Commerce. Incidentally, they do take individual memberships... your help is needed. Give some thought to this organization today and act NOW.

* * *

It has been some time since I have wanted to stand up and cheer. However, I think now is the appropriate time. When I heard Mr. Earl

Warren is resigning from the Supreme Court I couldn't help but think we were at last headed in the right direction. However, do I see political implications in this unexpected move at this time?

I should say I do.

If he had waited until the elections, we might, and I say again, just might, get a real live, knowledgeable Chief Justice of our Supreme Court. As it is, President Johnson will have the toughest job of all during his tenure in the president's seat, and that is to find someone as bad as Warren.

At this time in our history our courts in the land don't know if they are coming or going. What is right today is wrong tomorrow.

Why do state cases have to go to the Supreme Court? And please don't tell me it is because they have smarter men on the bench in Washington. It has always been my opinion that the Supreme Court should only try cases that affect us nationally.

By accepting cases handed up from the states, they are taking away "States' Rights."

July 3, 1968

Where have you been shopping lately? Remember the stores in West Fargo are here to serve you.

We all know that not everything can be bought in our own home town BUT, before you buy that needed item, take a look at prices in West Fargo. At first glance that item might look like it costs more. Take an extra minute and read the fine print.

Last week a fellow was bragging about buying fertilizer for his lawn elsewhere, paying a little less than what he could buy it for in West Fargo. He didn't check what the small print said. If he had, he would have found that he received just half the regular ingredients of ordinary fertilizer. The rest was filler to make the bag look nice and big.

It behooves us to buy at home when we can. We can trust our merchants to give us what we pay for and, I might add, it will be with a smile as he is loading it in your car. I have yet to see someone from the big fancy stores carrying merchandise for the buyer.

Shop at home and you will find your merchants are well able to support the city with the things that are needed to make our city what it should be. A merchant who is making money has a little more time to think about why he is making money.

He knows it is the people who live here who support him. He wants to keep the people here who are here and at the same time bring more people to West Fargo. He, in turn, is willing to invest in his city.

THE ANSWER TO ALL THIS IS SUPPORT YOUR HOME TOWN MERCHANTS.

July 24, 1968

May I put a plug in this week for our correspondents? They, I am sure, get people up in the morning and maybe call them out of bed at night to get that extra bit of information that you leisurely read Wednesday evening or Thursday afternoon in the *Pioneer.*

* * *

I must tell you as I was making my advertising rounds Saturday morning, a friend of mine leaned out his door and asked where I was going so fast. I hadn't given it much thought up to that moment, but I figured if he was worrying about how fast I was going maybe I had better worry about how fast I was going!

He informed me that he hadn't found a way to take it with him, so he was saying the heck with the business and was taking off for Colorado for a few weeks.

You know that sort of thing gets a man to thinking. Right away I had a pain I hadn't noticed before, so when Roy Johnson invited me into the West Fargo Drug for a dish of ice cream I accepted and the pain went away. There must be a sequel to this somewhere but I can't think of it just now.

* * *

Over the weekend I had a visit with one of my relatives who has worked for the welfare department in Mille Lacs County for the past twenty years. She has a new University of Minnesota graduate working in her department. My relative told me that the new member works well but she cannot spell or punctuate. It's lucky she didn't take a post graduate course – she might not have been able to work well either, and that would have been the livin' end.

***

Always With'em

It seems to me we are getting an awful lot of talking done about the park. If we could just put some of this lip action to work on some real action, wouldn't it be wonderful?

Received a telephone call from Herb Tintes last Wednesday. He said vandalism in the park is getting out-of-hand. Tuesday night, July 16, vandals struck again! They piled the picnic tables three high and broke the overhead door off the park shelter.

Now listen to this... a reward of $25 has been posted for any information given to the Cass County Sheriff's Department leading to the arrest and conviction of anyone damaging park property. Herb is also adding $25 to this reward making it a total of $50.

Last week the city commission tabled a request for protection of the park for further study. If we all keep studying this situation much longer, two things will happen: there won't be a park to worry about or it will be too d— cold for the kids to go out there to break things up.

August 21, 1968

This is just a short note in relation to your safety. How safe do you feel when you go to bed at night in West Fargo? Do you leave your car outside the garage? Do you put your lawn mower away? Do you lock your doors?

If I were you I would start checking into these things, for the man who protects you in West Fargo is also looking after 1,448½ other people at the same time.

There are two more policemen and they each have 1,448½ other people to look after also. When you add these all together you have three policemen looking out for the rights of about 4,345 persons in West Fargo.

If you get robbed, hit over the head, or your car smashed into, just remember the policeman that comes to your aid has 1,448½ others to take care of in West Fargo.

It wouldn't be hard to find out what he is paid. I can tell you most of us wouldn't take what he gets when it comes to salary. He doesn't work just 40 hours like you and me. One of the fellows over there works 45 hours a week. In addition to this, he puts in 104 hours a month in the office. Do you know this comes to 71 hours a week he puts in on duty?

Now why don't you call the police department and ask what he is paid a month?

There are two solutions to this problem. We can all move to Barnesville, Minn., where they have three policemen to protect 1,600 people, or we can appear at the city commission meetings and ask why we don't give our police a better break.

If YOU don't show at the meetings, please don't blame the police department when something happens to you or YOUR family.

* * *

I was all primed this week to add my two cents' worth in relation to the Republican convention.

However, after reading Ken Anderson's editorial in the *Cottonwood County Citizen* in Windom, Minn., there is not much I can add to his thoughts. Besides, if I wrote what I thought about the whole affair, I am afraid I wouldn't be half as nice about it. Mistake, mistake, mistake... is all I can say about Agnew for Vice President.

Here are publisher Ken Anderson's thoughts on the subject:

WILL IT BE HAROLD STASSEN IN '72?

"It didn't seem possible that the Republican Party could make two monumental blunders in a row. But it has happened and the GOP might as well kiss the 1968 election goodbye and gear up for '72 – if the party is still in existence.

"The nomination of Richard Nixon and an unheard-of running mate by the name of Agnew makes it a foregone conclusion that the Democrats will be spending four – and possibly eight – more years in the White House. It really won't make much difference whom the Democrats nominate now, because we're afraid the 1968 GOP race will be another exercise in futility.

"With men like Rockefeller, Lindsay, Percy, Hatfield, Brooks, etc., waiting to give the GOP a new image with new ideas in a changing world, the Republicans went for a lackluster candidate like Nixon who has little or no appeal to the young people or the Negro population. Not even a solid majority of Republicans will back the former vice president.

"And with only 27% of the voting population being in the GOP ranks, what chance does Nixon have of winning in November?

"None, is our guess.

"Not only did the Republicans pick the wrong presidential candi-

date, but they completed the fiasco by naming an unknown with no popular appeal as a runningmate. Thus what little chance the GOP might have had of winning with Nixon went down the drain.

"We think it is to the credit of the Minnesota delegation that it opposed the nomination of Agnew as vice president. It at least shows a little individuality in a convention that had all the earmarks of being rigged from the start.

"History has a way of repeating and it looks like '68 will be that year. It was Goldwater in '64. Now it's Nixon in '68.

"Who will it be in '72? Harold Stassen?"

* * *

And Jim Fitzgerald of the *Lapeer* (Mich.) *County Press*, writes that "The first joke to spring from the GOP convention: The Republicans are changing their emblem from an elephant to an owl: 'The GOP ticket is Nixon and WHOOOOOOOOOO?'"

* * *

A note here in regard to the paper and Red River Valley Fair issue the *West Fargo Pioneer* published last week. The paper that arrived in your mailbox or you bought at your local newsstand was the culmination of approximately two and one half months' work. It is also the largest paper ever to come out of this office.

The last four days before publication, the staff worked almost around the clock to get this paper to the presses in Hawley on time.

This is not meant to create comment or concern from the public about how hard we work at the *Pioneer*, but rather to commend the staff of the *Pioneer* for a job very well done.

* * *

Say! Does anyone know what a TOYOTA is? Have been asking around but no one seems to know.

Sounds like a small Japanese skyscraper to me.

Someone said it's a new kind of snowmobile. It's certainly not a motorcycle because I haven't seen anything with that name running around.

Maybe I'll be able to tell you all about it next week!

* * *

Now here's something for you all to think about.

Last Wednesday I took a trip to South Dakota for a short visit with a farmer brother of mine.

I asked him what he thought about the 60 cent barley prices and he proceeded to tell me the following:

In 1929 our dad bought a $1,500 new combine and a new $900 tractor. Wheat at that time was $1.23 a bushel.

In 1968 the same type of tractor with about the same power costs $7,000 and a combine with the same swath costs $14,000. Wheat is $1.30 a bushel.

Another thought he left with me... In 1947 wheat was up to $3.00 a bushel. Bread was 18 cents a loaf. Wheat is now $1.30 a bushel and bread is 32 cents a loaf.

WHAT'S THE ANSWER, AMERICA?

September 4, 1968

You kind hearts and gentle souls received a shock if you watched the goings-on at the convention in Chicago Wednesday night on TV. Being somewhat of a hawk myself, I didn't give it much thought until the police started using those clubs. The big eye showed thousands of police and National Guardsmen. Now why couldn't they surround the place and stand firm. Nothing can get by those guards and police when they stand shoulder to shoulder. BUT... to chase people all over the landscape is another cut of the cloth. Shame, Shame, Shame on Mayor Daley. Let's hope he is the last of his breed.

Thursday evening I talked to our tired and harried Mayor Lashkowitz of Fargo who had just returned from the convention in Chicago, and these are a few of the impressions he gave me. In his eyes the big political conventions cannot possibly do four years' work in three days. Both the Republican and Democratic conventions need a complete revamping. He said that people were fainting all over the place, food was hard to get, hours were late and long and this was especially hard on the older people. In the mayor's words, he faults and indicts the whole convention system.

In relation to the hippies and yippies and stop-the-war people, he said they threatened to burn the town down, waved Viet Cong flags and broke the law. This, he said, is why Mayor Daley cracked down and hard.

Always With'em

Mayor Lashkowitz said not to rush to quick judgments, that there is a great deal of unrest in the country, but we must have respect for life and property. Also, he stated that there is a big generation gap, and in the communication between the old and young that must be improved.

* * *

Before the big freeze, I would advise those citizens who like real beauty to take a trip to North Dakota State University to see those beautiful flower beds. Much hard work has been applied, so let's all enjoy the sights. Man seems at times to foul up a lot of the beauty in the country, but I think this time he did a pretty good job.

* * *

South Dakota, once the land of the pheasant, is no longer THE LAND OF THE PHEASANT. We traveled over most of my old haunts a week ago and did not see a single one! I happened to have been born and raised in South Dakota, and I know where to find pheasants, but the sad tale now is there are few, if any. The point I am trying to get across is when you add a bit of greed on the part of the Game and Fish Commission, there is not much left to worry about. Selling licenses in a land that has very little game to shoot is one thing, but killing off the little game that is left is another story entirely.

October 2, 1968

We had no idea that the second Tuesday in October the West Fargo Fire Department intended to have their annual drive for funds to carry them through the next season. Roger Olson, West Fargo Fire Chief, and a friend of his came by last Saturday and informed me that it was time to kick in again. All this happened at an opportune time for me in that I intended to say something about our fire department this week anyway.

May I start by saying that over the past year I have gained considerable respect for our West Fargo volunteer firemen. I have followed them through rain, snow and blizzard to big and little fires. I am at last getting a little smart about following these fire calls. Used to grab my hat and run for camera and car. Now I pick up the phone and find if this trip is really necessary. BUT the guy who gets no pay and in many cases little thanks, in rain, sleet, snow or what have you, GOES ANYWAY.

REMEMBER, the next time the siren sounds it may be your house I'll be taking a picture of for the *Pioneer*. So when that smiling gentleman calls at your door, keep in mind that some very dark, stormy night you may need him very badly. If you don't give him anything he will be there to help you anyway. That's the kind of guy he is.

* * *

Those of you who took time out to watch the Homecoming parade last Friday should have enjoyed yourselves. I think the kids did a terrific job.

A special cheer for the High School Band! They played and marched beautifully. And aren't those new uniforms something? I think we can all be proud when our West Fargo High School Band marches by, in that most everyone in our city has played some part in the purchase of the new uniforms.

* * *

On walking into the West Fargo State Bank this past week I noticed a brown blob on the floor. I drew the attention of one of the fellows in the bank to the fact that they didn't keep their feet very clean or the floor wouldn't have that spot on it. On closer inspection it was noted that the caller who left the familiar blob had recently visited our famous West Fargo Stockyards. Whereupon my friend at the bank said with pride, "We're happy to see such as this on the floor, for to us it looks more like gold than anything else." As the saying goes, the customer is always right.

* * *

Received a note this week from the Horace Fire Department. In that I have a soft spot in my heart for all Volunteer Fire Departments, I think I might just put on those old dancing shoes and head for Horace Saturday evening, Oct. 5. Seems that the boys are having a ball or rather intend to put one on. In any case, they need to raise some money to keep truck and fire hoses available and ready in case someone smells smoke. The Ball will be held at the Horace American Legion Hall. Music is to be furnished by Hal Kenny and his Orchestra. I might add here that no one will go hungry as lunch and refreshments will be served.

* * *

Always With'em

My young daughter, on demanding to know the facts of life recently from her mother (after being told just what was what), finalized her questions by asking, "Say, Mom, does Dad know about all this?"

November 13, 1968

A letter comes this week from Grove Wills of Eveleth, Minn. He sent an article David Lawrence had written recently.

All far-seeing Americans will thoroughly agree with Lawrence who, in our opinion, is one of the better writers and thinkers of his time. He expresses his opinion regarding the national election procedure of this country. Here it is:

"Sometimes when there is a transition from one president to another, policies are stalemated. The interval between Nov. 5 and Jan. 20 – nearly 11 weeks – may not seem long, but inaction in government during two and one-half months could have serious consequences. The outgoing administration doesn't want to initiate changes, and the incoming administration doesn't feel it should assume responsibility for decisions before actually taking office. The inevitable result is delay and procrastination which could prove disastrous in a crisis.

"Some day the American people will demand a revision of the present system so that the transition will be made quickly, as is the case in the parliamentary systems abroad. With the size of the American economy and its involvement in world finance and trade, and with a gross national product of over 870 billion dollars, it certainly does seem risky to have to wait two and one-half months after election day before a new administration comes into power."

* * *

Saturday afternoon I took my family on a trip to downtown Fargo. It has been my opinion that usually I could find some place to park. However, I certainly had a couple more thoughts coming.

I circled and circled. Naturally, there were no parking spots in front of the stores but in that I am a determined character, I headed for a parking lot. At each lot there was a sign informing us they were full.

About this time I began to get a little frustrated and you fellows know what happens then. What else – a fight with the wife.

Now there must be some kind of sequel to all this – STAY HOME AND SHOP IN WEST FARGO.............

* * *

Over the past twenty months since the *West Fargo Pioneer* came to town, we here at the *Pioneer* have wondered just how our big neighbor in Fargo felt about us. Yes, I am talking about the *Fargo Forum*. As most of you know, a big paper like the *Forum* could shut a small weekly like us out in not many months. My first contact with the big paper was nothing but pleasant. I was informed that West Fargo needed a paper and we just filled the bill.

Three weeks ago I finally got up the nerve to walk right into that building at 101 North 5th and introduce myself. Talked to a lot of the fellows up there who make things go. I couldn't have been treated nicer.

December 18, 1968

I cannot help but take typewriter in hand and explain our front cover. We at the *Pioneer* have for many months been thinking of what we could do in relation to the paper for Christmas. We have gone many routes to find just the right thing to tell people in Cass County and West Fargo how much we appreciate their support.

The *Pioneer*, you may remember, took its first faltering steps one year ago March. In all cases, it has been run and nurtured along by people with very little experience in this type of newspaper production. In fact, the owners of the paper a little over two years ago didn't know a "pica" from a "pig." However, all this talk is neither here nor there.

What you see on the front cover is Christmas as most of us know it. We remember it probably much as the little girl will remember this tree and this Christmas. Later we watch our own children as they play around the tree. Much later we dream our dreams of how it once was.

So, as you again view the front page picture, in a way it is like your life at Christmastime passing before you.

So, in this manner, may we take this opportunity to wish everyone a lifetime of wonderful Christmases.

* * *

When was the last time you ice fished? I went ice fishing ONCE. With all this talk about ice fishing accidents, I thought I would tell my story. Some time back a friend of mine by the name of "Porky" Thompson invited me ice fishing. Porky lives in Barnesville and has for many years.

To make a long story a bit short, he and I ended up on Lake Lizzie in his ice house. You who have been in an ice house know that it is dark inside – like a stack of black cats. You sit on a couple of boxes and look into a square hole and wait for fish to come by.

There we sat hardly breathing because you are not supposed to make any noise. After a half hour and nothing had happened, a guy like me gets restless. Besides, my posterior was getting cold.

I started to stand and stretch. I heard a crack... my heart skipped about four beats. I said, "Porky, what the h__ is that?"

There being no immediate response from Porky, I took off for the door. The catch was I had forgotten which way to run for the door.

In that this ice house was papered generously with tar paper in the inside, I tore off about fourteen yards of tar paper trying to find an opening to the great land of freedom.

By this time, the water was boiling up out of the hole and the cracking was something terrific. I reached for the roof but the darn thing was too high. As I was taking my eighteenth leap across the room I noticed that Porky was still on his box. I also noted his stomach was going up and down like at least thirteen Santas.

He reached up and with a flick of his wrist the door flew open and at that time a little ol' truck huffed by.

Now I want to tell all who are invited to go ice fishing: Always keep one hand on the door.

January 29, 1969

Recently it has come to my attention that fox in our country are being run down by snowmobiles; also he is hunted from airplanes.

If there is anything that grits on my conscience, it is running an animal to death. Is this fair play? Is this sportsmanship? In fact, is this humane in any manner of speaking?

JUST KEEP KILLING OFF THE ANIMALS, "MR. MAN," AND YOU WILL SEE THE DAY YOU WILL PAY AND PAY AND PAY.

* * *

Say! They tell me postage is going to seven cents! It takes two days to get a letter to Moorhead and three days to Valley City. I'm sure that with this raise, the postal department can hire more people to move the mail faster, providing they don't run over each other in the already large crowd of postal employees.

* * *

Each week there are about three or four papers that miss the addressing machine in Valley City. Now out of 1,800 mailings we don't consider this a bad record.

However, if you happen to be the unlucky person on the addressing end, please, please give us a ring. We want you happy.

ALSO, when you complain, we know you miss us and we love to be missed.

* * *

Had a short talk with Roy Larson, our representative from the 21st District. He tells me very few letters are coming to him concerning goings on in Bismarck. Now, if any of you don't like the way North Dakota is being run, drop him a note.

REMEMBER, how in heck is he going to know what you are thinking if you don't tell him?

* * *

I call on the news media in our nation to avoid any extensive publicity on riots, hippie shenanigans, sick hooligan parades like the one at the inauguration, and the Chicago fiasco.

I hope you don't think all the yelling and cussing in Chicago last summer would have gone on it if hadn't been for lots and lots of TV cameras.

I also say, use no names of those who plan to overthrow the nation. Keep in mind that there is no "Black Panther" if there is no news to carry his name around.

February 12, 1969

Those of you who take the *Reader's Digest* will note a small American flag attached to the inside pages. In my opinion it is about time we started flying "Old Glory" again. I have it pasted on my car window. I could go on for about eight pages about what I think of the way our flag has been treated over the past few years by our young people. I would, however, like to ask one question of the people who take this new outlook on life in our country... WHAT IS THIS FREEDOM FOR WHICH THEY ARE WILLING TO SELL OUT OUR NATION?

* * *

After some discussion with our treasurer and editor, in late April or early May the *Pioneer* will publish a PROGRESS EDITION. As far as we know, nothing as ambitious as this has ever been undertaken before in West Fargo. It is our plan to tell everyone about the development and progress that has gone on and is going on in West Fargo and area. We will talk about new business, new building, new plans for our city and the opportunities and advantages of living in West Fargo. To make sure we put our best foot forward we are hiring a professional photographer to shoot a great share of the pictures.

March 5, 1969

I note in the paper last week that Sandee Paulsen, our cute little high school reporter, and our esteemed editor kind of got into it over this thing called "Bop Music"... or is it called Ditty Bop, Rock, Bee Bop or something else? Darned if I can begin to keep up with all this fancy music that keeps coming and going nowadays.

To tell the truth, folks, when I read what Sandee wrote and then read what Dave, our editor, wrote, I thought I had bilingual people on the staff. I sure couldn't figure out what either one was talking about so just assumed it was a foreign language. Now that proves two things... I'm getting old and I'm certainly not keeping up with the latest in fancy, dancy music.

As most of you know by now, I happen to lean toward classical music. At least I can keep up with that as it has been around for some time and I do like to hear those old tunes over and over. I would like to mention here that more people attend classical concerts in our nation than organized professional baseball games, and this has been going on for many years. Also that every third record sold is classical. I'm sure we old folks are not buying all these classical records, so I would assume a good share is bought by, yes, you guessed it, those wonderful teenagers.

* * *

The U.S. Post Office will soon raise (or so they tell me) postage to seven cents for first class letter mail. When this happens don't raise heck through the window of the local post office. A letter to your Senator is the answer.

A good example of what is being done around the country is displayed by a Mr. Murray who is located in Oklahoma City, OK. He delivers what is commonly called "junk mail" by the post office. A lot of it is very colorful and sometimes very interesting. He delivers this mail for $11 per hundred less than the post office. Incidentally, he is doing financially very, very well. Sears, Wards, Penneys and others are real sold on his mail delivery method.

Good old American ingenuity is sometimes much better than super special organized organization.

I find lately that as I grow older I am constantly bothered by dropsy and heart trouble. Yes, now the truth comes out... I drop into a chair and haven't the heart to get up.

April 2, 1969

I couldn't help but notice as I read Saturday's *Forum* two articles almost side by side, one headed "Protest March Planned," and the other "Minot Man Dies in Vietnam." It seems to me there is a story here.

I heard it first aboard our ship, the "Santa Catalina," during World War II. We were outward bound for the Persian Gulf with a load of 3-inch gunpowder. At that time we were having coal strikes in our own country and we were all very bitter. I think my pay was about twenty-one dollars a month and I felt that I was a bit out in the cold in that the miners were wanting $3 to $4 an hour.

My commanding officer at that time had a very good answer... "I do not believe in what they do or what they (the coal miners) are saying, but I would give my life for their right to do and say it."

Lawrence Robert Esser, 21, Minot, N.D., was killed in action this past week in Vietnam. One would wonder if he gave his life so that Tom Davidson, conscientious objector, serving two years in non-military service at St. Luke's Hospital, would have the right to conduct a protest march in downtown Fargo Saturday.

Always With'em

* * *

Most of you know, I'm sure, that Roy Larson, owner of our Jack and Jill grocery in West Fargo, is back at the old grind. In a talk with Roy Saturday I asked him how he liked returning to work in the store after three months in Bismarck at the legislature. It took Roy about three seconds to tell me that being back was like taking a vacation. Seems that the pace is pretty fast in Bismarck, lots and lots of work, work, work. All in all, it is good to have our 21st District representative back in town. Good men like Roy are hard to find. Lucky West Fargo, I say.

* * *

This is the month of taxation. My tax man told me the other day there are only two nations in the world who tax greater than the U.S. Germany and England hold the honors.

However, more and more we hear of the middle class tax revolution. In other words, the ordinary guy paying the taxes nowadays will make it a point to earn less instead of more. You hear every day of people who do not want that raise because it will mean less take-home-pay. Keep in mind the first rule of Communism... TAX THE PEOPLE INTO SUBMISSION.

* * *

As most of you know, there is a flood in our town. Saturday I had worked all day carrying sandbags for our dike in West Fargo Industrial Park. Sunday morning I was up to fight the battle all over again.

In our front yard stood an elderly gentleman looking around. I said to myself, "Just another 'looker' come to watch me in my hour of despair. He looked like one of those fellows who have seen many years of hard work... there were calluses on his hands and deep lines in his face.

He walked with a bit of a stoop as he investigated first one side of the house and then the other. He stood for a long moment looking at the water lapping at my back door.

His next appearance came in the form of a soft rap at the kitchen entrance. In an apologetic tone for disturbing me, he said, "Sorry, Mr., but I came to see if I could help."

The picture at the top of this story shows him loading sandbags into the wagon. He worked until ten Sunday evening.

And I don't even know his name.

May 28, 1969

This one is more sinker than hook and line. Last Wednesday the publisher of this paper took the afternoon off and went fishing on Pelican Lake.

Boy, did those pork chops taste good when I got home that night!

* * *

Talking to the West Fargo postal authorities this week brought to my attention the large amount of pornographic literature coming into this post office. It is not ordered, mind you. The people who send this stuff get names from lists that are sold from company to company. OUR SUPREME COURT HAS RULED THAT THIS TYPE OF LITERATURE IS ART. I have always been under the impression that art could be viewed without the viewer having to blush.

This mail coming into West Fargo has doubled in the past year or so. WHAT CAN YOU DO ABOUT IT? WRITE YOUR CONGRESSMEN!

* * *

Talked to a friend of mine Saturday in New York (via phone). I was much surprised to learn he is leaving his position there. Being president of a corporation, one would wonder why he would want to leave. When asked why, he said, "Tired of the rat race." Having been through the mill there myself, I fully understood what he meant.

I asked him what his plans were. The clincher was this. He does not want to go to work in any big city. Looking for a small, sleepy town, I would suspect. He was raised in a small town in Colorado. As the saying goes: once a small town boy, always a small town boy. The grass can be very green on the other side of the fence, but who wants to walk through all those weeds at the same time. North Dakota looks better to me every day.

June 4, 1969

Now it seems to me there must be some other way to spend one's time than turning stop signs and street signs the wrong way in West Fargo. There is a rash of this sort of work going on and has been for the past three or four weeks. If anyone knows who is doing this, it should by all means be reported to the police. A stop sign turned the wrong way can cause a serious accident or maybe a death. Consider when you report someone turning a stop sign you may be saving a life and that life may just be your own.

It has also come to our attention that cars running in and out of the Sheyenne Plaza area after closing hours are causing considerable damage to windows... in the past month to the tune of six hundred dollars. Parents of West Fargo and area, talk to your young people. A car speeding away from a window area can throw stones. These stones break windows and big plate glass windows cost lots of money.

* * *

I don't know if anyone else does this or not, but at 5:30 when TV news comes on, if at all possible, I'm in front of the set. Up until the past month in the middle of the news when the ads come on I turn to the other station. In this way I have been watching news for the full half hour without the ads thrown in. BUT you know what? Now those darn stations are having their ads come at the same time in the news program. Now I leave one station in a burst of Fab and end up on the other in a tub of Ivory Snow.

* * *

Last Tuesday morning I watched our men of the West Fargo Fire Department whose sad duty it was to grapple for a body in the Sheyenne River. A few weeks ago the Department had faced the same situation. They are to be commended for their efforts. Please keep in mind these men who come to your aid at the mere dial of your phone. They work without pay the year around to keep your home safe from fire or flood. There will be a time during the year when they will need your help. A few dollars given to our Fire Department is the best investment we make in our city.

And last Sunday afternoon the West Fargo fire whistle blew and yours truly took off after the big red engine. The whole procession ended up at the West Fargo train depot. You know what we all did? We waited for the train to bring the fire to us! Seems that during the trip into Fargo somehow a flat car caught fire. I'll bet that is the first time in history that the West Fargo Fire Department waited for the fire to come to them.

* * *

A battle happened Sunday morning with the young daughter. Seems that she had her own ideas about what she would wear to church. Her mother won the battle but daughter got the last word... said that wearing what she was wearing made her feel like "a string bean in a watermelon patch." Anyone for church?

July 2, 1969

We had a visitor at our house Thursday, Friday, Saturday and Sunday... a very charming fellow, and a very good friend of mine from the days when I traveled in the music business.

His being somewhat of a world traveler, we found he had some unusual food tastes.

Took him fishing Saturday and ended up with a nice mess of sunfish. He loved the sunfish but also insisted we fry the heads, livers and roe. We were informed that that is the best part of the fish. Have you been offered a fish eye lately? I was... last Saturday night.

What really throws me is that he learned this way of eating in Japan. AND to think I always thought those Japanese soldiers during World War II were just getting the leftovers when their supply ships would float barrels of fishheads ashore for their men. Here they were getting a great delicacy all the time...

* * *

Yep... a new camera. No doubt you will note a lot of pictures in the *Pioneer* lately. Yep, this newspaper bought a new camera.

When I asked the man how much it was, I nearly fell over. However, he went to explain further that it awakened you in the morning, tossed you into the bath, got your breakfast and took pictures...

* * *

Gee, I hope Senator Ted Kennedy, if he gets to be president, doesn't leave the scene of the accident. It could very well be you and me he is leaving.

* * *

The only disadvantage I can see about our trip to the moon is that we can't use the expression, "He couldn't do that any more than he can fly to the moon."

* * *

Know what? There's a guy singing over on Channel 11 on Thursday nights that puts the bead-bouncing, long-hair-in-the-face, rear end shaking, poor diction singers in the music business to shame. His name is TOM JONES.

* * *

I understand that week before last Henry Newgard locked the keys to his car in the trunk of the same car.

I have heard of people having to break the window because of locking keys in the car... but how do you break a window to get into the trunk?

August 6, 1969

Last Sunday I took the kid (our daughter) to her uncle's farm in South Dakota. In that she loves to go barefooted and for some reason has an aversion to water, I admonished her about a little water on the toes before going to bed.

I started my lecture by saying, "Now, Kathy, life on the farm isn't like being at home in West Fargo..."

"Yeah, Dad, I know. We don't have air conditioning at home."

Oh, these modern farms.

* * *

One evening this past week I was diligently attending a most juicy steak on the charcoaler when a voice behind me said, " What'cha doin' out here?" Turning I noted a slim little fellow behind me, hands in pockets, a curl drooping down over the forehead and an inquisitive grin on his face. He came in height all the way up to the middle button of my shirt and his name is Mark Walz.

Now being somewhat of a steak charcoaler from 'way back, I was a little insulted that I had to go into any explanation about what I was doing. However, the great one consented to tell his little friend he was cooking a steak.

"Mighty funny," replied the little one. "I thought you lived in a house that at least had a stove inside."

* * *

Friday evening I was just finishing locking the door to the *Pioneer* office when two young fellows came walking by. Being a friendly cuss myself, I said hello. They both stopped and asked the way to get to the highway south out of town. I asked them where they were going and they said, "Des Moines, Iowa." We decided that they had to take Hwy 81, and I volunteered to take them out on the K-Mart road and head them in the right direction. On the way the wife and I started asking questions. We found they were just out of the service and had hitch-hiked from Oregon. In that it was 9:30 p.m., I asked if they had had their dinner. Both said "No." I then asked when they had eaten last. "Yesterday" was their answer. I then said, "Of course you have money to buy something to eat." They said they had spent their last money to fill a fellow's car with gas that had given them a ride. In that the only thing they had asked for was directions out of town, the least I could do was buy them a hamburger. On investigation I found I had a dollar and fifteen cents (I told you before there is no money in the newspaper business.) To make a long story short, I cashed a check, gave each three dollars, took them to a hamburger joint and wished them well. The sequel to all this is their hair was short, they asked for no handouts, their plans were to return to college. Both had a look of good American strength and were not afraid of the future. I also might add that they both smelled like a couple of goats, and you would too if you had hitchhiked a couple thousand miles.

September 3, 1969

Those of you who haven't grown at least a little stubble by the big Round Up Days kick-off on the 12th day of this month had better stand by for a fine. Last year they hauled me off to the jailhouse and fined me. Don't remember how much it was, but they took my picture and I got a lot of bad publicity.

But I'm a stubborn cuss and have refused to grow a beard again this year. As the saying goes, "a fellow always finds a loophole." Yup, stopped in the other day and had my hair cut at Wilson's Barber Shop and also bought myself a "No Beard Permit." It only cost 50¢ and now I'm free as a bird – at least for the time being. Some of those Jaycees are sure to think something up.

Incidentally, these permits can be bought in every barber shop in West Fargo.

September 17, 1969

Since we started our space program I have often wondered where our government found that special kind of people who man our space rockets. Over the past four months it has come home to me that they are right here in our midst, passing us every day on our sidewalks. In our case, they are upstanding young men in our city and surrounding area who give of their time and efforts to make our city and county a better place in which to live... to make known to everyone that West Fargo is not just another town.

I have seen these young men working, working, working to make West Fargo Round Up Days the best and biggest ever. They have done just that! We all can be grateful that we have people who are not afraid to step forward and MAKE THINGS GO. At this writing I know not if there was any money made by these willing hands, but I do know that we have Jaycees in our town like no town EVER HAD!

* * *

It always gives me pleasure when I can write about someone who goes that extra mile. That man is Luverne Eid, chairman of Round Up Days. I personally know that he has not let anything get in his way to make our recent celebration successful. He not only has worked night after night but in many cases when it was required he worked all night! We have returned to our office at the paper (he has his own key) many a morning to find Luverne still slaving away to make things go on the Jaycee project.

A good man to have on your side, you lucky Jaycees!

* * *

I look back with nostalgia now that Round Up Days are over. However, I must add that in a way I am also happy. I can now get my hands in my pockets... darn, those cowboy pants are tight!

October 1, 1969

I happened by West Fargo Fairway (formerly Brekke's) Friday just in time to see Ron Ladusaw chase a little white dog from his place of business. The dog wasn't to be kicked out with a couple of hands beating together to make a big noise. Before Ron got back to his job at the check-out, the little white fellow had come in the other door. Never did see what the final outcome was. Last I saw of Ron, his coattails were flying down the produce aisle with a flash of white leading the way...

* * *

The school nurse called my wife last Thursday to report that our daughter wasn't feeling well and we had to keep her home for the rest of the week. On the way home I asked her what was wrong. She said that she must be allergic to something in school. As an afterthought she added, "I think it must be books..."

* * *

Last week when I went to the post office Mary Stensatter wanted to give me a little gray cat that had wandered in to look over the mail situation. They put him out the front door and he went right around and came in the back, so she was sure they had a kitty for good. In that we have ONE cat and I have made it definite with our daughter that we DON'T NEED ANY MORE, I kindly turned down her offer. However, I guess everything wasn't lost. That evening when all the kids came from school the cat picked out one he liked and went home with him. End of cat story.

November 5, 1969

This past week my young daughter was examining my thinning hair. "Gee, Dad, you know you would make a good fill-in for a pumpkin." Now I wonder why she said that.

* * *

While I am on the subject of small folks... I was talking to Jay Lindgren the other day while delivering printing to his dad, Randy Lindgren of Lindgren's Hardware. His answer to my query concerning his mother's using the envelopes I was delivering... "Yeah, my mom, she does everything. My dad, he just works."

* * *

Always With'em

Now here is one lucky guy. Rodney Reith, who used to manage Brekke's Fairway and now travels for a wholesale food company, makes a regular stop at Wilson's Barber Shop for his haircuts. Now Rodney is not in the habit of coming out on the long end of everything, but lately he has been shaking the barbers for his haircuts. To date he has come out on the best end of the deal seven times. Hey, Orlon, you had better check those dice! Rodney says he's going to be a customer of Wilson's Barber Shop forever.

* * *

A call was received week before last at the *Pioneer* office. Seems that four West Fargo boys traveling down Business 94 came across two older ladies in distress. They had run out of gas on a busy highway and were just a little nervous... more so in that the traffic is heavy and fast in the section of Falls Mobile Home cut-off. The boys stopped, inquired what the trouble was, drove to the nearest gas station, got gas and returned, started the car for the ladies and went on their way. Now lots and lots of cars passed, but it took some of our hometown West Fargo boys to let us know someone had to care.

December 10, 1969

In a short visit with Mayor Clayton Lodoen Thursday, he stated that he was quite distressed with actions of the NDSU personnel who attended the flood control meeting Wednesday night. He thought it mighty fine that they take an interest in what is going on in relation to flood control for this area. However, it wasn't his intention to call a meeting only to be insulted and shouted down at every turn.

The meeting was called to make West Fargoans more aware of what had been done and is being done about Kindred Dam. Chairmen of eighteen organizations had been invited. Few went home with any concrete information as the meeting was taken up with pointed questions from professors and students from NDSU. One student who seemed to have plenty to say is a resident of the state of Iowa, another from the country of India. Another student said he wanted "to build a fence around the whole Kindred Dam area and let it sit forever."

* * *

Hey, kids! Please don't steal that Christmas tree bulb. It is plenty tough enough on us old guys to climb those ladders, teeter around 'way up in the air to make our city beautiful only to have the bulbs removed and smashed on the street. Kind of discouragin', I would say. Wouldn't you?

* * *

Last week the wife and I were to dinner with friends at the Galaxy Supper Club in Barnesville. My friend asked me what I was going to do with all the money I am making at the paper nowadays! I told him that I was making plans to take it with me when I go to heaven. The little woman (my wife) spoke right up and said that if I left right now I would have no problems at all in that category. (Oh, how right she is.)

* * *

I was stopped by a West Fargo mailman the other day. The guy had a point. "Gee, it sure is slippery in front of some of these houses." I would also appreciate it very much if people would keep their walks shoveled on these icy, cold days. Also, it might just save them from a lawsuit if a friendly neighbor comes to visit and breaks his neck.

* * *

A note here from the police department and fire station. I have been asked to remind people to please not call these two places to find out where the fire is because it cuts off real calls from the firemen who need to know where the fire is located.

One lady during the big fire at Red River Grain last week called to complain that all the noise of the fire engines kept her awake. This very lady might be very glad to hear them some day!

Always With'em

The 1970s

January 21, 1970

I was so proud of our West Fargo Jaycees Sunday I couldn't quit smiling. When I saw hundreds of cars coming from every direction to the Snowmobile Derby they had worked to promote, I knew their efforts hadn't been in vain. I don't think many people outside of the Jaycees and their wives realize the work involved in a production of this kind. We at the *Pioneer* saw some of the action in that they used our offices for final work. A lot of midnight oil was burned in the completion of plans. OUR YOUNG MEN OF ACTION IN WEST FARGO DID IT AGAIN.

* * *

Friday I had a call from the telephone company. "Come right over," they said. "We want to talk advertising." The very word makes my blood cruise twice as fast, so before I had my gloves on I was out the door and on my way.

After giving the man a big sell job and he agreeing it was just the thing they needed AND being a salesman who knows when to quit selling, I picked up my hat and headed for the door. At the door I couldn't help but ask one more question. "Say, how did you ever find out about the *West Fargo Pioneer*?" The reply, "We have a young lady who lives in West Fargo and sold us on advertising in the paper before you got here."

An added note here... Northwestern Bell wants to tell West Fargoans about their touchtone telephone system. Read all about this in a series of ads to appear in the *West Fargo Pioneer* in the March editions.

* * *

I can't help this... have to say it no matter what... no one is going to keep me from it... it now has to come out.

Have you folks in West Fargo been noticing that our grocers are competing with grocers right down the line in Fargo and in some cases OUR PRICES ARE BETTER? I keep telling you gals to shop West Fargo first.

February 4, 1970

In response to the letter to the editor from Oscar Lykken in Kindred last week... Mr. Lykken intimated people from Kindred are caught in a speed trap going through West Fargo.

Checking with the West Fargo police, we find that just three tickets were issued to Kindred motorists in 1969... one to a driver who fell asleep traveling on 4th Avenue E. and was involved in an accident... one for reckless driving between 5th and 6th Avenues on Sheyenne St... a third for speeding and the charge was dismissed. All three tickets were issued for occurrences in the city of West Fargo streets, none on Business 94.

To further reply to Mr.Lykken's opposition to the Kindred Dam... he should have read the front page report the *West Fargo Pioneer* carried in the January 14th issue. This report is to the point and answers a great share of the questions on Kindred Dam.

* * *

This past Wednesday a man by the name of Dave Hamm came into the *Pioneer* office. He looked like a businessman to me. In that he wanted to talk about a new ladies' ready-to-wear business in our city, I was most interested. He said he had talked with the Chamber of Commerce and they were most helpful. I suggested he talk with other businessmen and would have taken him around to introduce him but he was in a hurry and had to be on his way. He wanted to know all about the *Pioneer* and right there he hit a soft spot in my heart and I couldn't stop telling how the paper was growing and how much the merchants and people of West Fargo had helped the paper and were continuing to help. He thanked me profusely.

The next time I heard about the guy was the next day when a friend of mine in Moorhead who used to be publisher of the *Moorhead Valley Times* called and told me the story. His new business wasn't quite what it was painted to be. It seems he was interested in starting a "shopper" in West Fargo. If you are familiar with newspapers at all, you know they have rough going when a "shopper" comes to town. The newspaper gets the news and the "shopper" gets the advertising. I don't have to tell you what happens to the newspaper. The city ends up with lots of ads but no news because a "shopper" only sells ads. It doesn't tell what is going on in your city and cares less.

Incidentally, the *Forum*, trusting this guy for what he said he was (ladies' ready-to-wear), rolled out the red carpet for him. Pretty hard to build a business on a lie, Mr. Hamm.

March 4, 1970

Thursday started out sort of questionable. I had set the alarm for 6:30 because I had to attend a Jaycee breakfast in Fargo. I very carefully turned the clock-set to 6:30 but of course didn't pull the lever for the alarm. The next thing I heard was my wife asking me if I didn't have some place to be at seven. I rushed to the phone and called Roger Fischer, our editor, as he was to go along.

"Say," he says, "we had better get on our horses – got to be there in ten minutes." In that I have told Roger very firmly that I don't like people being late for anything, I was sort of stopped. I opened my mouth to give a great, long explanation but nothing came out. Besides I didn't have any time for explanation. We arrived at the breakfast, late of course (Roger didn't rub it in), and I figured maybe it wasn't going to be a bad day after all because I had enough to pay for our breakfasts. Usually I get where I'm going and I have no money to pay my way in.

My luck failed me miserably by nine o'clock when I arrived at the office. The high school paper which was to be sent to Valley City to be run on the presses was still lying right there in the office. Guess who was supposed to put it on the bus Wednesday night so we could deliver it to the school Thursday. Right then I started to rev up for the day. I picked up the phone, called Valley City Press. The guy at the other end says, "I been to the bus depot three times to get that d— paper paste-up and it still hasn't come!"

Now I figured if I didn't tell the wife who had explained to me very carefully the night before how important it was to get the high school paper going to Valley City, I would be in the clear. I could drive that 55 miles there and back in a little over two hours and she wouldn't know the difference. FIRST, however, I had to deliver the mail to her eager hands before I did another thing. As I stepped inside the door at home before I speeded towards my destination, says the other half, "I hope you put the high school paper in the mail last night." Right then the fur began to fly. While all this was going on the phone rang – it was our gal, Jean Hust, who comes in on Thursday and runs the office and types up news for next week's paper. She had the flu and couldn't come to work.

Always With'em

That didn't help things at all because there stood my wife with dope in her hair in preparation to going to the hair fixers. (Thursday and Wednesday are the only days the wife gets off from the office in that she works every day the rest of the week and this includes Sunday.)

THE END CAME WHEN I REACHED VALLEY CITY AND FOUND I HAD LEFT BEHIND SIX PICTURES WHICH WERE SUPPOSED TO GO WITH THE PAPER. LEFT THEM IN WEST FARGO.

To make this story shorter, I later found the way the bus schedule worked out, I would not have had to make the trip at all, but there I was in Valley City.

The day finished in a complete foul-up! I was to take pictures of the girls' bowling league for a special bowling issue that will be in the *Pioneer* next week. Two cameras I figured would do the trick, one Polaroid and the other a 35 millimeter job. All went well until I looked at the Polaroid pictures. They were one big blur. 'Course I figured, in that I didn't have my glasses, they were just fine until one cute little gal looks over my shoulder and tells me they are what I thought they weren't. "Don't worry," says I, "my trusty 35 millimeter is really what picture-taking is all about."

As I stepped up to take the last picture, I ran out of film in both cameras. ALSO, as I leaned down to pick up my Polaroid I had laid on the floor I got a Charlie horse in both legs. I didn't think it just the thing to sit down in the bowling lanes and at the same time I couldn't stand up. A quick look at the gals showed me they were all watching my shenanigans. Then over my shoulder came a helping hand and a sweet smooth voice saying, "Can I hold your camera for you?"

Whew, what a day!

April 8, 1970

You will note smeared print, color that doesn't seem to fit the page and just not a very clean-looking paper in Saturday's and Sunday's *Forum*. Those of you who might lose your patience just keep your cool, for I'm sure the *Forum* people are losing theirs. No one can know how frustrating it is when adjustments on a press won't bring out a clean paper. The *Forum's* problems are tenfold because their press is ten to fifteen times as big as other presses in this neck of the woods. It is new and unfamiliar to men running it. In a few days the *Forum* will have a bright, shiny new look so stand by for the best in future issues.

* * *

You folks who do now and then read the crazy things that go on in this column might remember that a couple of months ago I convinced our daughter (11 years old) that a canary was much better than a dog. In that we already have a sassy cat and 20 fish to take care of, I figured I made a pretty good deal. To compound the deal I convinced "the kid" that good grades also went along with a canary. The grades did just fine and, of course, then came the hard part. I had to buy a bird, a cage, cuttle bone, two kinds of bird seed, a special water tank, gravel feeder, and then things got real tough for I had to also find twenty bucks.

Saturday was the golden day for that is when "Tweety Bird" came to stay at our house. The kind man at Stonegate Kennels guaranteed that Tweety would sing his heart out if we bought some super special canary seed that makes birds sing even if they didn't want to.

We put Tweety in the guest room and waited for the song to start. He squeaked a couple of times and grew very excited about something in the corner. Yep, you're right. There sat Sandy, that sassy cat, with a most pleased grin on her face and a light her eye like I have never seen before. We convinced Sandy right off that dinner was not being served in the form of Tweety. Still no song came from our canary. I became convinced that no matter what kind of seed that bird ate, there would be no song.

So that things fall into place here, I might mention that a guest showed up at our house Saturday. In that there is so much junk in "the kid's" room she can hardly get in there herself, we had to leave the bird in the guest room. I was sure he wouldn't be disturbed as that bird didn't sing anyway. At five o'clock Sunday morning Tweety suddenly recovered his voice. The house rang with canary bird song. To make things worse, he seems to have his record stuck. Now he won't shut up; he sings all the time. That nice man at Stonegate Kennels sure was right about that bird seed but now how in heck do we shut that darn bird off?

May 13, 1970

Let's make this a back scratching affair!

I think everyone in West Fargo knows by this time that the Chamber of Commerce of West Fargo is in trouble financially. A meeting Friday morning didn't settle very many problems in relation to money except that it had to be raised if the Chamber were to continue to exist. I offered to form a committee to raise the money and the offer was accepted. Personally, I think I happened to be the last straw or they wouldn't have grabbed on so quickly.

In any case, the sequel to this little story is I had a call from Mr. L. S. Pierce of Pierce Mobile Homes of West Fargo on Saturday morning. Mr. Pierce wanted to have coffee and talk about the Chamber's problems. I hurriedly called Paul Vance, our president, and then picked up Roy Larson on my way to meet Mr. Pierce. The three of us met with Mr. Pierce and his sons, Richard and Carl. We explained some of the problems facing the Chamber, whereupon we were given a check for $300 for 1970-71 dues. There is one string attached – Mr. Pierce explained that he hates to be alone in this venture. The other 150 businesses in West Fargo are also urged to support their Chamber. The Pierce Mobile Home people explained that they live here and want West Fargo to have a Chamber of Commerce because it is extremely important to every business in our city.

Soon all businesses in West Fargo will be asked to support their Chamber. This will be done by a personal visit from a representative of the Chamber. LET'S MAKE IT A ROUND ROBIN AFFAIR. IF YOU BUSINESSES CAN DO SOMETHING FOR THE CHAMBER, THE CHAMBER CAN DO SOMETHING FOR YOU.

* * *

Last week Herb Tintes informed me that bids would be let on a project for the park. He told me where the meeting was to be held and at what time. I discovered after that there were not enough people on our staff to cover all the meetings going on the night the Park Board met. Not that the Park Board isn't important but we just couldn't make them all, so made arrangement to get the facts later. They are to be found in this week's paper instead of last week. I hope I'm forgiven, Herb.

June 24, 1970

Between the days of Tuesday and Saturday last week the Withams had their vacation. This may not seem like a long time for a vacation to some people but for us it was a millennium.

We, of course, took our kid with us. You would have thought there were three kids in the back seat with all the different kinds of noises emanating from that direction.

Our destination was Winnipeg, and I must say that everyone should make this city at least once in their lifetime. They of course have many things that a large city in our country has, but with a different touch. As for "the kid" I'm sure she enjoyed herself but not without adventure. An introduction to a Polynesian restaurant our first evening kept her on the go (for the ladies' room that is) most of the next day. However, her first great adventure was getting lost in the Hudson's Bay store.

I started in one direction looking for her and the wife the other. In my search I became intrigued with the cigar counter. They sure go all out for cigars in Canada. In any case I had to buy one and light up right on the spot. In the interim the wife was becoming more excited and ran on to me standing around blowing smoke rings. After giving me a short, quick piece of her mind, as an afterthought she said, "Incidentally, you can't smoke in this store." I don't mind looking for lost kids but no one is going to tell me to throw a brand new cigar away. We put a couple of messages on the loudspeaker and I went to the mezzanine to await the "lost." Her mother discovered her coming down the escalator as she was going up. Seems that "the kid" had covered all six floors about 14 times. She was bedsheet white with two red eyes in the middle. By this time we had used up our allotted shopping time and as we proceeded out the door I dropped my cigar into a waiting receptacle that had a sign over it saying, "No smoking in this store." How come they don't put those signs where people can see them?

* * *

Father's Day came to me in Canada this year. My daughter bought me a 42 inch belt. Seems that my being 36 inches around the waist has nothing to do with the size of the belt. When the clerk suggested to her that the belt might be too big she said that she was sure I would grow into it. How much faith can one kid have?

* * *

I noted as we passed through Grand Forks a very large sign proclaiming that city as the fastest growing one in North Dakota. I guess they have never heard of West Fargo.

Always With'em

July 1, 1970

The wife sure learned why there is not a lot of smoking of cigarettes in Canada when we were there week before last. Cigarettes 70¢ a pack! The poor girl has cut down to five cigarettes a week since she got home.

Another thing I liked in Canada – most of the radio stations play good music. If I don't get blasted out of my seat by American stations I think they have gone off the air.

* * *

My background being a farmer, I have wanted for years to have a garden, not a big garden but one I could "putz" around in after work. The catch there is there is never a time in the newspaper business that you call "after work." About the time I grab the hoe I have a call from someone who has a question that I don't have an answer for. Such is the life of a newspaperman. In any case, this year of all years I determined to have a garden. It all started when I spotted a special sharp pointed hoe at Lindgren's that my Uncle Ross always said was the best for gardening because it cut out weeds and left the radishes.

Tony Walz who lives across the park from me has the best little tractor for digging garden you ever saw. Five bucks and I had a nice garden with the mulch thrown in. Rushing into Lindgrens, I was told that the hoe had been sold the day before. Clarence tells me that the hoe had been there for two years and no one wanted it. Now he had two sales in the last two days AND why didn't I buy it when I complained about the price day before yesterday.

After the hoe episode I bought seeds. Of course I bought the seeds I like – radishes, peas, beans, and just for good measure, three packs of radishes. Why? Because I like radishes. I then proceeded to plant those seeds in what I thought were nice straight rows. In the process of planting, the other half of the family came along and wanted to know why I didn't plant carrots. I didn't tell her that I don't like carrots and that it was my garden and that I was going to plant in it what I pleased. Instead I took the trip back to Lindgrens and bought some carrot seeds. To this day those carrot seeds haven't come up. Can't tell you why – they just didn't come up.

When that little ol' garden began to grow, the other half had a very fine time. "Say," she says, "I thought you used to be a farmer. Look at those rows – they are so crooked a snake couldn't follow them." I just kept right on hoeing.

I will say one thing. I shall have tomatoes before anyone in this here town. Yep, about all they have to do is turn red. Suppose I should 'fess up that when I bought the darn things from Hemms Greenhouse they already had small tomaters and blossoms like heck. I sure couldn't see raising tomatoes in my basement all winter long just so I could put them out in the garden at planting time.

One thing for sure – to say the least I have radishes, radishes, radishes. The darn things have taken over the whole garden. I can't begin to eat them fast enough. I have given them to the neighbors. I have walked on them to keep them from growing, but nothing will deter them from being the most beautiful radishes in Cass County.

August 5, 1970

You who felt that lifting weights and doing push-ups are just the thing to keep you in top physical condition should have spent two bucks and visited the National High School Rodeo this past week. These kids have the pep and vitality that is sure longed for in us oldsters.

To top things off, their appearance is a little misleading. They are polite, considerate, clean, and all-around good-looking people. Yet, they are as tough as they come and back off from nothing, and I mean nothing. When I saw 16-, 17- and 18-year olds climb onto those mean-looking bulls, I decided right then and there that we have a breed of kids in our country that can't be beat.

We had three young rodeo cowboys staying at the Witham ranch all week. They made their own beds and kept their bunkhouse in topnotch condition.

I don't think I impressed one that came home Friday night. When I asked how things went, he said that his calf got up (meaning that after he had roped and tied the calf, it escaped and ran away). I, thinking that he had made a big hit, said, "Gee, that's fine." Then I saw the look on his face so I followed with, "You mean that ain't good?" He put on his hat and walked away.

* * *

This past week, as a gesture of good relations, the *Pioneer* gave away special free souvenir editions at the rodeo. Wednesday morning, soon after the newsstands were filled with *Pioneer* papers, I noted a young fellow carrying three. He came up to me and wanted to know if I wouldn't like to buy one for 10¢.

I told him no – but then he said, "How about a nickel, mister?" I guess there is always a way to make a dime if one really tries.

What makes me feel bad is why didn't I think of it first...

September 2, 1970

Has your pocketbook felt a little skinny lately?

Here are 32 million reasons why. In last week's *Parade* magazine in the *Forum* a short article explained that the United States had paid $32 million to non-combat Filipino troops in South Vietnam. The catch was the money went not to Filipino troops but to the politicians. The worst of the whole situation is our government has been trying to keep this information from the American people. Now if you had just happened to have not reported a few income tax dollars that good ol' Uncle Sam thought he should have, WHAT DO YOU THINK WOULD HAPPEN TO YOU? In other words, if some guy in the Philippines gets away with it, it is okay, but on the home front LET'S MAKE 'EM PAY.

Now $40 million is earmarked for Cambodia. Looks like our government has found a brand new rat hole. What the heck – the 32 million dollar rat hole must be full!

* * *

Last Saturday I saw Ione Lindgren going down the line squeezing cantaloupes in one of the local grocery stores. I couldn't resist saying that that cantaloupe didn't look like Charmin to me. If Ione thought it funny, she didn't say so.

October 7, 1970

I note with some interest the water problems Fargo is having. I also recall we didn't hear much from Fargo or Mayor Lashkowitz in relation to the Kindred Dam when the issue was hot. During all the fuss, the *Pioneer* published an article expressing concern about water conservation. At that time no one seemed to be concerned about water needs in the future for Fargo except the *West Fargo Pioneer.*

We now hear many strange noises emanating from Fargo concerning water. Some reports claim the river hasn't been so low since 1936, and the fish are dying. Mayor Lashkowitz is very concerned about a shortage of water. He is even talking in terms of diverting water from the Sheyenne River to the Red so that Fargo will have enough water.

I will tell him this. I will be glad to channel the water to Fargo that ran through my house for five weeks during the flood a year ago. The mayor didn't seem very concerned about water conservation at that time. What I could suggest, but maybe I shouldn't open an old wound, is we build a dam somewhere in the Kindred area and save the water for that dry day in the future.

There will come a day when Fargo is going to be searching far and wide for water. When people get thirsty, they aren't going to give a damn what the Sheyenne River looks like and the thirstier they get the less beautiful that river is going to look...

* * *

We at the *Pioneer* shall miss our front line help– namely Mrs. Elaine Coggins. She is presently ensconced in St. John's Hospital where she is recuperating from an operation. Mrs. Coggins is our "girl Friday", who keeps a ready smile for people who have occasion to visit the *Pioneer*. She types news copy, answers phones, makes up ads, helps put our paper together for the press, takes full charge of the stationery department, empties waste baskets, makes coffee each day – and I guess I'll stop here before someone comes along and hires her away from us!

November 4, 1970

Checking with the West Fargo Police Department Sunday morning I find that, mostly, West Fargo kids had a good time Halloween with practically no disturbances. I also heard that things really came apart in Casselton with plenty of destruction.

One couldn't be happy about Casselton's misfortune, but I must say I, for one, am proud of our West Fargo youngsters.

I might mention here that I don't know if I'm so proud of the older people or not. Three pins were found in three bags of M&M candies. People who do this should be in an institution as this sort of thing makes no sense at all. Children eating this candy could end up in the hospital on the operating table.

Always With'em

At 3:30 Sunday morning I was called out to take a picture of a one-car accident beside Falls Mobile Homes. Seems that some young fellows couldn't quite make the turn off Business 94 onto the service road. They took a very big NSP power pole and all with them. I would say damage to the car was over a thousand dollars.

I might add here that while in the police station I read a report that came out from Yarmouth and Boston, Mass., Sunday. Seems that the militant young have a new thing going there. They hand a policeman a suitcase to hold while they step into a store for a moment. The suitcase is filled with chemicals which explode and burn the policeman to death. Living in West Fargo is pretty good living, I would say.

December 2, 1970

Notice of the week: My wife, that gal who goes on a diet every once in awhile and twice in between, lately has taken to stewed tomatoes. Don't ask me why, because I can't explain but I can tell you what she told me.

Ladies who wish to drop a pound or two, put this in the back of your mind to use as a last resort. She cooks and eats those stewed tomatoes to lose weight, not because tomatoes take anything off or put anything on for that matter, but she just plain hates stewed tomatoes. She takes one look at those hot tomatoes and hands them over to me. I haven't mentioned this before – but I love stewed tomatoes. The reason I haven't told her I love stewed tomatoes is because I want her to think I'm doing her a big favor by eating the tomatoes she can't face.

This in turn gives me the privilege of an extra beer at my favorite pub when I'm a little late for dinner some evening.

This secret I would like to pass on to all you guys who would like that extra beer on the way home, but the heck of it is your wives probably love stewed tomatoes. Sorry, guys, but this works only for me!

* * *

Saturday I went into Lindgrens to sell Randy Lindgren an ad. He was busy with a customer at the time so he made the shortest speech to me I have heard in many a day.

"Are you buyin' or sellin'?" he says.

I'm a lover of short speeches, but a golden eagle goes to Randy this week.

* * *

Just a short note here... We got just a bit fouled up last week on the colorful ad of Northern Freight. The same ad is running this week with correct prices and they are bargains to behold, so all you folks get in on the ground floor and save yourself some real bucks.

January 6, 1971

All is excitement around the *Pioneer* office nowadays. By the time you read this, hopefully there will be new photo-typesetting equipment to take the place of our Just-o-writers. As many of you know who have visited the *Pioneer*, our Just-o-writers look like two very intelligent typewriters. I can say they sure are intelligent enough to go on the blink every time they are bumped or moved an inch. We always had to call in a repairman to get them back in shape.

BUT now they tell me that all of this is behind for our frustrated operators... everything will be done photographically from now on.

I would like to explain what the new machine is all about but, to tell the truth, if they brought an old cardboard box filled with straw and told me it was our new equipment I would have to believe them because I have never even seen what we have bought. In any case, if that man with the new machines gets here this week to install them, drop by and listen to the darn things tick... we won't know what makes them do that but you might as well listen right along with the rest of us.

* * *

Some high school bands just can't win. This seems to be the situation with the West Fargo High School Band when it comes to band calendars.

Everyone worked hard to sell the calendars. Everyone worked hard to see that things got to the *Pioneer* on time and correct. The *Pioneer* sent the information away to its printer on time and all assumed everything was going smoothly... UNTIL, as the saying goes, "the boom fell."

We are sorry to report that the West Fargo Band calendars will not be delivered until the last of January or very early February. From what we have been able to glean from the deep secrets of the printer's office, the dating on the calendars will probably start with February.

We are sure this is going to make a lot of people who bought band calendars in West Fargo unhappy. We accept your disappointment and chagrin. Please accept our sincere apologies for a job not very well done...

– The Publisher

* * *

An orchid to our street department. Hardly had the snow stopped blowing Monday afternoon before they were cleaning up our streets. When everyone looked out Tuesday morning, lo and behold, where they had gotten stuck the night before the snow had all been cleaned away.

February 3, 1971

Yep, I did it all on my own. Last Tuesday afternoon I parked on the north side of the street from the post office. I had noticed the "no parking" sign before, but last Tuesday, anxious to get the afternoon mail, the parking sign sort of slipped by my eyes and mind. The result was a parking ticket.

So a word to the wise for those picking up mail at the West Fargo post office... your mail may just cost you two bucks if you park on the north side of the street.

* * *

I note where the governor of Minnesota cut fifteen million from the budget of the University of Minnesota. Ain't it heck, now some of those fancy Dan professors might have to attend class and do a little teaching. Too long they have had student stand-ins while they were toasting their feet at home writing a book. You can write your book on your own time, Mr. Professor...

* * *

I see the *West Fargo High School Packer* put out a special drug issue this week. I don't think it settled any issues, but I will say the kids sure had their say. Never having smoked a joint (marijuana) I can't say if it is good or bad. I don't know if it speeds one up or slows one down, but I do know this battle concerning "grass" is going to go on for a long time. After all it's already been here for about 10,000 years. I just like the feeling of being able to say I've never used any kind of drugs that weren't prescribed by a doctor. How about it, kids?

* * *

Recently I received a parking ticket for parking on the wrong side of the street at the post office. This week our esteemed postmaster, Harlan Boyer, received one but mine said words to the effect that I had better get right down to the police station and pay up. Harlan's was just a bit different.

Evidently he had parked in the wrong spot at the wrong time and raised the wrath of another driver for sure. This driver issued his own kind of ticket and this is what it said.

"Parking Violation, Time 3:30, License Number – North Dakota, Make of car – Mercury; This is not a ticket, but if it were within my power you would receive two. Because of your bullheaded, inconsiderate, feeble attempt at parking you have taken enough room for a 20 mule team, two elephants, one goat and safari of pygmies from the African interior. The reason for giving you this is so that in the future you may think of someone else beside yourself. Besides, I don't like domineering, egotistical or simple-minded drivers and you probably fit into one of these categories.

"I sign off wishing you an early transmission failure on the expressway at about 4:30 p.m."

March 3, 1971

I know everyone will believe this when I tell them because the publisher of this paper quite frequently is off on cloud No. 9. In any case, the event took place at the basketball game this past Saturday night.

I was invited to sit with Henry Newgard and his wife to watch the game. After we were seated Judge and Mrs. Ralph Maxwell arrived and sat right behind us. After Mrs. Maxwell sat down she made the remark that there was a green Pontiac station wagon parked with its lights on and they couldn't be turned off because the doors were locked.

Mrs. Maxwell, being a conscientious woman, didn't let the problem drop there. She asked for a pen which I gave her and proceeded to write a note to be read over the loudspeaker. Several of us then convinced Gerald Pierson, who was sitting in front of us, to deliver the note to the people in charge of the loudspeaker. Gerald, being a gallant gentleman, climbed over 20 people and delivered the note.

A moment later the note was read over the loudspeaker. A light in my brain lit up about this time and I sheepishly climbed over the same

20 people Gerald had just climbed over and went out into the street to turn off the lights on the green Pontiac station wagon which just happened to belong to, of all people, the publisher of this paper...

* * *

Don Goerger, who lives in Horace and is one of our favorite people who comes to fix our typesetting machines when thing go wrong, has been on vacation for the past two weeks. Don went to Corpus Christi, Texas.

In that he hadn't had a vacation for three years, he was looking forward to lots of fun and relaxation. One small cloud arose on the horizon before leaving – his paycheck didn't get to him before taking off. That wasn't so bad, as his thinking was clearly directed toward the place that I had informed him was a land of sunshine and happiness, having spent some time there myself.

Monday morning our machines were on the blink but we weren't worried as we all knew Don was to arrive back on the job. An unhappy Don came into the office. I couldn't resist asking how his trip turned out.

He informed us that three hours after arriving someone picked his pocket... it rained and was cold and foggy every day he was there... he had planned two big days of fishing and he didn't even get a line wet... and on the way home a motorcycle ran into the side of his car on his way through Minneapolis. End of story.

April 7, 1971

I want those of you who regularly read the *Pioneer* to take a real good look this week at the print. We folks at the *Pioneer* think it is really big stuff because it all comes from our new photo-typesetting equipment. To turn out this kind of print we use two machines. One is called a recorder and then there is a big mystery box we call a photo reproducer. One machine punches lots of holes in a narrow strip of paper and the other machine reads the holes and then reproduces the holes into real type one can read. Now that is as simple as I can explain it and besides that is all I know about the darn thing so if you want to know any more about what goes on in the typesetting department of the *Pioneer* you will have to come and see for yourself.

* * *

I see where Senator Javits is trying his darndest to shift the blame for the My Lai incident back on Lt. Calley. Isn't it wonderful that we have such intelligent, upstanding senators in Washington trying to preserve the purity of the whole nation? What Senator Javits is really saying is "Let's visit the sins of the nation upon one man and we'll all be free of any responsibility." After all he is only "one" and there are almost 200 million of us so let's just put him on a rockpile for the rest of his life so we can forget that we sent him to Viet Nam in the first place.

* * *

I missed the picture of the year last week. One of our ladies who waits on people at Lorentzens was dressing the store window. As she stepped to the far end a wire from overhead caught her wig and gave it a merry whirl through the air. I won't tell who it was – you will just have to go in and ask for yourself.

I also missed another picture at Roy's Jack and Jill. Rushing in to buy some hamburger last week, I spotted a little guy all the way in the popsicle freezer. Only his feet were sticking out. By the time I got my camera he had found his favorite flavor and was on his way.

May 26, 1971

I was impressed and pleased this past week to see a portion of our high school young people ready to do something about a school program they wanted to keep. They have not only put up quite a squawk, they have had meetings, made decisions, and are making a working effort to keep their program. I am talking about the modular scheduling used in our high school program. The high schoolers felt deeply enough about this to wash cars to raise money to be donated to the program.

It takes about $9,000 a year to support the program. The school board, as everyone knows, has made cuts or are in the process of making cuts in school money demands for the coming year. The reason for all this? Because at a recent mill levy vote the people turned down the eight mills the school board said they would need to run the schools for the coming school year.

There are two ways people who support our West Fargo schools find out where their investment goes and what it is used for in the everyday life of our schools. These are legals read in this paper and news read in this paper. At times there is real news in your school legals we don't always get when we attend and write up a school board meeting. When we catch this news as it comes to us delivered by hand or mail, it is read for things we think are of special importance. In the public interest we will continue to do this. It is my personal feeling that if the school board had told people what they wanted the money for, the eight mill levy would have passed with flying colors. Trying to find out what the money was to be used for was not an easy task. This paper, in desperation, attempted to find out exactly where the money was to go and got no solid answers.

The people in this school district will support their schools. They did not go to the voting booth and turn this mill levy down for meanness. They went there and marked NO on their ballot because they want to know where their money is going.

In this era of high taxes, the average guy on the street says HELL NO. He pays through the nose every day to a federal government who, in some cases, wastes and, yes, squanders his money in every stupid project some crackpot in Washington can think up. Pick up any daily paper and you can see taxes are going to be a lot higher in the next five to ten years. The one bright spot I do see comparing our state to national policy is that the men and women we sent to Bismarck this year did a darn good job of holding the line. If you don't think so, take ten minutes out and read what's happening in Minnesota. Even the governor raised his pay over there.

May I end by saying to our school board: I'm not intimating that you are squandering our tax money, but tell the people exactly what you want and why and when the mill levy elections come along you'll get it.

June 2, 1971

Just a note here in relation to the progress issue you now have in hand. We had planned a much bigger issue but at the same time we all forgot that there are employee vacations. The result is that old Father Time caught up with yours truly. I can't run as fast as I used to and now people holler at me when I go down the street, "Say, what's that stuff flying around in back of you?" I refuse to tell them that that's just my rear end dragging along on the ground stirring up what little dust they see.

Anyway that's the best excuse I can think of for not getting out a forty-page progress edition this year. But, as the saying goes, there sure as heck is another time coming.

* * *

This past week we finally got our garden in. I wanted to plant it the week before last but the wife said that it wouldn't do well if it was planted before Memorial Day. I didn't agree with her, of course, but I waited just the same. The result was that our kid planted the garden for us (when no one was looking). She also had the help of another little girl in our neighborhood. What was planted in the garden? Darned if I know!

I am sure that we have radishes because the radish envelope is empty. Where they are is another question. Somewhere in that well-turned ground I have been informed are peas, beans, carrots and cucumbers. I lost count of the varieties when the gals got into a fight over how to plant radishes. I happen to like radishes very much but I know that I will never be able to find them in what I thought was going to be my garden.

The one thing I did have a hand in was the tomatoes. I have three beautiful plants. I raised each plant myself. By that I mean I raised them up from Hemm's Greenhouse tables and took them home and planted them in my garden. I watered them and covered them up when I thought they might get nipped by a light frost. I have them all hoed up nicely... not a weed in sight.

Granting that my kid doesn't step on them... the worms don't cut them off... we get enough sunshine to make them grow... the hail doesn't strip off the leaves... and the slugs don't get at them... I might in eight weeks have tomatoes. You know, this life of a tomato farmer like me isn't easy. Just think of all the things that can happen before I have the pleasure of picking my very own tomato. It's so discouraging I may next year turn to raising dandelions. Boy, the guy who is raising those things sure does a good job. You should see my backyard, and I didn't even ask him to plant them there.

July 21, 1971

I don't know about the rest of you garden lovers, but I had my first ripe tomato Sunday. Granted, it was a bit small, but it was a tomato all the same and right from my tomato patch. Incidentally, that tomato plant that Hank Newgard gave me which is supposed to grow ten feet tall is still growing like mad and I see green tomatoes all over the darn thing. However, I can see right now that I'm going to have to put up a strong fence to keep the monster from growing all over the yard. The other three plants (regular kind) with all this rain think they have to feed the whole world the way they are getting ready to put out the tomatoes. Yep, I think for sure this year I'm going to be the tomato champion of West Fargo. Guess I'll just keep track of how many tomatoes one plant produces and sort of hold it up as an example for all garden lovers to reach for.

* * *

I talked with Roy Nelson at Selland Motors Tuesday and also Larry Lorentzsen at Lorentzsens here in West Fargo. They had both spent the Fourth at Medora (not together). Both men couldn't say enough about the good time they had had at one of North Dakota's leading tourist attractions. The setting of course is most beautiful and from all reports the musical that is presented in the open air was also excellent. While people watch the musical, wild deer, antelope and buffalo roam through the hill area back of the show on stage. The people who are behind this project have been wise to blend the whole attraction into the land and not, as in most cases, the other way around.

In the not too distant future, the hard work of local people in our Bonanzaville project will pay off as well. It would be impossible to count the hours and work that have gone into Bonanzaville up to this time.

August 18, 1971

Took my daughter with me on ad selling rounds in Moorhead this past week. These are thoughts from a 13-year-old. There were plenty of comments like, "Gee, Dad, this is sure hard work. How many miles do you walk in a day?" "How come they don't all buy ads, Dad?" "How come you thanked that last guy, Dad? He didn't even buy an ad." "That sure was a small ad that man bought. Didn't hardly pay to take your time there, did it? "Dad, what time is it?" (11 a.m.) "I'm hungry. Let's stop and get a Kentucky Fried Chicken lunch."

* * *

Had my hair cut at Wilson's Barber Shop last week and was visiting with Orlan Rokke about his vacation trip to Yellowstone Park. I guess he sure isn't excited about going back. Seems that the place is plumb full of "hippies" and their dogs. Nine of them camped behind their camper and it was two days before he could tell one from the other enough to know there were three girls in the group. They all dressed in bib overalls, all had long, long hair. He said that on the road one guy was lying down with his thumb up in the air hitching a ride. Seems also that the gas stations out that-a-way are interested only in one thing, your money. They just fill it up and hold out their hand... have to be asked to wipe the windshield.

September 1, 1971

We asked a non-working hippie recently, "How do you eat?" He smiled and responded, "My friends feed me. I've never been hungry."

"Where," we persisted, "do your friends get what they give you?" He smiled again, waved his hand and said, "Maybe they have wealthy parents."

That may be the story in some cases – but it's not the whole story. Bill Fiset wrote recently in the *Oakland* (Calif.) *Tribune* about how you, as a working taxpayer, are financing hippies. Fiset gave the case of a specific hippie:

"He boasts that for 50¢ he buys $28 worth of food stamps... Each week he uses the stamps to buy exactly $27.51 worth of groceries and gets 49¢ back in cash as change, the maximum amount of cash he can get on a purchase.

"Then he adds one penny for the 50¢ to get his $28 worth of stamps for the next week. The fourth week of the month he sells his food stamps to friends for $15 cash. Thus in a month he's paid out 53¢ for $112 worth of stamps, for which he gets $83.53 worth of food and $14.47 in net profit in cash."

From the food stamp saleswoman: "Can you imagine how this adds up when you have 15 hippie kids living in a commune house, all doing the same thing? No wonder they laugh at the Establishment." No wonder welfare programs are in trouble.

You may be taking a hippie to lunch – without knowing about it. And the hippies are certainly taking you for a ride.

October 13, 1971

A false alarm was turned in to our fire department at 4:15 Sunday morning. The caller said there was a fire at 912 Sheyenne. In the small morning hours the people who put out our fires and save lives don't question the exact position of a fire, they don't look up the address to make sure there is such a address as they know the caller could easily make a mistake. They just go and risk their lives. JUST REMEMBER THIS, YOU WHO TURNED IN THE FALSE ALARM: THE NEXT ALARM YOU TURN IN MAY JUST BE THE ONE THAT SAVES YOUR LIFE OR YOUR HOME. The volunteer firemen who come to your rescue will still not stop to look up your number to see if it all is a silly hoax. Let him rest for the real fire that is sure to happen. He will be thankful he can and you too can rest easy for he is as close as your phone.

* * *

Honesty is not lost after all. I had begun to think for sure that anyone who ran into your car while you were not in it and could be confident that no one would see the situation would just consider that was tough luck for the owner of the car. Not so according to Loran Pazcowski, owner of West Fargo Drug.

While his car was parked in the Herbst lot in Fargo, the door of his car was pushed in and damaged to quite some extent. When he returned, naturally he was disturbed until he found a note on his windshield. The note informed him who had run into his door and also gave a name and address for him to contact. He followed instructions and learned that he could get his car fixed and forwarded the bill. When this was done, he received a check back for the entire bill from the doorcrusher, with a note explaining that he was very sorry for the inconvenience.

November 3, 1971

It has been my contention for years that people should pay their way in life or go not so expensive a route. I feel most strongly about this when it comes to nations around the world that we pour billions of dollars into year after year. It has been proved over and over again that this buys no friends. In fact, it has bought more enemies than friends. Therefore, this past week I agree with the Senate killing the foreign aid bill. To have to support countries for years means one thing and that is they are not going to help themselves if we keep helping them.

It has been going on so long, in fact, that they have come to expect the money as if we owe it to them. We support the UN with 33 percent of the entire budget besides giving gifts. Russia hasn't paid their membership for years because they became miffed over a minor issue, but good ol' Uncle Sam doesn't have the right to speak up and say "the hell with it – let someone else pay the bill for awhile." What makes me so mad is that I help pay this big giveaway with my taxes.

* * *

The Lawrence Knutsons had one pup too many at their house. When the "tricks or treats" kids came around Sunday night, they dropped the pup in the sack of a little boy with a big grin. I wonder how much Pa and Ma grinned when they saw what their little "tricks or treats" guy came hauling home.

December 1, 1971

I was talking to Gene Johnson a few days ago. Gene is one of our state highway patrolmen and had just invested in the C and C Grocery on Business 94 just east of West Fargo. I was curious about his investment so asked a few questions in regard to the business. Gene came right back with a quick answer. "If you had eight kids, Don, you would invest in a grocery, too."

* * *

You might have read an article on the front page of the *Pioneer* last week titled, "When a Road Becomes a Headache!" The road I am referring to is County Road #17, which runs to Harwood from West Fargo.

Now, in the article Roger Fischer, editor, had to stick with the news angle only. I don't have to. The road in question was plowed up in late summer and early fall in preparation to resurfacing. After it was nicely plowed up and made into a very fine mess, the county decided they didn't have the money to finish the road until 1973. No one evidently gave a thought to the people who live on this road, and if they did they certainly didn't give a damn or they wouldn't have plowed it up in the first place. It seems to me that if I were a county commissioner I would have waited until I had the money to finish what I started.

Today while driving over 13th Avenue to the West Acres shopping center, I noted the county out there nailing little red pieces of cloth to the road. I don't know what this means, but usually a newly surfaced road appears after the little red flags go down. Now, if I were the people who live on County Road #17, I would raise a little hell over this maneuver. In fact, one of these years there might just be another election.

We hope to bring you pictures in the spring when things get really sticky on this road after the rains come down. We might even get a commissioner to pose on the road for us.

January 5, 1972
WE NEED YOU

A special note in relation to your hometown paper, this *West Fargo Pioneer*. We arrived in West Fargo in March of 1967. Since that time your weekly paper has grown from a struggling 750 subscriptions (which we have to thank the West Fargo High School Band for selling) to a circulation at this time of 2,700.

We are still growing and, in fact, as most of you know, have grown out of two offices because of extra space needed to serve an expanding paper.

It is our intention to make the *Pioneer* an interesting, newsworthy publication. Not that you can't find things of interest in the paper now, but we are always searching and working to make it even better.

To make it better in the new year of 1972 we need you who look us over each week. If you see something we are missing, let us know. Start by filling in and returning the questionnaire below.

This paper was made possible by the merchants who advertise and the people who read it, so we want to hear your suggestions. It can only make us a better publication.

In closing, we are here to serve our city the best way we know how. In the next five years I look for West Fargo to grow dramatically in size. My hope is that the *Pioneer* can be of some assistance in respect to the friendly, clean town that it is today.

* * *

WHAT NEXT, MR. NEWSMAN?

I was rather amused this past week watching newsmen in Peking squirm and complain that they couldn't get any news from the president's people there or the Chinese people. John Chancellor made a real point of not having his own way concerning news coverage. Could it be a very small taste of what life could be for Chancellor if he were a newsman working for Mr. Mao?

This is just another example of the short-sightedness of the men and women who gather news in our nation. I definitely say not all news-gathering people are this way, but certainly many self-appointed feel they are above the common herd. A pox on all those so-called news-gathering elite who write what they think we should digest out of New York and Washington. As the saying goes, "You can fool some of the people some of the time but not all the people all the time."

April 5, 1972
STILL GOING STRONG

I see the war protesters are still raising a bit of heck in Washington. Now, they chain themselves together to get attention. I also see where a couple fellows were killed over the past week in Vietnam. I don't intend to condone the Vietnam situation, but I wonder how many died on the highways last week in our nation.

One would think the demonstrators would really get to something with some meat in it like the 700 who died in auto accidents in one day on our highways last July 4. These figures should give them something really super special to chain themselves together about.

* * *

SOMETHING DIFFERENT

As most everyone knows, we have a new piano and organ store in our city of West Fargo. Saturday I was in to see Obert Tenold, the owner and manager, and was plumb intrigued by a new electric organ he just got into his place. Turn a switch and you have all kinds of rhythm. No work at all. I used to play the drums and no one ever invented anything like that for me.

* * *

LET THEM STAY THERE

There is much talk about letting our draft dodgers come home from foreign countries. Of course, I'm a little tough about this. Remember these are guys who left when the going got rough under the guise of saying the war was not right.

I can say this much... I sure wouldn't want these fellows protecting my back if we were invaded from two sides at once.

I say no thought should be given to their return until every prisoner of war is home.

May 10, 1972

A week ago I had an opportunity to meet and visit a short time with Chet Reiten. Chet, as I'm sure you already know, is seeking the Republican nomination for Governor of North Dakota. At this time he is mayor of Minot but he is covering thousands of miles of the state countryside visiting with the people of North Dakota

In my book, he has all the qualifications for governor. I am not going into his background, but rather give you my impression of the man as I see him.

He is a man who has made his own way – what he is today he has earned. Being born on a farm has given him a basic philosophy, not only about life but what it's like to work hard with one's hands. A college degree in agriculture has given him an important foundation to work from, if he is to have the highest office in our state. Making good in the business world of our state impresses me, as this will help him in decisions where our cities bump up against our farm and cattle people.

He explained that after being married he and his wife had moved ten times in eleven years. Any wife who would put up with this many moves has to be someone special. I'm convinced his wife, Joy, must be one of these people.

A final note – he appears to me to be a man of great common sense, and I would say an asset like this is hard to find.

June 7, 1972
ABOUT "THE KID" AND THE COLLIE

Saturday was a special day at our house. "The kid" took the collie pup that has suddenly grown into a full grown small elephant out for a walk. This isn't anything unusual on the surface of this little story, but it doesn't stop there. "The kid" decided that a nice walk or run in the big park across the river would be just the thing. All went well until another dog showed up... on the other side of the river. The collie being interested only in making friends took one big leap and ended up in the

Sheyenne River. Cold and bedraggled, she was pulled from the river and, of course, "the kid" had a problem... the dog was one big bundle of wet mud and something had to be done.

Ma and Pa not being home, that problem was handled in the normal way at our house. If you are dirty, you get into the bathtub. The dog being sort of "people" at our house, what could be more natural than that the dog should be put into the tub.

After the bath you can't put the animal outside, so she stays inside. In fact, the dog is much smarter than anyone living at our house... she proved it by moving right in and taking over the living room carpet... she proved it by moving upstairs to "the kid's" bedroom... and was still proving it the next morning when I peeked into "the kid's" room only to find the dog in bed, all four feet up in the air with her head on the pillow. Incidentally, the little girl pal, Mary Walz, that "the kid' had invited to stay overnight, ended up on the floor in a sleeping bag.

I thought I had seen and heard the last of that adventure until I got into the bathtub Sunday morning. That darn dog sure must have dragged in at least half the sand from the river and, believe me, also the scratchiest sand...

* * *

VACATION

Last Wednesday for the first time in five years the Withams decided to take five days off. Yep, and I must say for the first 500 miles yours truly, in his mind, was still in West Fargo at the *Pioneer* office. (I don't know why I worried as things went along very well without me.)

In our travels we visited Buffalo Bill Historical Center in Cody, WY. Anyone traveling this summer in the direction of Cody must take two hours off and go through the museum. This is truly a beautiful insight on the old west as it really was. In my opinion it is the best of its kind picturing early days of the west.

August 9, 1972

"What is a Fargo Forum?" This question came from a little fellow entering Stop and Go Sunday morning to buy what his mom told him to buy.

I must mention this the next time I talk with Bill Marcil, publisher of the *Forum*.

* * *

BE THERE NEXT MEETING!

I had a visit with Barney Dirks, president of our local Chamber of Commerce, this week concerning attendance at our once-a-month evening Chamber meetings. We all know it is easier to stay home or go to the lakes the evening of the meeting, but it is more important to be in attendance. Our city is growing faster than any other city in North Dakota. Things are going on of great importance to the future of West Fargo. Come to the meetings; there are things you have to say and things to be done. The Chamber of Commerce of West Fargo needs your ideas. Only in this way can we have the kind of city we want to live in and have our children grow up in. Keep in mind the next meeting – August 15, 7:30 p.m. at the M & J Steakhouse.

* * *

SPOTS ON MY CAR

Walking out the front door of the *Pioneer* office last Friday, I noted about ten thousand little black spattered spots all over my nice, newly washed blue car. Boy, was I disgusted and started wiping madly to see if they would come off. I breathed a sigh of relief as they began to disappear one by one under the rubbing of my thumb. As I stepped back from the car to observe my thumb work, Gerry Walz inquired as to why I was so concerned about someone else's car. I turned around to answer her and noted my car standing across the street.

September 6, 1972
SIDEBURNS! WHO, ME?!

My wife told me the other day that I looked old-fashioned because I don't wear sideburns. Now I never thought much of anything could improve my looks. When you're born with a "hang-dog" look there is very little you can do to escape what God put there.

Like this past Saturday night... I went overboard with a bright red shirt and white tie. I thought things were pretty classy until I took off the shirt and discovered my red shirt had quite a determined nature because my undershirt, shorts and a few other items had also turned red.

Anyway, it took my wife about a year to get me into a red shirt, so I suppose one of these days I'll be sporting sideburns. We "old bucks" will do anything to spruce up a bit. After all, I'm still not too old to notice a well-turned ankle.

October 4, 1972

Monday morning I couldn't figure out why my razor wouldn't shave my whiskers. I strongly suspected "the kid" had been up to something again. Sure enough, I find my razor cleans her fish tank just fine. Just think... when "the kid" goes away to college, my razors will always be sharp, the radio will play good music again, I can watch my favorite TV shows, the cat won't get her tail pulled, the dog will depend on me to play with her, the mom of the house won't have to be so quick on the draw, and I will probably grow old and fat and bored.

* * *

Talk about COME HOME, AMERICA, the people in our nation had better wake up to what our congressmen in Washington are doing and bring them home and I MEAN FOR GOOD.

Now here's a tidbit for all of us to chew on.

Congress is never on the side of cutting taxes when it comes to spending on ITSELF. In the past five years it has almost doubled its own annual budget. It used to be 180 millions; now it is 300 millions. All this goes to bigger staffs, higher wages, better pensions. Staff salaries up to $40,000, pensions can go up to $34,000, members' salaries $42,000 plus fringes, and most likely up to $50,000. Two new office buildings, parking garage which will cost 133 millions. A new rug $32,000, drapes $22,000, and, of all things, chandeliers at $45,000. Now keep in mind, all this is to go into one room where House members lounge... CLOSED TO THE PUBLIC.

November 1, 1972

Next Tuesday several million Americans will take that most important trip to the polls to cast their vote for many and assorted politicians who will either be voted in or out of office.

It has always been our privilege to cast a vote. If the majority doesn't like what is being done, we go to the polls and throw the rascals out. Let us hope we still value our freedom enough to go to the polls.

I am afraid Americans today — especially young Americans — cannot understand what freedom really is. How can one understand what not having freedom is when they have never really been without it.

IF WE DON'T VOTE WISELY WE MAY ALL SOMEDAY HAVE THE UNHAPPY EXPERIENCE OF LEARNING WHAT FREEDOM IS ALL ABOUT BECAUSE IT WON'T BE HERE ANYMORE.

December 13, 1972

Saw the old movie, *The African Queen,* the other night on TV. As the movie progressed, I kept wondering why they can't make a movie like that nowadays. I guess the producers are as smart today as they were when *The African Queen* was produced. The only thing I can figure is that people who go to movies now are willing to put up with second class productions.

I might add that I think sex is here to stay but the movies today beat everyone to death with it.

* * *

LIFE

The end of this month will see the end of a magazine that has been around most of the lives of the people in our own home town. *Life* magazine will come to an end December 29.

It isn't that I have been a regular subscriber, but I guess during the years of its existence I have always taken every opportunity to read it. They say they could not battle TV which presents, in a way, the same thing that *Life* did... a series of pictures. Where *Life* has been up-to- the-week, TV is up-to-the-minute. All this, in combination with postal rate hikes, dictated the magazine's death.

While we're on postal rates, I might mention that every delivery service which handles any kind of packages or mail does so at considerably less cost to the customer and at the same time makes money. How the post office can continue to lose money by charging exorbitant rates must take at least a thousand experts.

November 15, 1972

Well, things were sure hoppin' around here at the office for a few minutes Friday about 3 p.m. Our gal Edna Lutes who writes the news from the senior citizens fell as she was crossing the street to bring in her news for the week. I might add that just as we were patching up two badly scraped knees, we had a three-car accident at the stoplight on the corner. Roger, our editor, was running to get a picture of the accident as I was running to get the car to take Edna to the clinic.

So goes life at the *Pioneer*.

* * *

SAME OLD STUFF

I note this week our nationwide news media, as in the past, again only told half the truth. Not that the part they did tell was a lie. It is just that they only paint half the picture... the half they want the public to see. I am speaking here of all the news about the arms the U.S. is shipping into Viet Nam. Our papers across the nation have been full of pictures and articles about the big build-up.

NOT ONE MENTION, HOWEVER, ABOUT THE BIG BUILD-UP NORTH VIET NAM IS BRINGING DOWN THE HO CHI MIN TRAIL!

* * *

CATCH THAT BALL!

For the first time this past weekend I saw a professional football game. Yep, went to Minneapolis to see the Vikings play the Lions. Stayed at a motel close to the stadium. Friends met us at the motel Saturday.

I must say that all the happenings from beginning to end were a big adventure for this country boy. In fact, I proved I hadn't been much of any place at all for several years because I proceeded to take the wrong road to Minneapolis. One would think that with only a couple of big roads leading to Minneapolis you could hardly miss. It wasn't easy... but I missed it. I took a road out of St. Cloud that I thought would be "peachy" and ended up driving all the way in on a single lane highway.

December 20, 1972
A GOOD NOTE

Walked out of the office Saturday and there was a young fellow putting a note on a car window. He asked me if I knew the car's owner. I told him I didn't and then he informed me he had hit the car with his car and wanted to let the owner of the car know what he had done. The damage was so slight I could hardly notice and surely the owner wouldn't have noticed for weeks.

In any case, it just goes to show we can be proud of our young people. They still "think" and they still "care."

* * *

WHERE ARE THESE CLOTHES?

It has been my intention for some time to get "the kid" to pick up her clothes when she comes home from school, or any place else for that matter. There are always shoes in one place, coat in another, hat in the corner and a little of everything everywhere. Lately, I was sure I had her stopped for sure. I carried every bit of clothes she left on the chairs or floor right down to the basement and put them in a large box.

Now I find she is happy about the whole situation because she always knows where to find her clothes.

January 31, 1973
RING, RING, RING

For years I have been grinning to myself when I pick up the phone book and see below the names of J.D. Wagner or John T. Brown a children's phone number listed. I always thought what a waste to have two separate numbers to one house.

Over the past months I have begun to learn just what it is to have a teenager in the house. They hang on the phone until you have to chase them off. They get mad and are going to leave home when you limit them on the phone. What is worse, as soon as they hang up, the phone rings and it is someone calling them back. It would be a real pleasure to tell all those cute young things who call that they have the wrong number.

Never know, someday I may be able to afford two phones. By that time, "the kid" will be grown and gone and this old man will be lonesome as heck.

* * *

IT'S HER DAY

Really out-did myself one day this past week.

Yes sir, it happened to be my wife's birthday. Not that I wasn't reminded in certain subtle ways. And not once did I come right out and mention that she was now only a year younger than I. The only thing I said was "Happy birthday" as she was putting the coffee on the stove in the morning. Also said it again as she was buttering my toast. And I gave her a little pat where it would do the most good as she was making the bed. All these little things tend to keep a wife happy and in a good mood as she struggles into her coat at 8 a.m. to go out into the cruel world to earn her share of the living. Yes, ma'm, I'm for women's lib when it comes to earning the living part.

However, as the day wore on I began to get the drift that my happy birthday salutations were not going to fill the bill and keep the little woman happy completely through one whole birthday. So I broke down and took her out to dinner, gave her a nice new pocketbook (in case she ever has any money to carry around). And you can believe this or not, but I took her to one fine movie (of my choosing, of course).

The sequel to all this, fellows, is if you're going to be spending any money on the little lady, make sure you get in on some of the goodies, you know, like seeing your favorite movie and having a nice, thick steak.

March 7, 1973
PEOPLE MUST BE EATING OUT MORE!

The wife and I were out with friends Saturday night for dinner at one of the local eating places. I must say every guy in town must have decided to take his wife or girlfriend out, because empty tables were sure hard to find. I certainly can understand now why so many new restaurants are going up all over the country. Seems that people just like to eat out more in this day and age.

* * *

NOTE

Orchids to those fellows (and gal) whose good thinking and fast-on-the-draw action saved the West Fargo taxpayers from many a sad day ahead by applying their well laid plans in Bismarck. What I'm talking about is their action, time and work in relation to West Acres staying in our school district.

June 13, 1973
THERE'S A NEW PAPER IN THE CITY

A special note this week to West Fargoans. By now you will have received the *Midweek Eagle* on your doorstep. It comes to you free of charge and is supported by advertisers. The *Midweek* includes Wayne Lubenow, Kay Cann on the arts, and Jim Adelson on sports. We think you will enjoy *Midweek* and its many weekly bargains.

* * *

THOSE! @*)$?@! MACHINES!

A short note here on errors that appear from time to time in the *Pioneer*. Please don't always blame it on the proofreaders because they can't catch everything. What I'm really getting at is we think man has machines to do the work for him and in most cases this is true. However, machines don't always do what they are directed to do. The result is sometimes a "w" that is supposed to be a "y" or an "e." The typesetting machines in our office will not even work off the same electrical line. A speck of dirt at the right place means a repairman has to call on us. We discovered recently that one of our overhead lights was too bright; the photomachine was picking up the light and giving us wrong letters in the type. At times, the machine we call a reproducer will make a short line in a column or a long line or leave the line out entirely. This really gives us a headache because we don't know if the machine that sets the copy is causing the trouble or the machine that is receiving the copy is the troublemaker. All in all, it is just one of life's challenges and we at the *Pioneer* take it all in good order. So if at times you see a letter upside down and backwards you can just say… that damn machine did it again.

July 4, 1973
OUR HATS ARE OFF TO HORACE

This past week a little city by the name of Horace, N.D., became a hundred years old. I say "city" because, Friday, Saturday and Sunday Horace was not any ordinary little town of a couple hundred people. It came to life in an unmistakable manner. There were dances, softball games, a queen's coronation, kiddy carnival and kiddy parade, rope pull, donkey baseball, pie eating contest, candlelight Mass, square dancing, old time dance, barbecues and these are just some of the things that went on.

I want to say right here that I have never seen anything better organized. Schedules were met, places to go plainly marked, and everyone of the committees knew what was going on and where it was to happen.

A special note here in relation to the parade. In my estimation, it was just excellent. The old cars, steam engines, horses, the gauchos from Fargo, the covered wagons, all helped to make it one heck of a parade.

Little Horace, we all take our hats off to you. We at the *Pioneer* consider it a privilege and an honor to have been invited to take a part in your 100th birthday.

* * *

QUACK, QUACK

Came home last week and three ducks were swimming around in the sink. Fourteen kids were standing around watching them swim as though they thought it a wonder of nature. I pointed toward the door and cried, "Out." Kids and ducks were soon on the way. I know what became of the kids, but where in heck did the ducks go? I'm afraid to ask, so will just let it go as one of those things that happen to all fathers.

August 1, 1973
ORCHIDS TO OUR FIRE DEPARTMENT

I was talking to Dick Fisher, general manager of Siouxland Dressed Beef, at Rotary. We were discussing the recent fire which had occurred at the plant and Dick indicated he thought the damages could be around $200,000. He was quick to comment, however, that if it had not been for the quick work of the West Fargo Fire Department and the willing help of men who work in the plant he thought it was possible that the whole plant could have been destroyed.

So, orchids again to our West Fargo Fire Department.

September 19, 1973
ROSES FROM WIFE CREATE PROBLEM TO BICYCLIST

Last week Otto Olsgaard's wife beat him to the draw.

On their 25th wedding anniversary she sent him flowers. They arrived at his desk at the bank in the afternoon and he sat there a little perplexed as to how he was going to get them home. Otto happens to be a bicycle enthusiast and rides back and forth to work each day. If I had only known all this was going to happen there would have been a picture in my column this week. I have never seen the vice president of a bank bicycling down the street balancing a dozen roses without their being crushed. In fact, I have never seen a vice president bicycling down the street with any kind of roses.

October 3, 1973
LIKE THEY SAY: LIFE IS WHAT YOU MAKE IT!

Oh, to be eighty. I always tell my wife... Don't sell the old boy short; he knows what's going on before it happens. We don't have many people around our house older than yours truly, but about once or twice a month my wife's dad visits. Freddie, as I call him, is nudging eighty, has a quick step and, in fact, when he really gets out on the road can just about out-walk any young whippersnapper in Barnesville, Minn. That's where Freddie was a depot agent for 45 years, or more, for all I know.

Freddie runs his own house in Barnesville, does his own cooking (and is getting fat) and about once a year falls into the basement on his way to check the basement drains. A rubdown with liniment and he is on his way again. He is completely indestructible; always takes a couple of "headers," as he calls them, every winter when he hits a slick spot on his way to the VFW for a "short one." It's a strange thing – when he takes a "header" it's always on the way there and never when he is coming back. Must remember that when I'm eighty. Better yet, I think I'll have the "short one" going both ways and then I'll never take a "header."

Took Freddie to the Galaxy in Barnesville a couple of weeks ago and I'll be darned if all the gals didn't flock around. Seems that Freddie can really shake a mean leg on the dance floor. My tongue was hanging out and my eyes crossed after a few times around the floor. Falling into my chair, I glanced out at the dance floor over my tall glass of ice water only to see Freddie on his umpteenth dance with the biggest grin on his pan you ever saw.

Was down to see Freddie last Saturday and, by garsh, the old boy had the brightest and shiniest teeth you ever saw. Guess he just plumb wore out the old set and is now practicing with the new set getting ready for a big, juicy steak that he hopes his son-in-law will come across with one of these days. Forgot to mention that he also bought a brand new red sportscoat to go with the teeth. That's another thing I must keep in mind when I reach his age – flashy teeth and a new red sportscoat go well together. Might mention here awhile back we visited friends at Pelican Lake. Freddie went along to see that nobody drowned. The lake was too darn cold so Freddie was the only one who ended up swimming in the lake. "Water's mighty fine," he kept saying, as he used a combination breast stroke, American crawl, side stroke, with a few whale-like rolls in the water thrown in.

December 12, 1973
CANADA: "AMERICANS ARE MOST GENEROUS"

The following is a clipping from the *Aberdeen News*, South Dakota.

I am including this in my column because many times we take for granted our relations with Canada. I think there are instances when she disagrees with us if for no other reason than to let us know she is there. And isn't it wonderful that only a peace garden lies between us? May our friendship last beyond a thousand years!

"LET'S HEAR IT FOR U.S."

Several months ago the *American News* published an editorial that had been broadcast from Toronto by Gordon Sinclair, a Canadian radio and TV commentator. It was offered to our readers as a morale builder at a time when bad news appeared to be getting great emphasis. Since that time it has appeared in many publications, including the *U.S. News and World Report* which offered it recently as a guest editorial. Several *American News* readers have requested that it be printed again. Here it is:

> *This Canadian thinks it is time to speak up for the Americans as the most generous and possibly the least appreciated people on all the earth.*

Germany, Japan and, to a lesser extent, Britain and Italy were lifted out of the debris of war by Americans who poured in billions of dollars and forgave other billions in debts. None of these countries is today paying even the interest on its remaining debts to the United States.

When the franc was in danger of collapsing in 1956, it was the Americans who propped it up, and their reward was to be insulted and swindled on the streets of Paris.

I was there. I saw it.

When distant cities are hit by earthquakes, it is the United States that hurries in to help. This spring, 59 American communities were flattened by tornadoes. Nobody helped.

The Marshall Plan and the Truman Policy pumped billions upon billions of dollars into discouraged countries. Now newspapers in those countries are writing about the decadent, warmongering Americans.

I'd like to see just one of those countries that is gloating over the erosion of the United States dollar build its own airplanes.

Come on, let's hear it!

Does any other country in the world have a plane to equal the Boeing Jumbo Jet, the Lockheed Tristar or the Douglas 10?

If so, why don't they fly them? Why do all the international lines except Russia fly American planes?

Why does no other land on earth even consider putting a man or woman on the moon?

You talk about Japanese technocracy, and you get radios. You talk about German technocracy, and you get automobiles.

You talk about American technocracy, and you find men on the moon – not once but several times – and safely home again.

You talk about scandals, and the Americans put theirs right in the store window for everybody to look at.

Even their draft dodgers are not pursued and hounded. They are on our streets, and most of them – unless they are breaking Canadian laws – are getting American dollars from Ma and Pa at home to spend here.

When the railways of France, Germany and India were breaking down through age, it was the Americans who rebuilt them. When the Pennsylvania Railroad and the New York Central went broke, nobody loaned them an old caboose. Both are still broke.

I can name you 5,000 times when the Americans raced to the help of other people in trouble. Can you name me even one time when someone else raced to the Americans in trouble?

I don't think there was outside help even during the San Francisco earthquake.

Our neighbors have faced it alone, and I'm one Canadian who is damned tired of hearing them kicked around.

They will come out of this thing with their flag high. And when they do, they are entitled to thumb their nose at the lands that are gloating over their present troubles.

I hope Canada is not one of these.

January 9, 1974
IT AIN'T REALLY TRUE

I'll bet because you haven't seen my column in the past two issues you thought you got rid of me for good. Not so, now that the big Christmas – New Year's rush is over. I'm right back on the corner checking for anything that might be of interest to my fellowman.

One thing I have to get off my chest right away (and I'm sorry I didn't write this four weeks ago when I first thought of it) and that is, I don't believe we really have an oil shortage. It is my feeling it is all a farce. I don't claim to be all-knowing, but deep down I have a strong suspicion there is a lot of music being played for us common folks. It is all a matter of our dancing to the tune the big oil companies and our government want us to dance to. Don't get me wrong; I'm not talking about the local gas pump operator. He's just as bad off as the rest of us.

* * *

KEEP AN EYE OUT!

Last week a fellow asked me to put a note in my column concerning kids in West Fargo running out between cars. Cars on the streets cannot stop in a few feet nowadays – too much ice everywhere. Also a note to you moms… dress them in colors the motorist can see easily in the daylight or dark. Remember, the kids will be going to school pretty much in the dark because of the time change.

February 6, 1974
ELECTION

In a few short weeks we will again go to the polls to elect our mayor. I would like to put my word in here for our present mayor, Clayton Lodoen. I have no way of knowing at this time if his intentions are to run again or not. However, I do know that no one works harder for the interests of our city than Mr. Lodoen and I'm sure sometimes at the expense of his own business.

* * *

Listening to our vicar's sermon last Sunday convinced me he has a point. He noted that there seems to be continual misunderstanding between a great number of parents and children. Johnny being picked up on a barbiturate charge, Mary running without her parents' blessing with a boy of questionable reputation, young Susie always complaining of not getting everything she wants.

Our vicar explained that there should be a school to train young people just married about how they should take care of their children when they come. We think nothing of taking golf lessons, or bridge lessons, but no one thinks of lessons on how to be a good father and mother.

March 6, 1974

Last week I had a field day because I happen to have a column and, of course, I can put anything in here I want (that is if my wife isn't looking over my shoulder). Last week she wasn't, so I went ahead and told the world what a wonderful alderman I would make for our big city of West Fargo Industrial Park. With all this power at my fingertips a guy kinda gets carried away, so I thought I ought to at least recognize that Charles Holter, Robert Winge, Mrs. Olmsted, Bruce Brubaker and Earl Sternberg are also running for the same post. Some are running for two years and others are running for four years. Your truly naturally is running for four years. There was a time I thought I should only run for two years because I wouldn't have as much time to get into trouble that way. But then again I figure I might as well be hung for a sheep as a lamb, so I'm going whole hog... let the tail go with the hide, as my Uncle Ross used to say.

* * *

THIS IS NOT FUNNY

Last Friday I was having a tire changed at Selland Motors when I struck up a conversation with the foreman. He showed me a car that had been sitting on their lot for three days. He happened to be concerned because there were a lot of eggs and butter in the car. On informing the lady who owned the car of the situation because of spoilage, she said she didn't care because she had lots more at home. The lady in question happened to be on welfare.

I was also concerned when watching the *Today Show* on Friday morning to see a fellow come out of the Hearst food give-away program for the poor with a sack of food under his arm and climb into a late model car and drive away.

Some give blood that others might have chicken whether they need it or not.

March 20, 1974
STREAKING IS NOTHING NEW

I have been watching and reading all about streakers the past few weeks and their "comings and goings," as the saying goes. Why, gee whiz, those kids think they got something. But just between you and me I have never seen so many knobby knees and hairy legs, and what really gets me is no hair on the chest. And I'll say something else right here while the typewriter is hot… I've been streaking from the bedroom to the bathroom at six-thirty every morning for about 50 years and no one ever took my picture!

April 10, 1974
THEY'LL HAVE TO PUT UP WITH ME FOR FOUR YEARS!

Running for an office can be a tiring thing, that is if you put anything into running. There is another way, however – move to a town that can be covered in 25 minutes on foot.

Now I didn't intentionally move to West Fargo Industrial Park to run for office, but now that I'm there it is kinda nice to know most all the folks in your town. In any case, I have a big announcement. As of last week I am now an alderman. Yep, for the first time in my life I'm in politics. Beat out my neighbor by one vote.

* * *

THIS CAN'T BE SO

Your pants are too short," said "the kid" to me the other morning. "Nope," I said, " I just had them cleaned and that makes pants shorter." "Nope," said Mrs. Witham, "the stomach is getting bigger... "

June 12, 1974
NEW VFW BUILDING

I had a pleasant surprise Monday afternoon. Paul Vance, who was Commander of our local VFW last year and is Vice Commander in the state this year, showed me around our new West Fargo VFW. I would venture to say that there isn't any better VFW Post building in the whole darn country. I was also surprised to learn they have 505 members, and that is nothing to look down on in our town. Better drop by and take a look. You will be proud to know what an excellent job is being done. Incidentally, they are open for business. Take the wife or girlfriend by to see what is going on. You won't be sorry.

July 31, 1974
SPEEDBOATS AND MY SAY

So there I sat all weekend watching the fancy speedboats going by and wondering why in the world anyone would want to hang on (for dear life) to a skinny little rope with his foot stuck into a six-foot piece of board. The heck of it was when I finally set down my cheap can of beer for a quick dive into the lake, the water was so churned up I couldn't tell it from a mud puddle.

Now I really don't mind those fancy speedboats if they stay out in the lake where old men like me don't swim. I do, however, have a vivid picture of losing my head by being run over by a speedboat just when I am surfacing from my dive into four feet of water. Not that there is a heck of a lot up there to lose, but I would like to keep what little I have for a few years yet.

What really burns me up about the guy who runs around the lake in a speedboat is the way he goes swishing by making all those big waves just when I have a nibble on my sunfish line. A couple of weeks ago I was

– 72 –

out on Little Cormorant trying to catch a couple dozen sunfish. Here comes a guy in a big old boat and darn near bounced me right out of the boat. It would have been much nicer if he had cruised by in a beautiful sailboat and I might have said, "A very good day to you, sir."

I don't want to appear here in print as a stick in the mud about fun on the lake, but I do think the sailboat over the speedboat is the coming thing. It doesn't kick up a lot of water or scare the fish. It takes advantage of the God-made thing called wind and saves on gas. It is quiet and serene and doesn't grate on the nerves... and best of all costs little or nothing after the original investment. I won't say the darn thing won't turn over in the water, but that is where the challenge comes in. If you can stay afloat and get where you want to go just by your own skill and ingenuity, you can call yourself an extra special person. Not everyone can make progress against wind and tide so that at the other end of the trip you can say, "By garsh, I'm pretty good."

Now that I have had my say about boats, I'll climb down off my soapbox, pick up my inexpensive can of beer (note I said "inexpensive"), lay back on my beach chair and let the motors roar.

September 11, 1974
IT'S NO RUMOR, WE HAVE A PRESS

To put rumor and speculation to rest, it gives me great pleasure to announce that in the not too distant future the *West Fargo Pioneer* and *Midweek Eagle* will be printed on our own press located right here in West Fargo.

Yes, we have worked hard to have the opportunity to write the foregoing sentence. However, the people who have had the most at stake here are the West Fargo businessmen. They supported a little struggling 8-page paper in 1967, when many a day even I wondered if the darn thing was ever going to breathe on its own. I guess they figured that if the city was ever going to be a city and not a suburb, they would need some kind of communication, and the *Pioneer* was the only thing they could think of at the time. In any case, I wanted to put the credit where it is deserved. I hope we have done the job... at least most of the time.

Our new press will be housed in a building in the new Westgo complex just west of town. It is a Goss Community web press and will be capable of printing a 16-page paper.

Always With'em

At this time they are installing and lining up the press. This should be completed within the next two weeks. Shortly thereafter our new, late model press... the first of its kind to be located in West Fargo and in the Fargo-Moorhead metropolitan area... will be off and running.

We at the *Pioneer* and *Midweek* are practically busting our buttons!

October 2, 1974

I ran into the good old American way this past week.

To make our copy stick to what we call paste-up sheets, we have to use a machine that will coat one side of the paper with wax. Naturally, we call it a waxer, and it is a little machine that is almost impossible to get along without!

To come to the point, the little machine is beginning to have thermostat trouble and that is where our trouble begins. I thought it would merely be a call to the local repairman at the company where we bought the machine. "Simple," said the voice on the other end of the line, "when the repairman comes to town I'll send him over." "When will he be coming to town?" says I. "Should be here within a week or two," repeated the pleasant voice. That two weeks turned into two months and we were still waiting for that man to come by and fix our little machine.

As time went by our waxer began to turn a very cold shoulder toward putting the usual smooth coat on each sheet of paper. In desperation I called the home office in Minneapolis where I met with all kinds of proper phone answering and overflowing efficiency. I finally ended up with a sexy voice giving me figures like I never had heard before.

"It will cost $215.00 for the repairman's trip up there – plus 15 cents a mile," she says. "Of course, that doesn't figure in the man's time spent on the machine."

"Holy smokes," I said, "I only paid $300.00 for the darn machine in the first place. Incidentally, how much does a new one cost?" "$450.00," came the reply.

Somehow her voice didn't seem half as sexy as I wrote down that last figure.

February 5, 1975
WITHAM JOINS WINTER DAREDEVILS

One would think that I would never miss a chance to tell the world what I think each week. I have a surprise for you… I plumb forgot all about my column this week. So this only proves that I'm human… not perfect by a long shot… still human.

When I was supposed to be writing for this corner, I must confess that I was in the ditch instead. One of the embarrassing points is that I pride myself in being a careful driver and, of course, I carry this same kind of caution to the 16-year-old daughter in no uncertain terms. The cause of my sojourn in the ditch was just plain forgetting that I was driving a high-speed car and not checking to see how icy the road was before I gave the footfeed that extra push.

I did get off lucky. Not a scratch on me or the car, but a definite dent in the right door, which I went to great pains to hide from my daughter. However, "the truth will out" as she heard me explaining over the phone to a friend of mine my great thrill of the day. The result, Monday night with every phone conversation my daughter had with ALL her friends (and I must say there were plenty of phone conversations) the big news of the day was, "Say, did you know my dad went in the ditch with the car and put a big dent in the door." I kept yelling, "It is not a big dent," but it doesn't seem to interrupt a thing, so word is out to the whole world.

If you're going to put a dent in the car and you have a 16-year-old daughter, fix it before you get home.

April 16, 1975
AN OFFICE OF MY OWN

In all the years I have been involved in the newspaper business, I have never had an office of my own. There was a time when I almost had an office, but when I checked the checkbook I found that paying the rent was probably more important. However, I must qualify the first sentence and say that the office isn't quite all mine. Our editor, Craig McEwen, really is the moving spirit in the whole affair. I would probably have gone on for years and never given it a thought until he brought up the subject. So he and a good friend of his got together and built the darn thing over the weekend. Craig said he was going to get away from Dusty, the office mascot, even if he had to build an office around his desk to keep that darn tomcat out. So I'm quite honored by the whole procedure to be included in the tomcat "keeper-outer."

May 21, 1975
A HELPING HAND

Orchids to the Fargo Post Office.

Last Thursday night some very important printing had to be delivered around the state by Friday. In desperation I rushed to UPS, but it was no go from there. However, they did take one box. I had 19 more to get out. We called the Fargo Post Office and they told us if we could be there by nine p.m. they would do their best. When we arrived, two very nice guys with the word "foreman" on their shirts came up to us. In that we had no postage and the windows were closed for the night, they put their heads together and came up with an idea. They would take money from one of their tills in exchange for my check, then in turn would use the bills in the change machine and then put them in the stamp machine and paste the stamps on the boxes. These fellows stuck right with us, even to the point of putting the money in the stamp machines and counting and pasting the stamps on the boxes. We made the deadline only because these fellows took the time and went the extra mile to help a guy in need. The Fargo Post Office can be well proud of these men. They were pleasant and cheerful throughout the whole ordeal.

June 4, 1975
THIS HAS GOT TO GO!

I am being told that the smell from the city sanitation lagoon is being cared for in the proper manner and that we should not be entertained by said smell in the future. It has always been my impression that a lagoon, when operated like it should be, does not smell. Now I may be wrong… maybe it is supposed to stink up the whole city. However, I do hope they have things in hand "smell-wise" by the time the VFW State Convention arrives here on Friday. I'm sure if we still have our lagoon aroma whirling about their noses they might just rename our city… and I'm sure it wouldn't be a name we could put on a signboard at the edge of town.

August 13, 1975
NO MORE GRASS!

The flood came and the flood left and took my backyard right along with it. What's left is absolutely nothing. Six feet of my backyard by now must be way up in Canada. The ground dried up and big cracks appeared. I must say, I don't think much will grow there for a year or two. However, I remember when a relative of mine lost two of his cows in the sweet clover after they ate too much. "There is never so much bad about anything but what there is some good. Now I don't have to milk them" It's about the same with me; now I don't have to mow the lawn for the next two years.

October 1, 1975
KINDA BROUGHT FORTH A TEAR

If you are a football fan you might have watched the Saturday game between Texas A&M and Illinois. The half time was taken up by the Texas A&M band. I understand it is one of the largest bands in the nation. What really stopped me were the haircuts. Yep, it took me back to the forties and fifties again. Each band member slick as a whistle. The marching, of course, was excellent and completely military. Kind of gave me a catch in my throat to see all that polish and the flourish of flags.

October 29, 1975
AND WE NEVER GAVE UP

I'm sure quite a portion of people in Pioneerland remember times and places of the hard time years of the nineteen thirties. I bring this to your memory because of the great changes that have occurred over the years since those times when maybe after working in the fields all week long, our fathers were just barely able to give us fifty cents. That wasn't spending money but a form of pay for the week's work. Dad and I cut hay from one o'clock in the morning until five because we couldn't stand the heat of the day. The hot winds blew for weeks on end without bringing rain of any sort to soak the cracked land. Corn planted in the spring failed to come up until the first rain in the fall. Winter's heavy snows reached almost to the top of the telephone poles. Cattle were fed thistles to keep them alive in hopes of grass in the spring to renew their lives.

Always With'em

I remember when lights had to be turned on in daytime in the streets of Britton, S.D., because the blowing sand blacked out the sun. I can still see the thistles rolling and tumbling across the land, piling up against the fences and holding the blowing sand so that even the fences were buried. My high school class ring would have cost five dollars, but there was no money to buy it. The horses were too poor to pull any kind of a heavy load. Their ribs showed through sagging skin. Grasshoppers darkened the sky, so thick was their passing. They ate everything, even making pitchfork handles rough to the touch because of their taste for salt from sweating hands. Rivers and channels across the landscape were devoid of water for months on end. To this day, when I cross a bridge, I always look to see if there is water passing underneath. Just a habit from the days of the thirties when the only sure crop was thistles and kids.

January 4, 1976
HOW MANY PAGES

Last Tuesday's *Forum* being ten pages, I mentioned this to my wife in that the *Pioneer* was 20 pages.

"Yeah," she said, "but they got those ten pages in one day and it took you seven."

I didn't say much about that remark, but there must be a lesson in there somewhere.

March 10, 1976

You folks who would like to know how the Post Office spends your money, here is just a very small example of how big shots up the line operate. The message has been sent loud and clear from Washington that the post office is plumb out of money and Congress won't give them any more. I can understand why Congress won't give them any more because they have a hard time deciding if they need another water fountain on the tenth floor.

Anyway, here is the story, so read it and weep, folks, because you are the guys who will be paying the bill.

The mailing out of the *West Fargo Pioneer* press over the past year has jumped from a few thousand copies a week to around 160,000 and sometimes as high as 200,000. This kind of mailing, in that it is also very bulky, makes it impossible to be handled in the West Fargo Post Office because there just isn't floor space. The result is, one large truck is sent from the Fargo Post Office to pick up the mailing at the press, by-passing the West Fargo Post Office, and also makes for one handling and quicker service at less cost for the postal service.

HOWEVER, now comes a directive from the big chief up the line, "Can't do that," he says, "because the *West Fargo Pioneer* might cheat the post office out of some mailing weight." How he figures this is one on me and I have yet to find out how it could be done. But anyway, even though we haven't cheated the post office, that doesn't seem to say that sometime in the future we won't, so without further ado everything has to change. Now we are to deliver all of our mailings to the West Fargo Post Office... which in turn will plug the floor space until the doors bulge. The guy who comes to pick up the mail has only a half-ton truck, which will make him run back and forth between Fargo and West Fargo four times. How about the cost of all this in time and travel?

If it weren't for the fact that here in West Fargo we have an exceptionally fine postmaster, I don't know what I would do. Anyway, what I'm trying to point out is, for the overtime and extra hauling in just this one instance, you, Mr. John Q. Public, are going to pay the bill! Multiply this by 10,000 times and now you have some idea of why the post office needs more money.

Wonder if the time will ever come again when the bureaucrats in high government offices will remember that they are public servants... and without little people like you and me kicking in our taxes they wouldn't have a job. And I would like to remind a few of these "hot dog" postal authorities in Chicago and Washington that we do pay postage for their services and we're pretty good customers.

And one more shot – it's my opinion that after a mess like Watergate, and all the reports of wasteful spending in our government, and everything else ordinary Americans have had to swallow the past few years, bureaucrats would be a little more careful who they try to keep from cheating. We don't do business that way... every grocery store that is paying for flyers gets theirs... and postage is paid on every last one of them. In our business when a customer pays us for our services we knock ourselves out to give him the best we have to offer.

April 7, 1976
OL' PA GOT UPSET

I mention here that ol' pa still gets upset when he sees his daughter crying. That very thing happened Sunday afternoon. First, I want to say when you have only one kid I'm sure you get concerned more quickly than if you have five or ten. The wife and I always worry when we see her taking off in her car for some "unknown to us" destination. You keep wondering if all will go well when you see her on her motorcycle. You hold your breath as she skips across the snowdrifts with her snowmobile and you worry plenty when she is on a horse for fear she will land on her head.

So naturally Sunday morning when she left with her boyfriend, her mother wanted to know where she was going. In that he is a carpet layer and had to work on Sunday, her mother said, "Don't go along because you will get in the way. He has to work and he doesn't need you along to foul things up."

Daughters nowadays don't listen as closely as they used to. She did go along; she did get in the way. She fell over a roll of carpet and broke her arm.

May 12, 1976
I WON'T MENTION THAT NAME!

I should really be hurt about this but I'm going to bear up under the situation anyway. Last Sunday's local paper had an article on the Main Street of West Fargo. They mentioned all the businesses but one and you all know which one that is because our business is in the center of that main street. Now I won't hold a grudge but on the other hand I won't use their name either. Ha!

* * *

MOTHER'S DAY

Well, I didn't do a darn thing for Mother on Mother's Day. Not that I hadn't laid the ground work for a present. The heck of it was I couldn't figure out what to give "ol' Mom." So being the practical soul that I am, I up and asked. Know what she said? Of all things, she wanted a tree and of course I thought that was just swell. BUT, being that I waited so long to get it, the time grew so short that I still haven't got the tree. To top it all off, I attempted to take her out for Mother's Day dinner and by the time I got going all the Sunday places that served Mother's Day dinners were closed. I wouldn't say I'm in the doghouse but on the other hand I'm so darn close to it I can hear the dogchain rattle.

* * *

A NUMB BOTTOM

Attended the North Dakota Newspaper Convention over the weekend. Lots of speeches and must say my posterior got so tired I couldn't wiggle. Meetings have never been my forte. When I have to sit for any length of time I sort of shake down into a nondescript lump and my mind refuses to absorb anything but a joke. In any case, I did sit up and take notice when they passed out some very nice awards to our people of the *West Fargo Pioneer.*

August 4, 1976
IGNORE IT AND???

We fellows who are getting a bit thin on top often don't give it much thought until someone diplomatically mentions it to us. However, in that my wife told me one day a few years back that I had always had a slight bald spot where I couldn't see it, I decided right then and there that I would ignore it... hoping of course that as the saying goes, "Ignore it and it will go away." I did just that and, by gosh, it did go away. NOT THE BALD SPOT. ONLY THE HAIR!

What I'm really getting at is in a conversation with Earl Brokofsky, our postmaster, last week we decided it would be quite tricky (in that hairpieces are expensive) if we bought one together. However, we would have to work out our church hours on Sunday morning. One of us would have to go to early church.

* * *

SWEEP, SWEEP, SWEEP

I was sweeping off our front walk one day recently when a fellow drove up and said, "I'll bet I know who you are!" "Who am I?" I said. "You're the boss," he exclaimed, "Only the boss sweeps off the front walk."

I have news for you, Mr. What's Your Name. I not only sweep off the front walk but I also keep the restrooms right up to snuff. In fact, if

I ever come to work and this is all done for me I'll know right then and there that I'm on the way out of the newspaper business because someone will have taken over the company while I was gone.

September 8, 1976
YES, I SAID THE POST OFFICE

Orchids to the postal department! A near disaster in our mailing set-up was avoided by the quick efficient service between West Fargo and Pierre, S.D. A mailing to Pierre on Wednesday arrived there on Thursday. A mistake in printing was discovered and a rerun necessary.

On calling the West Fargo post office we were assured by Earl Brokofsky a rerun mailing would arrive the following Monday. It did, and a serious mistake was corrected before the Tuesday deadline.

November 24, 1976
I LOST THE BATTLE

Thought I would mention this week that the squirrel that has been stealing the birdseed from my feeder has definitely won the battle. I've greased the birdfeeder pole he climbs up. I wrapped the tree in tin so he couldn't jump across from the tree. I sawed off all the limbs so he couldn't swing over the birdhouse and land on the roof. Now he scoots up the nearest tree and runs across to the tree closest to the feeder and drops down from only the good Lord knows where, and always ends up in the birdfeeder.

I have now bought a large sack of peanuts to scatter on the ground. My plan is to get that darn squirrel so fat he can't climb the tree.

* * *

EVERY MAN SHOULD HAVE ONE

I'm sure most of the fellows I know own a special TV chair. Mine happens to be green and just fits what I plunk in there every evening about news time. I love my green TV chair. My wife always knows where to find me, which is one of the weak points of not having wheels on it, but, all in all, I'm happy where it sits.

To go along with every TV chair, a fellow needs things to keep him company. I happen to have a two-tiered end table. It holds my beer stein, both *Time* magazine and *World News*. In a special place I have my "church key" to open stubborn beer bottle caps, fingernail clipper, a comb to keep our long-haired cat happy, eyebrow tweezers to keep my fingernails clean. (They're much better than a fingernail file.) Also, one must never forget to have a box of nice, soft tissues in case a tear-jerker movie comes on. Then, just back of the piano, I keep a handy TV tray.

I can't think of much more an old guy like me needs unless it's a wife to do his cooking and I already have one of those.

February 2, 1977
PRAYER FOR A LONG AND HAPPY LIFE

The demands of each day tend to put pressures on each and every one of us. There are times when I find myself seeming to run a hundred and thirty-two miles per hour into nowhere. Then there are always the bills, taxes, and all the rest of everything in everyday living (including the kids) which grind on our nerves. We, at some time or other, wonder where we should turn next to get out from under these burdens we carry.

I have a card which reposes on my office wall. These words may help. I know not the author, but he has a point!

* * *

PRAYER FOR LONG HAPPY LIFE

Slow me down, Lord. Ease the pounding of my heart by the quieting of my mind. Steady my pace with the vision of the eternal reach of time. Give me, amidst the confusion of my day, the calmness of the everlasting hills. Break thou the tension of my nerves, and with the soothing music of the spring streams that live in my memory, help me to know the magical restorative power of sleep. Teach me the art of taking "minute vacations," slowing down to look at the flowers, chat with the friendly, pat a dog or read a few lines from a good book. Remind me each day of the fable of the hare and tortoise that I may know that the race is not to the swift and that there is more to life than increasing speed. Let me look upward to the towering oak and know that it grows great and strong because it grows slowly. Slow me down, Lord, and inspire me to send my roots deep into the soil of life's enduring values that I may grow toward the stars of my great destiny… in Jesus' Name. Amen

April 27, 1977
LADY GOES EXTRA MILE

I reserved space in the "Always With'em" column this week to pass out a special Orchid. There is a lady in our town who has gone the extra mile and I think West Fargoans should know it.

She has always been available when needed to make calls for all those special meetings we like to have. She has written for clubs, and mimeographed like mad for people who needed everything at the last minute. It was a rare case when she was not at hand to answer questions at ALL Chamber of Commerce get-togethers. In the hot days of the Red River Valley Fair you would find her smiling and pouring water for thirsty people who happened by the Chamber booth. I watched as she patiently put up with a small hot office on our Main Street during the summer and wore sweaters on the cold winter days when those breezes seemed to blow right through the place.

People who worked with her on projects knew everything would go O.K. because things didn't slip by unnoticed. She picked up the loose ends! On top of a five day week and a ridiculous pay scale, she was always pleasant, always had a smile and, most important of all, she was always on time. I can say this for sure: Without her the West Fargo Chamber of Commerce would not be alive. Arlene Franchuk went the extra mile! Arlene is taking a well earned rest, but you know what? If you check around I'll bet a dollar or two you will find her doing something for someone somewhere for nothing!

June 1, 1977
WHO KNOWS

Got a call from *Newsweek* in New York on Tuesday afternoon. Seems the magazine found out that youngsters in the West Fargo schools were testing out Pop Rocks candy. They wanted to know all about what was written in the *Pioneer* and wanted pictures. They didn't promise to use any of this but, who knows, they might and, if they do, you certainly will hear from me!

* * *

IMPORTANT

Don't forget school board election Tuesday, June 7. You will also have an opportunity to vote again to have your school proceedings published. This is important to you who live here and invest in the school district through taxes. KNOW WHERE YOUR MONEY GOES!

July 13, 1977
DO YOU HAVE THE WRONG JOB?

Did you know that every fifth American works for the U.S. government, state or local government? Keep this in mind in case you want to change jobs. These people make on the average of $4,500 more each year than you and I who have to work and worry about making a living and keeping the boss happy. They can retire early, work to get Social Security and collect two retirement incomes for the rest of their lives. They get more sick pay days off than you and I, and longer vacations with pay. Now if you really want to live it up, all you have to do is run for Congress where your pay will be about $57,000 a year or more plus a nice little stipend for your office force of $1.5 million a year. The United States Chamber of Commerce claims this is not true, but what is true is that it's closer to $2.5 million. You also get 26 free trips home each year and lots of other little goodies thrown in to keep you happy. Now if you think your senators or representative deserve all this, why don't you drop each a line and tell him so. I'm sure it will ease his conscience.

September 7, 1977
KIDS, DOGS, GARAGES AND DOOR OPENERS DON'T GO TOGETHER

I have always thought having a door opener for my garage would be just the thing for an old guy like me. Over the years I intended to buy one, but that extra buck never seemed to be there when door openers were on my mind. In the interim of time, "the kid" got a dog, which I thought was swell but, of course, the dog took over the garage. After that came a fence to give the dog running room. One thing led to another and I still don't have my garage door opener.

The main reason is that when the door would open, the dog would come out and when she gets out the whole countryside knows about it because she knocks every kid sixty pounds and under flat. Not that she would ever think of biting them, but that darn dog loves kids. The only way she thinks she can show real love is to knock them flat, then give them a big sloppy kiss across the nose. Of course this scares the kids to death, the parents get all excited, and police are called and yours truly has to start talking himself out of paying a fine. To prevent all this (it happened to me a couple years ago), I now call the police as soon as I find the dog has escaped. Next call is to the sheriff, then all four schools and last, but definitely not least, Bev Walters of KFGO. She knows our dog, Ginger, and also knows what havoc a hundred and twenty pound friendly collie can do in an unsuspecting neighborhood like West Fargo.

In any case, I thought I had better explain why I have no garage door opener. Opening the door without a firm hand on that dog only spells disaster. I do have a way out in the future. "The kid" has bought a lot and I know darn well she will build a house there some day. As far as I'm concerned the sooner the better. I have now saved enough money to have my very own garage door opener. The dog belongs to "the kid" or "the kid" belongs to the dog. I don't know which, but I do know when she builds her house the dog goes! I have explained this to "the kid" and she tells me this is fine but I have to build the dog run. If I do, then I won't have money for my door opener! Kids, dogs, garages and door openers don't go together. I think I'll go next door and talk to my neighbor. He's got a door opener, no kids, and no dogs. He does have a couple of cold beers in the fridge. That I can talk about.

November 2, 1977
A SHOE EXPERIENCE

Recently I have gone into a shoe business, only for myself, that is. I found this super-duper place to order shoes. The advertising said that they have "the best shoes in the world." They said that there was nothing else in the U.S. that even began to come close to their quality... leather lines and all that good stuff.

My super-duper shoes came week before last. They were four sizes too big and the wrong color. Anyone can make a mistake and nothing stops me, so I sent them back and ordered a different design. After all, they might have been completely out of the first pair of shoes I ordered and they certainly would not want me to go barefooted!

In any case I must say they were prompt with their order. I received the second pair of shoes. They were the right color and the right design but were for *two left feet.*

My wife always said I walked like I had two left feet. That guy who picked my shoes sure read her mind.

December 14, 1977
ALL IN ONE DAY

There stood Gordon Spidahl, manager of Gordon's Standard Oil, with a very pained, perplexed look on his face. "Do you want a story?" he says. Well, I'm one guy who's always looking for an extra special story for my private little corner which a few of you people read each week. You will notice, I didn't say a lot of people, but you must bear with me because it's one of the few things I have in life that's really all mine. My bank has most everything else.

To get down to brass tacks, this is what happened to Gordon, all on Friday, mind you.

First, he loaned out his pickup and received a call later from Moorhead. Seems the fellow who borrowed it broke the drive shaft. Second, some fellow who needed air in his tires backed into the west glass section of his front office and pushed in the whole side of the building three feet and, of course, broke all the glass and studs. Third, his new emergency haul truck was sitting waiting for a traffic light to change, a car came from the opposite direction and smashed in the front end, driving the left front wheel under the engine. Fourth, his second emergency truck was out helping someone when they broke the power take-off. How all this could happen to one man in one day is hard to explain.

I really hated to bring up the subject of what I had come to see him about, but in that I have braved the lion in his den many a time before, I put on my best selling air and said, "Gordon, I think what you need is a Christmas ad and a New Year's ad." With that pained and perplexed look still on his face, he said, "I'll take both." As I went out the door, he said in a small voice. "Better make 'em little. After today, I don't think I can afford much for Christmas."

January 4, 1978
THE TRIP BACK

Coming back from Hawaii isn't the same as going over. Going, you are full of happiness and a few other things that you get on the plane. Coming back, you are sunburned and unable to look a pineapple in the face. Also, if you are unlucky enough to get a wiggle wart for a seat partner, getting a catnap is next to impossible. I might mention that you should never take a night flight home from Hawaii. Those seats are not in any way designed for sleeping.

When we boarded, my wife took the window seat. Well, what the heck, who can see anything at night anyway. The third seat was taken by wiggle wart. She also talked, which made it worse. Every time I would doze off she would wake me with some question. She even complained about her dress being too short. She wasn't bad looking so I didn't mind that, but when she put her feet on top of the seat in front of her I about fell out of mine.

One other thing I did bring home that I hadn't expected was the most super cold I have had in years. Anyway, I'm back in the swing of things and from all reports everything on the home front went better than if I had been here. It's heck not to be needed.

* * *

NO MORE WORRY

I note that haircuts have gone to five dollars. However, one can always look at it this way: when haircuts were four fifty, that fifty cent piece could wear a hole in your pocket. Now you won't have to worry about that.

* * *

THE LIGHTS WENT OUT

Last Monday while sitting in my green TV chair, I heard an awful racket in the living room. Having the door closed to keep out the vacuum cleaner noise, all the uproar didn't come through very clear. In that there were a few cuss words thrown in, I thought I had better check things out. I found Mrs. W. looking at the bottom of the vacuum with an "I'll be damned" look on her face. It seems she got too close to the Christmas tree and sucked in twelve feet of Christmas tree lights before she could shut the machine off.

I only made one mistake. I asked, "Why did you do that?"

March 8, 1978
MOVINGEST PAPER

Someone asked me the other day how many times the *West Fargo Pioneer* has moved. It didn't take me long to tell him five times. Not that moving five times is anything special, but I'll bet we're the movingest paper anyone has ever heard of. Five times in ten years is very unusual for a newspaper. However, no matter how many times we have moved and no matter where we moved, people always seemed to find us. That always gives me a good feeling because it means a very important thing to me. It means we're needed and being needed is an important thing in this world today. I'll add another thing. A guy can't help but love a town that sticks with the hometown paper. As I have told many who asked, there's no great amount of money in this business but it sure gets in the blood.

I remember a young lady we had working for us part-time back in 1969, keeping up what few books we needed. She said to me one day, "Don, we have all our bills paid up for this month." I thought that was something special because from the day we started the paper in West Fargo, I always owed someone more money than I could pay. I couldn't resist asking if we had any money left. "Yes," she said, "we have $5.00." I'm sure our business isn't by any means the only business that only had $5.00 left at the end of the month in the history of business, but it sure as hell made an impression on me.

I might mention here that a good wife who works her tail off is worth her weight in gold to a new business. The "gold" part may devalue but it is only because she is losing weight working to keep your business above the flood of bills and collectors that go along with having something you want to call your own.

All in all I note our business has grown primarily because of good and loyal workers. I have been mighty lucky in this category as we still have people with us from the day we opened our doors in 1967. I have learned a lot from our work force over the years. It always gives me a twinge of pleasure and pride when one of our people says to me, "Don, why don't you do it this way? It's quicker and costs less." These are the things that count. The business grows in this kind of atmosphere.

I well remember when we decided to start the *Midweek Eagle*. It was known as the *Moorhead Eagle* to begin with because that's where we laid the groundwork. I'm not going into the blood, sweat and tears route we took on the road to making the *Midweek* what it is today. I can say that many a night I awoke in a cold sweat. I guess the blood and tears came during the day. I didn't have time to stop and take notice.

Our biggest financial step came when we invested in Davon Press, which prints our *Midweek* and *Pioneer*. This part wasn't the big worry because we knew that we had something to put on the press to keep us in business. In any case, we had the impression that it about ended our adventures into the printing world. However, for the past year we have been in the business of printing all the music programs for United States and Canada for Community Concerts out of New York City. This entails some one and a half million programs which, I might add, keeps us with our nose to the grindstone. We also ship the programs to some eight hundred cities, the right programs to the right cities at the right times. We find that there is a big print world out there and we might just be able to compete with some of the best. Of course, that's the impression we like to give ourselves.

You now have a bird's-eye view of our ups and downs in the world of print and newspapers in West Fargo. Who knows what grand adventure might be just around the corner, and we at *Pioneer, Midweek* and Davon Press might just step around and take a look.

July 12, 1978
SPECIAL NOTE

It has always been my contention that good men are hard to find ... more so, kind and honest men. Randy Lindgren, who passed away a week ago, was one of those people. Here was a man who took a real interest in his city and the people who live here. He was also kind to this paper in the early years of its beginning in 1967, many times, I know, advertising when it was more in the interest of the paper than his hardware store. He approached most everyone he came in contact with in the same fashion, always lending a helping hand when needed. He shall be sorely missed.

August 16, 1978
TWO TERMS ENOUGH

Politicians over the years have been held just a little bit in awe by the American public. However, in the last 30 years people are becoming more aware of just what a politician is, and is supposed to do. Education is responsible for some of this new feeling, but I would say TV, radio, and newspapers have brought to the public the facts of what a politician is supposed to represent. This window on the political arena holds in glaring view the good and the bad concerning those we send to Washington.

I can proudly say most of the maneuverings and plain bad conduct exposed have come about through the news media. I think most of us have also suspicioned that, for some reason, being a representative or senator has somehow become a vocation. In my opinion, a senator or representative in Washington is there to serve the people. Some do, but most don't. They go there to make a career out of their post. Keep in mind, a great many have never owned or run a business. Their business is staying in Washington, by hook or by crook, probably more the latter than former.

I have an answer for a lot of the problems. *Limit their terms.* They get too entrenched and too many things come their way too easy after 15 or 20 years. I do think it is wrong that representatives only serve two years. Running for re-election is no easy job when it has to be done every second year. I don't think the representative can settle into his job and do it as he should. I also think six years in office for a senator is too long. Four years are plenty.

And now comes the clincher which could change things in Washington forever (and really give the people in our nation a break). Limit terms to two terms only. Then they should drop out and give someone else a chance. As I said before, being a politician should not be a vocation. I think Ted Kennedy heads this list and 400 others are right behind him.

January 10, 1979
BON-BONS CAUSE VISIT TO VET

Much to my surprise I found out that New Year's Day doesn't necessarily mean that the New Year's celebration is over. We invited Ginger, our big collie, into our nice warm house because she is always so happy to come inside. Of course, we also think she is cute because of the way she looks at us out of big brown eyes, also the way she teases the cat by running her long nose through the cat's fur and then jumping back when the cat takes a swat at her. However, while the dishes were being done in the kitchen, we noticed that Ginger was very, very quiet in the living room. Investigating, we discovered Ginger in the process of licking up the last of the chocolate bon-bons. All went well until the next day when odors began emanating from one collie dog and even Ginger couldn't face it. Seems that what goes in must also come out. It all came out. It was the way it came out that made life challenging for Ginger and all those who got near her. The end result was a trip to the vet where they have a guy who will put up with collie dogs who eat bon-bons. Something sure must have gone on because we didn't see Ginger again for 15 hours. When next we invited her into the house, she came trotting in all fluffed up and beautiful with a big grin on her face just as if nothing at all had happened.

January 31, 1979
DUNCAN WRITES ABOUT LIFE

Recently I read a book, "I REMEMBER," a 128-page book written by Russel Duncan of Fargo. Russel told me his grandchildren were always asking him what things were like when he grew up. Instead of giving a long dissertation on his early life, he decided to write it all down for them to read.

The book starts with his birthday of August 5, 1910. He was born on a farm near Calvin, N.D. From there he explains his early years and experiences on the farm. How he grew up and all the things a little fellow would experience in those years. He reminisces about sickness in the family and what they did in the early years for colds and all the illnesses that we cure in a day or two nowadays.

A quote from the book as a sample:

"My father and I went to town one day shortly before Christmas with a load of grain. I heard my mother and father talking before we left for town. Mother told Dad to cut off a good-sized branch from a tree on our way home. Sure enough, on the way home while I held the lines, Dad went into a clump of trees where he cut off a branch which he put in the sleigh. I had no idea what he wanted that branch for – I was puzzled but didn't say anything.

"When we got home we went out to do chores. When we came in to supper, my mother and the other children seemed especially happy. I wondered why they were so happy. They said, 'Come into the front room.' I went in, and there to my surprise was the branch we had brought home in the sleigh. It was all decorated with different colored crepe paper and pieces of cloth. To me it was beautiful. That was our first Christmas tree. I can remember it as well as though it were yesterday."

To those of you who lived through the '20s, '30s and '40s in North Dakota, this will bring memories most vividly. He paints his stories as they are with no fancy words and no great explanations. If you would like to live these years again, or to those who would like to know what it was like because you are not old enough to know, I urge you to write or call Russel Duncan. His book is $4.95.

March 14, 1979
SCARED OF THE NEEDLE

For some time now I have been getting the needle from Mrs. W. because I haven't gone to the doc about my bursitis. Frankly, that's just what I'm scared of: the needle. I'm told the darn thing is about a foot long and when the doc pulls it out of his scabbard it automatically sharpens like a World War I bayonet. For years, I stood in line when I was in the Navy, waiting for the needle. If I bent over, they shot me in the arm. When I stood up they shot me in the butt. It was always my impression it was supposed to be the other way around.

In any case, for some time now I have been exercising my bursitis and hoping for the best. Sometimes I think I'm winning the battle and at other times I'm not so sure. I do know that I can't scratch my head with my left hand and that tells me I'm not heading in the right direction.

So yesterday morning I appeared in Doc's office. "There he stands in his robin's-egg-blue shirt," said Doc. He was right about that. But getting in a shot myself before all the proceedings, I said, "Doc, I have to be out of here by 10:30." "No sweat," said Doc.

So two minutes later he was checking me out by whacking me on each elbow with his little rubber hammer. "Hmmmm," said Doc, "they're both dead." A decision was made to take a picture of what was happening underneath my hairy shoulder. "Say," says Doc, "this is going to be in black and white. If you want color in your picture you will have to go over and see Arden Glanzer of Northwest Color." "That's O.K., Doc. I don't plan to hang it in my living room anyway," says I.

As I was in the process of buttoning my robin's-egg-blue shirt after the pictures, Doc asked, "Why do you have to be out of here by 10:30?"

The truth had to come out. "Doc," I said, "a friend of mine and I just made a deal on a case of whiskey and I have to meet him at 10:30 to close the deal!"

August 1, 1979
PEOPLE COME ONLY TO OPPOSE IDEAS

I attended another flood meeting July 23. The only thing I can say about the meeting is there must have been about 75 people in attendance. The meeting concerned a diversion levee around West Fargo and the Kindred Dam (dry dam). I am thoroughly convinced that the people who show at these meetings are there only to object to everything that is going on. If someone would come up with a good idea that concerned the interest of everyone I would fall off my chair. One guy kept saying he has lived north of West Fargo for 25 years or more and he knows that the Corps of Engineers is wrong about a diversion levee around West Fargo. It's no good because it would flood their land twice as much as it is flooding now. Another guy said if the dikes broke in West Fargo that would be fine because it would give the people in the Harwood area time to get ready for the flood and they could handle it when it arrived in the Harwood area. It was learned later that when the dikes break in West Fargo it would take approximately an hour to flood the city. Mayor Lodoen said he didn't think West Fargo could hold out for more than 10 years to keep the flood out. In my opinion if we hold it back five years we will be mighty lucky.

I still say, and I will repeat it again, the government is not going to help us out of this flood mess in the next few years. We cannot depend on our government to help us in the next 20 years and maybe later than that. The people who are affected by flooding cannot and will not get together to demand anything from Washington. They are too worried about just themselves. To hell with the other guy.

WEST FARGO MUST MAKE PLANS IMMEDIATELY TO PROTECT THIS CITY FOR THE FUTURE. I SUGGEST WE MAKE A ONE-SIDED DIVERSION LEVEE. IT WILL PROTECT WEST FARGO AND WILL NOT BE CONTROLLING ANY WATER TO ANYONE'S DISADVANTAGE. I say this in the interest of our city. We must do something and we must do it now.

In relation to the Kindred Dam (dry dam) they talk about mitigation lands, rare species affected, and threatened and endangered species affected. When the water is up to my knees in my house I may still worry a little about rare species, but when it gets up to my chin I'm going to say to hell with mitigation lands, rare species and anything else that has something to do with my house going down the river.

October 3, 1979
IT'S GREAT TO BE A JOINER

I have never been much of a joiner in my lifetime. In fact, I learned to watch how much I got involved with by watching others when I was in the concert business. I ran into guys who belonged to as high as 10 organizations or more, and not only that but in many cases they were president of several. They were so busy running from one place to the other that they had to place their work and living second, just to halfway keep pace with all their volunteer work. Now don't get me wrong. I think it is swell that people give of their time and efforts. However, some people let themselves get too involved and the results are not good. I think people should give some thought to what they would like to help with and then get in there and fight the battle.

I happen to have been invited to join the Lions in West Fargo. Now I didn't have to join the Lions, but my "drinkin' buddies" were over there, which in fact isn't quite true, but we do have one hell of a lot of fun. In the first place we only meet every other Monday night and that doesn't butt into much time in my business world. It also starts at 6:30 and is out at 8:00, which gets me home in time for Monday night football. I do have to admit that there is also work involved as each year we go on the hook for a couple thousand dollars to raise money for eye glasses and many things which augur well for our community. We never have much money to kick around, but it is all used to do some good some place or other. At the end of the year we are broke and then have to get out and sell those light bulbs, brooms and candy, etc., to raise more money.

When I joined Lions I started right off having a ball because of all the singing that goes on before the meal. In fact, I had so much darn fun that I ended up "Tail Twister." Now this is a guy who collects little fines when things don't go just right, especially if you come to club without your button. That job was O.K. and when that was over I thought I was in the clear for some time because as far as I was concerned I did one superb job. Little did I know that that job wasn't the end but the beginning. One thing led to another and now yours truly is president. I thought when you were president all you had to do was stand up at the podium and tell 'em what a "hotshot" you were and also see that everyone else did all the work.

Not so at all. The fellows you ask to do things seldom if ever refuse. What they didn't tell me is I have all the worries.

December 12, 1979
INTRIGUED BY STORY

Visiting with one of my relatives in St. Cloud last week I was intrigued by this story. She was evidently waiting in a parking lot when suddenly a car from across the way backed out and ran into the side of her car. She got out of her car to face a little grayhaired lady who was demanding why she hadn't moved when she saw her backing up. My relative retorted by saying that she couldn't move that fast and besides she hadn't seen her backing up. The little grayhaired lady said, "Well, I didn't see you either, so I guess it's both our faults."

Don & Betty enjoy the holidays with their granddaughter, Morgan, and daughter, Kathy.

Daughter Kathleen, son-in-law Brad Brinkman, and granddaughter Morgan smile for the photographer.

Don, the cameraman, caught his family in this one, Kathy, Brad, Morgan and Betty.

Always With'em

Always ready to pitch in and help promote the company, Don and Betty take a moment to pose for a picture, showing off Don's FM Greeter *t-shirt.*

The Sheyenne Street building housed management, editorial and news assembly, advertising sales, and graphic design for the West Fargo Pioneer, Midweek *and numerous in-house publications.*

In 1984, Davon Press, Inc. moved into their new facilities located at 615 West Main Avenue, housing a new "four-high" press which was added to the existing five-unit press for more color capability.

On these web presses, skilled craftsmen produced the Midweek Eagle, Midweek Plus, West Fargo Pioneer, *and other in-house publications, as well as numerous commercial, college and church materials.*

The Withams have lived on Sommerset Drive in West Fargo since 1996.

Don and Jake snuggle up in their favorite chair.

Dusty, an earlier feline, was the "office cat" that quickly adapted to doting treatment to become the Witham household pet.

As owners and publishers of the West Fargo Pioneer *and its subsidiaries, Don and Betty made it a point to attend as many local and state-wide events as possible.*

Don and Kathy at the employee-sponsored 25th anniversary of the publishing of the West Fargo Pioneer, *begun by Don and Betty on March 15, 1967.*

Kathy and Morgan at Don's favorite restaurant.

Don and a weighty catch.

The 1980s

March 5, 1980
U.S. WASTE COSTS

The rest of the world keeps talking about United States' waste, and to quite some degree I would say they are right. I think most of this has come about in the last 20 or 25 years. In that the raw materials were available, we all got to tossing products in the waste that were still to some degree usable in some fashion.

It always bothers me to see so much paper wasted, especially in the newsprint end of production. Take a look at pens, pencils, all kinds of fancy foods, shaving gear. It's all wrapped up in very expensive plastic and process color cardboard. This all costs money and materials. In the end you find it in the garbage.

Living through the depression of the '30s taught me to keep an eye on waste. I remember knocking over a 10-gallon can of tractor fuel. My dad said, "My garsh, there goes another dollar down the drain." It was the money that hurt then. Only in the past five years have we given enough thought to the consumption of fuel in relation to money. Now a gallon of gas is over $1.15 and now we begin to think about money in relation to fuel. The catch was my dad didn't have the money to buy another 10 gallons of gas for the tractor. Everything we did in the 1930s was in direct relation to saving the materials we worked with because it meant having enough money to buy more. A chicken not completely eaten was turned into soup. The clothes were patched, re-patched and then another patch put on the patch. We churned our own butter in a tumbler barrel. It was then placed in a crock and stored in a dugout in the backyard. To keep them fresh, eggs were placed in oats and they, too, were stored in the dugout. My shirt collars were turned to add extra wear. My socks were mended many times. Most of the summer time we needed no socks at all. Old papers were not tossed. They ended up as insulation between the walls. I don't have to tell you where the old Sears and Montgomery Ward catalogs ended up (that little outhouse in back of the house).

Always With'em

Nails, screws, bolts of all kinds were saved and used again another day. Cigar boxes became a special chest for marbles and other valuables.

We must stop and think that materials we came in contact with in those days were properly used and reused. There is an end to things we use today. We must now learn the value of the packaging we toss, the energy we have wasted, the many and varied foods we consume, the clothes we wear. If we don't, as a saying we used on the farm, "the chickens will come home to roost."

March 26, 1980
"TAB" SIZE IS REAL IMPROVEMENT

Taking a look at our new paper last week (new in size and design) leads me to think that I should have done this long ago. However, I should make a correction here and explain that I really didn't have anything to do with the new design. Mrs. Witham and the girls in the backshop, with help from our new editor, Kim Koppelman, did all the work and worry about design, etc. I sort of stood on the side and "oh-ed" and "ah-ed" about everything they did. In that way I wanted them to realize that I was around and did care that things didn't come out upside-down and backwards. After the front page was all pasted up and ideas were coming from everyone about how the "new look" should look, I thought I might as well put my oar in the conversation. You know what? That was a big mistake. They all looked at me as if to say, "How come you're climbing on the bandwagon now?" I knew right away what I should do. That was steal quietly away. Which is what I did!

In any case I still have the column and I can sit here at my 60-year old typewriter (which was given to me in 1968 by Cliff Ellingson (who used to own the little round red and white liquor store on Main) and write anything I want. No one can stop me on that score because I own the whole darn paper.

April 18, 1980
NO INTEREST ON SOME MARKET INVESTMENTS

Nowadays with savings going down the drain and everyone trying to save a buck or two, people are going to the money markets to save money at interest rates that at least stay somewhere near inflation. However, the Federal Reserve Board doesn't see it that way. For some reason, known only to them, they are now requiring the money market to deposit 15% of the amount by which that fund's net assets exceed the amount of the fund's net assets as of March 14, 1980. Such deposits will not bear interest. In other words, a certain percentage of investments in money markets will pay no interest. In times when the government is encouraging people to save their money in the interest of defeating inflation, this kind of maneuvering is very disconcerting. Just another case where the government permits you to get ahead on one hand and then takes it away on the other. People in this nation will some day learn that it is our government's intention to concentrate the money they make in Washington and not in the people's pockets. FIRST RULE OF COMMUNISM: TAX THE PEOPLE INTO SUBMISSION!

May 2, 1980

It's a rare thing when I make an effort to open fishing season. However, when I do, I have the common sense to go with some guys who would like to catch enough fish to have a meal. If the fish do not like what we offer them as bait we say, "The heck with it," and have something else, like steak or good things like that.

This past weekend I applied some of that common sense in relation to fishing and opened the season with some fellows just like that. Really what I think this past weekend was all about was some guys getting together and having fun. We bring out all our old jokes, the good ones and the bad ones. We eat steaks and all the things that go with it. We spend a good hour hooking all the right bait to our line. We haul a boat 30 or 40 miles (one way) to the lake. We swear a lot because there are no girls around. (That seems to emphasize what we have to say to each other.) I must say we don't talk business and we don't have much to say about politics. In fact, I can't remember much that we did talk about so you can see that what we had to say wasn't very important. I guess, in my case, that is what opening the fishing season is all about.

I can say we didn't catch any fish. We didn't fall in the lake. We didn't drink too much. We didn't get involved with any girls or look for any. We didn't get in any fights with each other or any outsiders. We didn't play cards so we didn't lose any money. We sort of sat around in the comfort of a cold beer. I wonder, does that indicate in any way, shape or fashion our ages?

July 16, 1980
TV SCHEDULE TO APPEAR IN *MIDWEEK PLUS*

A few months back an idea began to germinate in the back of my mind in relation to cable TV in our area. I'm not in any way playing down our four local channels as they have given years of good entertainment and information. However, as this idea grew, I began to wonder how the *Midweek Eagle* or the *Midweek Plus* could assist (and at the same time make a buck) the general public with weekly information. Beginning the first day of August and every Friday thereafter you will be able to open the *Midweek Plus* and pick out your favorite channel, local or cable, from a complete guide. It will be called *"Television Plus"* and will enter your home through the delivery system of 180 newscarriers each and every Friday.

I urge everyone to let us know what you think of this new innovation to our *Midweek Plus*. If there are changes we should make, we welcome your suggestions.

In the meantime, we'll just keep plugging away, bringing you the news of what your local merchants are presenting for your particular taste or need.

October 22, 1980
SQUIRREL CHOOSES CAR FOR STORAGE

Top this one. A week ago while driving my car, every time I turned a corner something under my hood and down around my front wheels would rattle. I talked to my friend, Warren Anderson, who does our CPA work. He told me he nearly lost the front wheels of his new car. They didn't tighten the bolts on his front wheels at the factory. He informed me his sounded about the same, so in a panic I drove my car right to Selland Motors where I know good work is always done. A call to my office later in the day informed me that my car was ready and they had cleared up the trouble. When I picked up the car, Tom, who checked into it for me, took me to the driveway to show me a pile of dog food pellets. Seems that some industrious squirrel had been stashing away food for winter or a rainy day, right on top of my motor.

* * *

Came home the other day and there sat a big gray squirrel right on top of my bird feeder munching away on my bird seed. How he got up there I'll never figure out. I have two baffles on the pole. I have since moved them further apart on the pole so we shall see what happens next. I have noticed lately a very small red squirrel who seems to be boss of all the big gray squirrels. I may just pay him off to watch my bird feeder.

February 4, 1981
RIVERSIDE FACES RISING EXPENSES

As most people know, I live in Riverside which, if you look carefully, is just across the street from West Fargo.

Our little town has for years been struggling to keep alive financially and keep its own identity and yet keep our collective heads above water in relation to those of us who live there. As time goes by and costs to have the things we want and need for Riverside increase, naturally our tax burden grows right along with demands. I am not, in this column, saying something should be done tomorrow, but as the months and years go by, I'm of the opinion that tomorrow is not too far away. We cannot afford our own fire protection, we have no city postal service, our children go to school in West Fargo. We are, to a certain degree, dependent on West Fargo for our police services. A new sewage system is now in the works, $220,000 to install and $40,000 a year to maintain. We are burdened with snow removal, street cleaning, garbage removal and sanitation services, park cleaning and maintenance. I have no idea what legal costs will be involved with upholding the new ordinance #83 banning nude go-go dancing and stripping in local taverns.

Riverside has grown, but I'm wondering just how much more it can grow. We now have approximately 450 people living in our city. Can they bear the burden of effectively and efficiently running the city in years to come?

The questions outlined here, I'm afraid, will become more pressing, causing continually rising taxes.

November 25, 1981
THE BUDGET HEADACHE

In that this column is being written on Monday, I'm fairly sure something will be solved by Wednesday when you read this column in relation to the country going broke. I would like to mention that the people of this nation voted in a man who said all along that he was going to save this nation from big government. Please keep in mind that we voted in Ronald Reagan to see that things are changed concerning billions being spent needlessly. People in many cases will have to tighten belts, but this is what everyone wanted, or at least most of the people, or we would have put former President Carter back in office.

In any case, now what has happened is Congress has monkeyed (purposely, I might add) until the last minute to present a budget to a president who has told them from the beginning he won't sign a give away bill. The screams are coming from far and wide that the President is refusing to sign a bill Congress has presented to him and now all the poor bureaucrats are going without pay, at least for a day or two. Of course, this completely upset the apple cart and they will have to go without that extra drink on the way home from the office. What really gets me is the bureaucrats turn right to the news media and they, of course, play it to the heavens because it looks bad for the President and THAT'S NEWS! AND THAT SELLS PAPERS! AND PEOPLE LOVE TO READ ABOUT BAD NEWS SO THE TWO GO TOGETHER!

Now we can kick the President out, and we can get a guy in there like Tip O'Neill or Ted Kennedy who will give everyone what they want. Of course, they have made their money and really don't need any more, so they will give your money and my money to the people who are doing all the yelling. Or we could do like they do in Russia – everyone gets the same amount of money, except the politicians, and then we all could be mediocre.

SPECIAL NOTE: Congress did get one thing done. It voted itself a raise!

January 13, 1982
A QUICK TRIP TO NYC

I took a quick business trip to New York City last week to sign some contracts. I find the Big Apple just as intriguing as ever. I also find that I don't have to jump from clean space to clean space on the sidewalks since they passed a law that pleases the ordinary guy immensely. That law makes people clean up after their dogs. They all come with their pooper scoopers and clean up after man's best friend. Of course, it's still worth your life if you don't know where you're going in the city. I think they should form a "Mugged Club." There would be thousands of members. They could pay dues and the next guy that got mugged could be paid accordingly to what he got robbed.

The city is expensive. Food in good restaurants very expensive, cabs not bad in cost. I have the feeling if one were to really try, and knew where to go, New York wouldn't be as expensive as one might imagine. In any case, for a short trip to New York, if you plan to have any fun, better take enough money to get in and out of the place.

May 12, 1982
IN CAME THE...

It all started when I decided that the river wasn't going to come visit me in my basement every year it got a foot over flood stage. Yep, I hired a guy to bring in a few loads of good ol' North Dakota gumbo to keep that river back where it belonged. When I make up my mind to fight, I really fight, and that means river or no river! In this case, my wife watched the proceeding with mixed feelings because for some reason she has little faith in my engineering ability. However, I knew what was what when it came to backyard flood protection because I mowed that damn lawn back there every year. SO IN CAME THE TRUCKS AND THE TRACTORS AND THE MEN AND EVERYTHING TO MAKE A DIKE. It took my neighbor, Tony Walz, half a summer to smooth the darn thing out because he does a super job of things like that. However, his tractor was little and the job big, but you know he really did a swell job. I stood back and looked everything over and said, "Behold, I did excellent with planning and everything!" My wife asked one question. "Now that you have diked the river out, may I mention you have also diked the rainwater that falls in our yard very definitely in?"

Back to the ol' drawing board I went. Another friend of mine, Ray Gerszewski, came to my aid with an idea about digging a hole in my backyard, putting in a sump pump and pumping the water back over the dike. That shut up the wife and my problem was solved, except for some reason every time it rained the sump pump wouldn't work very well because it plugged up with dirt. The result was the water came in to my house like always. The solution was to keep the pump clean and, of course, that required my standing on my head with a very small can scooping out the mud from the bottom of the sump pump hole.

The very next year after my big dike project, up came the river at flood time. I stood back and viewed the whole scene with complete confidence that I would remain warm and dry. However, the river kept right on rising and rising and rising. I thought it might be a good idea to put a row of sandbags on top of the dike just in case! The closer it came the more concerned I became, so I put another row of bags on top of the dike.

About this time, the neighbors began gathering in my backyard and it didn't take them long to lend a hand in relation to the sandbags. They could see for themselves that my downfall was also their downfall. If I got flooded, the whole town of Riverside got flooded. Before it was all over 5,000 sandbags had been placed on my dike and seven sump pumps were working day and night. The wife and I took turns watching the pumps and in general keeping the water world from caving in on us. The neighbors also began walking the dike just like in Holland. This went on day and night for nearly three weeks.

Needless to say, I got plumb fed up with loss of sleep, pitching sandbags, walking dikes, working pumps and everything that goes along with a spring flood. So it wasn't long before IN CAME THE TRUCKS AND THE TRACTORS AND THE MEN AND EVERYTHING TO MAKE A BIGGER DIKE! Now the darn thing is so big I can't get my tractor mower to come over it so I can mow my backyard. When I'm in my rec room, all I can see is a great green mound running through my backyard. Can't see over it! And I know when the next flood comes and the river starts to rise, I shall stand back and view the whole scene with complete confidence that I will remain warm and dry. And I shall be reminded again by my wife that I'm still diking the water in as well as out!

October 20, 1982
THE THREE R'S

It has been my thinking that most teachers are sincere in their feelings and association with the students they teach. I have faith that most of our teachers on a national basis have the common sense to keep their union, the National Education Association, in line. This will augur well with the children they teach and themselves as a whole. However, the following is from the *Heritage News Forum* by Edwin Fuelner.

TEACHERS STRIKE OUT

While fewer teachers ushered in the new school year last month by illegally walking off their jobs, it was not due to any change in policy by the huge teacher union, the National Education Association.

Once a staid professional organization interested in imparting knowledge to kids, the NEA today means muscle. Muscle for politics. Muscle for doing battle with school boards. Muscle for just about everything, it seems, but teaching Johnny and Jenny how to read and write.

Which is what has parents fed up and, according to author Burton Yale Pines in his new book, *Back to Basics*, demanding an end to open classrooms, permissiveness, and sociological claptrap, and a return to reading, writing, and arithmetic.

But don't think the NEA is going to take this lying down. Union officials see the back-to-basics movement as some kind of right-wing conspiracy. And at the union's big 120th national convention this summer NEA President William McGuire rang the alarm.

McGuire told his flock in order to combat the "onslaught" from the right "you have to organize, you have to fight, you have to put your shoulders to the grindstone of the political and legislative lobbying process."

In his keynote address he said, "educational excellence without political power is not a practical possibility; political power for educational excellence is a professional responsibility."

Accordingly, the first set of "educational excellence" items on the convention agenda dealt with the international peace movement. The delegates approved a statement advocating a nuclear weapons freeze. Members also approved an unusually long seven-point plan to put the NEA in the forefront of the women's rights movement.

The ironic twist, of course, is that as the educational community has gotten more politically savvy, "educational excellence" has undeniably declined. Why, for instance, should the NEA spotlight the nuclear freeze movement as a priority issue when problems of student delinquency, declining test scores and functional illiteracy are plaguing our educational system?

How are parents to have any confidence in the teaching profession when even a superficial glance at what they as a collective body consider to be important shows broad international issues instead of rudimentary basics like how can we help our children to be intellectually better equipped to deal with a complex world?

Not all teachers are failures, of course. One teacher of my youth drummed a lesson into my head that I will always remember. She did so by making me write it on the blackboard several thousand times during a semester.

The message: "Persistent perversity provokes patient pedagogues producing painful penalties."

Instead of chasing right-wing boogeymen and flexing their political muscle, perhaps McGuire and Company would do well to write those words down on paper – substituting the word "parents" for pedagogues.

January 26, 1983
GLOSSY REPORTING PREVAILS

It's a rare thing today to hear anything on the bright side of news media information. Turning on to the so-called super TV news commentators does something to my opinion of what's going on in our nation. However, looking behind the headlines of what the commentators play up, one finds they don't tell the truth. They tell only what they want you to know. Talk about Russia and how they guide their news media, we must look certainly with a jaundiced eye towards what TV is saying to us today. When there is a certain amount of truth in our news, it is so slanted that one gets the impression that they think the people of our country are just plain stupid.

I am of the opinion that hard news in our country is a thing of the past. As news is presented today, it is embellished and made into a glossy picture of what the commentator intends to present. In turn, the more he glosses over the truth and the more he expounds on what he thinks, the more famous he becomes. Commentators today are almost like movie stars, recognized wherever they go. They don the covering of something special in our society. Keep in mind, folks, they are no smarter than you and I. They only give that impression.

I want to say our own local TV people do give a good accounting of what is going on in our area. It is pretty much down the line and is what they say it is. They are to be commended.

As I see it in the future, TV commentators on a national basis will, in time, be called to task to prove in court that what they tell us is really the overall picture of what it's all about! Thank God, the country takes what they hear in this area of news presentation with 14 grains of salt.

February 2, 1983
NOT OLDER... BETTER!

There have probably been 40 million words written on growing old. I haven't noticed that I'm heading in that direction other than little things that indicate as much. Like when I say, "This old duffer still notices a well-turned ankle" no one disputes the word "old duffer." When I mention that "I'm only 44" they look at my thinning hair and give me that certain look. Most are polite enough not to say anything. They just smile and change the subject. I usually follow through with words to the effect that I might be 46 next year, just depends on how I feel.

I do get the impression that I might be just a little older because our 19 year old cat is looking more like a rag mop each year. Also she doesn't spend nights out of doors anymore, just sniffs the morning air when I open the door and returns to the heat register. Why I say all this is I seem to do a lot of the same things as the cat. When the alarm wakes me, I make a quick trip to the bathroom and return to bed. I open the door in the morning and go back for a sweater to put under my coat. On the way to start the car I take little, short steps when I get on the ice. When I get in the seat to start the motor, from somewhere comes a short grunt. I'm certain it isn't the car, so it has to be me. Could it be that I'm really a little over 44? However, I can still click my heels like I could a year ago and I know I jump just as high when I'm doing it. I still do 20 push-ups in the morning and about as many sit-ups.

All in all, I think all this boils down to one thing. "You're only as old as you think you are." Maybe next year I'll be 42!

March 16, 1983
SOME ADVANTAGES TO TAB SIZE PAPER

The past two years and more, you have been receiving the *Pioneer* in tab form (that is as tabloid, about half size of ordinary newspaper).

Always With'em

There was some gnashing of teeth at first because it looked like the *Pioneer* was just plain smaller. However, now that people are used to it, we hear no more complaints. It is less expensive to put out a paper in tab form and we have eliminated filler, which really doesn't interest anyone.

Something on the side here, and to some advantage when you are reading the paper in the bathtub, keep in mind that you don't get the bottom part wet because it isn't as long as an ordinary paper. I said that with tongue in cheek, of course, but, all in all, a tab makes for easier reading. I have also noted that several other papers in the state have gone to tab form. It is easier to put together and the news can be concentrated, which is good for the reader, as well as the paper itself.

April 27, 1983
SHE READS MY MIND

As we were getting ready to go for a ride in the country last Wednesday, my wife said to me, "Now don't put on those funny-looking tan pants." She seemed to know what I was thinking because she was in the other bedroom when she said those challenging words. In fact, I had my hand on those funny-looking pants when she made the remark. I am firmly convinced that our wives make a determined effort from the day they marry us to read our minds. Now I'm not one to come all apart over her being able to read my mind. However, it is a little disconcerting when I appear in the morning wearing something that doesn't match with pants, coat or tie. She says, "I just knew you were going to wear that tie with that coat and it certainly doesn't match at all." I spent four years, one month and 11 days in the Navy and no one ever told me I was color blind. As the years go by, maybe blue does really look black to me and maybe green matches purple for all I know, but I'm still in there pitching to please the little woman.

I used to wear size 16 collar shirts. When I started buying 16½ collar shirts, who should right away notice? Yep, you guessed, the wife was right there telling me my collars were too big. The catch to all this is now I don't take her along when I buy shirts! I figure breathing is much ahead of a tight collar. I do wear a tie most of the time, so much so that my brother-in-law swears I wear them to bed. If that's so, I'm the best dressed guy in town when I get up in the morning.

October 19, 1983
UNHAPPY RESULTS FOR YEARS TO COME

Pointers to consider and think about after January 1 when your phone bill goes up!

Congress will vote to hold down local phone rates.

There will be a $2 charge per line for local phones.

A $6 charge for businesses, but not if they have only one line. (I don't understand this, but who knows about the government!)

A surcharge will be put on all users of private telecommunications, also on long distance carriers.

Revenues will be used to subsidize rates for the poor and help pay for services to rural areas. Congress feels phones are a right... not just a privilege.

Rates of increase for individual users will depend on location.

Business will pay more for Watts lines, private-line services, toll-free numbers.

Long distance directory assistance calls will soon cost 75¢ each.
Special Note: If those of you who read this can make head or tail out of what will really happen, you are a wizard. This is a tragic case of government interference in business which will cost the American people billions. When you pay more for your telephone service in the future, you might ask those people who represent us in Congress WHY? All this big changeover in telephone communication in our nation will have unhappy results for years to come.

December 7, 1983
A FEW PILLS, A HOT SHOT, AND A LITTLE BED REST

"You're coughing again," says my wife. Yep, that's right, I am coughing. Now there is a time to cough and there is a time to hold that temptation in and not cough. When the wife is around, it is a good time not to do those things. "Call Doc and get something to help," she says.

I can remember when I was a kid, my mother used to toss me into bed with about 14 blankets, six hot water bottles and lots of hot lemon. The crowning point was mustard plaster. Darned if I know how she made it, but it sure as heck heated me up. About the time I thought I was going to float out of bed with all the sweating I was doing, she would come and dry me off, put clean dry clothes on me and tuck me in for a good, long sleep. I think it cured the cough and cold, but I sure went through heck reaching that point.

Nowadays, a few pills and a little bed rest and (if you take care of yourself) you will be up again in no time. However, if one gets a nice head cold, one really should learn to enjoy it. After all, you don't have to put up with a cough and you have a wonderful excuse to stay home. You can sort of snuggle down into the covers of a nice, warm bed or bundle up and watch TV, catch up on all the soaps. To smooth things out later in the day, a small shot of brandy does wonders (maybe two) just for health's sake. Around 5:30 or 6:00, it's time for dinner. I would think a nice pan of crisp fried chicken, washed down with a gentle wine, topped off with good black coffee and maybe a small, heady, after-dinner drink, should finalize the day just fine. In the morning, if you don't feel top notch, do the same thing over again, only substitute steak. Maybe the chicken didn't agree with you!

January 4, 1984
RESOLUTIONS?

I have been thinking of New Year's resolutions that I should make. First off I tried to think of the resolution I made last year so I wouldn't repeat. Now that I think of it, I don't remember that I made a resolution. If I did, I am sure that I failed miserably to carry it out. In fact, I don't think I made one the year before either. However, this year I'm going to make three or four if I can think of any that will do me any good.

First off, I promise not to kick the cat. In that we don't have a cat, I don't have to worry about that. I promise not to get up until the wife gets up because she always turns on the light. That way I know I'll get my shoes on the right feet and that makes me pleasant to work with all day. I'll not park my car so close to the neighbor's driveway that he can't get out of his garage. I'll try not to shoot the sparrows off my nuthatch feeder, that is unless my wife is not watching. Next year I will put the Christmas tree lights up right the first time so my wife won't raise heck because they are upside down and backwards. If the Sheyenne floods like past years, I promise not to stand on my dike and swear because my sump pumps don't work. I will not stand by the window and wait for the neighbor's cat to cross over into our lot so I can shoot him with my BB gun. However, I might hide behind the garage and wait for him instead.

That way he will have half a chance to escape before I can shoot him twice instead of three times. I promise not to remind the barber again when I used to get haircuts for 50¢. I told them the other day that they used to open the door when they saw me coming. Now I'm lucky to get an appointment when I telephone. Times sure change. Maybe I'm getting old, but I don't think I cuss out the politicians as much as I used to. I know darn well they aren't doing a better job. However, I promise not to think about them any more and maybe they will go away. In any case, I have promised to give the church a little more in the coming season so that will put me in better with the fellow upstairs, I HOPE!

March 21, 1984
ALL FOR NOTHING

Recently I wrote a column on insurance in relation to flood protection in West Fargo. Needless to say, I was NOT PLEASED TO FIND PEOPLE IN OUR AREA WILL NOT BE REIMBURSED IF THEIR BASEMENTS ARE FLOODED. Yet we must pay for flood insurance, which in turn makes the insurance we must buy each year absolutely worthless. Our federal government takes this money we pay for worthless insurance against our will. We have no say whatsoever. You can write your representative or senators about this, but it seems this is one way the people must pay no matter what the outcome.

I did write to Senator Andrews and he investigated this new law. I will copy the paragraphs here so those of you who are interested can get a firsthand idea of the thinking behind the actions of Congress. It looks to me like when someone in Georgia gets flooded, you and I help pay the bill. I object to this, because when we get flooded in West Fargo it is rare that anything is flooded except our basements for which we get nothing.

I appreciate very much Senator Andrews investigating this for me.

The following is from Richard Grehalva, Customer and Information Services of National Flood Insurance Program.

"Despite improvements in flood plain management, and previous rate increases implemented for the first time in 1981, the NFIP continues to require a heavy subsidy from U.S. Treasury Funds. In order to moderate the amount of subsidy and yet keep the insurance reasonably priced, the Federal Insurance Administration has had to utilize a combination of rate increases and coverage restrictions. These policy changes cut back the coverage for property whose replacement is less essential to the fundamental goal of returning the building to a habitable condition. In an attempt to achieve this goal, new and renewal policies will not cover finished walls, floors, ceilings or other similar constructions or improvements to a basement area."

March 28, 1984
FREEDOM OF CHOICE

I was reminded by my neighbor Saturday that next Tuesday is voting day! I hadn't given it much thought one way or another. . . it really isn't a very important day. We will be voting for mayor of our city and a few other things. However, Sunday on national TV I witnessed people in another country ducking bullets and facing threats to their lives to rush to the voting polls. When they got there, not all of them had the opportunity of voting because the authorities did not have the proper facilities to take care of all those who wanted to vote.

Monday morning I stopped by our city hall and picked up an absentee ballot, in that I cannot get back to town in time to vote. It reminds me that I served four years, one month and 11 days in the Navy during the war to have the privilege that I almost forgot. At times, I am completely frustrated by what the outcome of elections generates. This goes all the way up to our federal government. The things Congress has done over the years borders on complete stupidity. Worst, all in the name of good government when it really is only politics. In my opinion, less than 5% of the people who make up our Congress really give a damn about the nation. I hate what they do to our nation.

I gnash my teeth over the way they waste our money. I have so little faith in what they do, I would prefer they do nothing. Yet I cannot think of any other way our government should be run. If it really is so bad, why are people from all over the world rushing to cross our borders to what they call the land of FREEDOM!

Yes, I shall vote on Tuesday. It is only a small sledgehammer to keep politicians in line. Let's all vote. Many sledgehammers make one hell of a noise!

April 4, 1984
CHANGES COME

Changes come and changes take place because of planning in many small companies today. However, in the company of Pioneer Enterprise, Inc., it seems that changes come on demand. By that, I mean we don't intend to change it; it just seems that when there is nothing else for us to do after we have painted ourselves into a corner, so to speak, we make a change.

The past two years an issue has been demanding our attention a little more each day, namely more room for people who run our presses for the *Midweek Eagle, Plus, Pioneer* and lots of grocery advertising. This past July, when I found I could not enter our pressroom through the usual door because of no room to squeeze through (I had to go around back through a little door), it dawned on me our time for change had come.

As it turned out, Roy Larson, my friend and standby chief encourager, suggested we build a nice, big building for our presses. Also, he mentioned that I would not have to skip through the storage room so fast to be sure the stacks of 1,000 pound rolls of paper wouldn't fall on me. To make a long story short, we started laying plans for a press building. It wasn't long before I began to hear rumblings about how nice it would be to have a big folder. I asked why that was so important. The word was it would put out papers twice as fast and save lots of night work time. Of course, this impressed me and then, for some reason, there came overtones of four more presses, only these would be stacked (in other words four presses high instead of four presses long). "What would this do?" I asked. They said, "You could then run 56 pages at once and include 16 pages of color. Think how glamorous that would be!" I don't go much for glamour, but I noted it would save two press runs on one publication and also inserting one paper into another after it came off the press.

So all in all, we have our shirt hanging out on the line and I do hope we don't lose it!

May 23, 1984
GETTING AWAY AND HAVING A BALL

There are times when young guys have to get together and have a bit of fun away from their wives. Such an event happened last Friday, Saturday and Sunday when five guys got together at one of their lake cottages. Note that I didn't add the word "young" in the last sentence. When we started counting up we found we were all over sixty. However, I want to say right here and now that guys over sixty can have "a ball." Yep, they can go to the local restaurant, dance hall, and what have you, just like young guys. Not only that, but they are smart enough not to get into any fights. We are smart enough to know when to go home, and smart enough to know that if you get into bed at a decent time you feel real good in the morning. All those things we did, so when it came time for fishing in the morning we were out there bouncing up and down with all the rest of the boats that were not catching any fish either.

I can say one thing. We sure caught most of the perch in the lake and they were all at least four and a half inches long, some longer. I know there were walleyes, because I caught one. He was at least seven inches long. It seems that we hit the lake season when the fish flies are in full bloom so I really caught a lot of those, mostly in my eyes and ears. When the wind came up, I found it is not a good idea to troll backwards because you are inviting wet feet and wet pants and wet seat and anything else that happens to be around. However, after three days of fishing we did get enough fish to have a Sunday dinner, so five old boys did right well at that!

I have decided that we should have written all our weekend events down and, more important, all those good stories so they wouldn't go to waste. After all, five old guys like us don't come along every day.

September 12, 1984
BEWARE OF GIMMICKS

The last 10 or 12 years I have been receiving letters from Carolyn Davis. She writes long epistles about how much I'm going to win if I just take two or three stamps off the letter she sends me and paste them on another page she has enclosed. Eureka! I'll win all the way up to $300,000. Fool that I am, I cannot resist opening her letters. The first few letters I received, I followed instructions. Lo and behold, I am now the recipient of about 10 or 12 years of paid subscriptions of *Reader's Digest*. In time, of course, I got smart. I now read very carefully all the fine print to make sure I'm not extending my subscription four to six years. I then make sure the stamps I remove from one page and paste on the other will only put my vote in for the $300,000. I'm sure to get something almost as good, like $100,000 in other prizes too numerous to mention on the colorful page I am reading.

I have no idea who Carolyn Davis is, but any gal who can write as many intriguing letters as she has the past 12 years I just have to meet. I have two or three pictures in my mind concerning her looks. One is a tall, skinny gal with a driving ambition to become president of either *Reader's Digest* or the United States. I'm of the opinion at least she could keep her foot out of her mouth better than the gal who is running for vice president of the United States at this time. In any case, I have another picture in my mind. I think she might be a short, fat gal with a very jolly laugh. She could be the type that slaps you on the back, tells you what a wonderful guy you are and, as you go out the door, turns to her secretary and says, "There's a sucker born every minute."

In the final analysis, Carolyn Davis probably will turn out to be a grizzled old man sitting behind his desk planning another attack on us poor subscribers who don't read all the letter and wind up with another four years of subscriptions to *Reader's Digest*. Incidentally, I did receive a check some time back. My excitement ebbed somewhat when I opened the letter with a 10¢ check enclosed.

December 12, 1984
CHRISTMAS COMPARISON

Now that Christmas is just around the corner, I'm comparing Christmas of today with those of yesterday. Naturally the weather hits about the same temperature, although it seems to me, in South Dakota in the '30s, twenty to thirty below was more the temperature. I remember this very well when nature demanded I had to trek through the snow to a little house in the backyard. Not only that, but I also remember the frost around the edges of where I planted my little, warm rear. In those days, I must admit, it was smaller. These days it seems to get bigger. In any case, we sure didn't have what we have today. Travel in the winter was about 16 miles to Britton, S.D. Our car had mechanical brakes, which always froze up in the fall and didn't thaw out until spring, so no brakes. That way going to town took some real judgment because you had to estimate when you were going to stop. If not, you ended up in a store front. I can also say you didn't have any money to pay damages because in those days there just wasn't any money!

Christmas, of course, was the big event of the year. The Fourth of July was second because it didn't last as long. I remember our first Christmas tree. My sister planned it while I was in town in Amherst, S.D. (four miles away). When I came home, the most beautiful tree I had ever seen in my life stood in our living room/dining room/kitchen and general gathering place for the family. Our original house had burned a year or two before and could not be replaced, so we lived in our garage. I remember that candles were used on the tree Christmas Eve. The little white church was, of course, the main gathering place on Christmas. They used a tremendously large tree. I always wondered how they ever got it into the church. We all received a mesh bag of Christmas candy and sang all the songs that go along with the event. Christmas was always very important to me in that it meant no school until the new year. In that school was in no way my forte, Christmas was the most important time of the year.

Christmas nowadays is sort of mixed in with Thanksgiving and New Year's. I don't approve of that, but I'll go along with the crowd, that is as long as it doesn't cost me any more than I'm paying already!

I still like Christmas at home. A lot of people go away at this time of year. Not I. Home fires are best. A few years back I spent Christmas in Hawaii. I won't do that again. Christmas happens to fall on the Chinese New Year's and firecrackers are the song of the day instead of carols. That I don't go for. Besides, snow is not what gets to me at that time of year. I like snow and bells and songs and red suits and long, white whiskers and happy times around a fire. This I wish for everyone!

January 23, 1985
MONEY TO WHOM?

At the risk of being criticized to quite some degree, I shall state here my thoughts and opinions of the starvation of people in Ethiopia. There probably has not been an outpouring of concern and money to people in another nation for quite some time as has been undertaken in our nation in the past few months. I know people mean well when they send a few bucks to Ethiopia, but I keep wondering if it isn't only a bandaid to a much larger problem. In the first place, it is a communist country. It's my opinion we have allies that need our help; they should come first! In that Ethiopia is a Russian ally, I keep wondering what Russia is doing to alleviate the problem. I also wonder why a nation that is producing food in areas that are sufficient in one place is not spreading the food to include the entire nation. It raises the suspicion that there is a reason for starvation. Could it be that this country of Ethiopia is intentionally doing away with their own people? Road blocks are continually in place to stop food being delivered where it can do the most good. Why is this? Last, we should ask ourselves what comes after the bandaid food delivery. Are we willing, and is our nation willing, to pour in not millions, but billions, to bring this nation back to food stability? The land has been stripped of vegetation, water is a real problem, transportation a disaster, and that is only the beginning. It will take years of work on the land to make it produce food that will, in some small measure, only begin to feed the starving thousands.

If we do all this for Ethiopia, what will our government tell our own people who are out of jobs and short of food? What do we tell the people of Mexico? Those of you who have traveled to Mexico in the past know what poor really is. Living in a tin hut with no water and a dirt floor is what it's all about in that country. This can be repeated twenty times over with countries that are allied with us. Can we tell them that they come second because we are busy helping a communist country? Giving some thought to where our money goes might be a very good idea.

March 27, 1985
BITE THE BULLET

My column this week involves a short article brought to me this week by a friend of mine. It was passed on by J. Vernon McGee. In one sentence it explains what can happen to our nation if we are not willing to "bite the bullet." Our president is trying to change the way we live so that our country will still be here for hundreds of years in the future. However as yet a free nation, we have the choice.

"Over 200 years ago while our nation was still a British colony, the noted English historian, Alexander Fraser Tyler, wrote about the fall of the Athenian Republic in these words:

"A Democracy cannot exist as a permanent form of government. It can only exist until the voters discover that they can vote themselves largesse from the public treasury.

"From that moment on, the majority always votes for the candidates promising the most benefits from the public treasury, with the result that a Democracy always collapses over loose fiscal policy, always followed by a dictatorship. The average age of the world's greatest civilizations has been 200 years.

"These nations have progressed through this sequence: From bondage to spiritual faith; from spiritual faith to great courage; from courage to liberty; from liberty to abundance; from abundance to selfishness; from selfishness to complacency; from complacency to apathy; from apathy to dependency; from dependency back again into bondage."

May 1, 1985
VIETNAM, STILL DISTORTED PICTURE

We've been hearing a lot about Vietnam the past few days on TV, radio and in the newspapers. The news media seem to delight in beating the people of our nation over the head with how bad we are because of Vietnam. The Congress is so busy blaming someone else for the war that they take no time to look at what really happened.

In my opinion and from what I can gather from the history of President Kennedy and the time he was president, he was only trying to help an ally. Our nation, since the First World War, has become involved in wars mainly in the interest of helping allies. Vietnam, in my opinion, was another similar situation. President Johnson, one of our worst presidents, through pride, led us into what eventually turned into disaster.

A vacillating, indecisive, imprudent Congress destroyed the moral fiber of our nation during the years of the struggle in Vietnam. The Congress gave our men in the field almost no support when they needed it most. All this only goes to prove that 535 men and women who compose our Congress make darn poor generals. When people of this ilk try to run a war from soft seats in a nice, safe, warm atmosphere, they tend to ignore the real challenge. What they can't blame on the military they blame on each other. The Congress of our nation should take the blame for Vietnam. The news media in the meantime, during the war, painted a biased picture of our side of the war, making it look like we were the villains and not the Viet Cong.

Only now our nation's young men who fought a useless war are given credit and recognized for their dying and bloodshed.

June 5, 1985
"COMPARABLE WORTH"

We are hearing more and more nowadays about a thing called "comparable worth." It would behoove a great share of us to understand what this is all about. If initiated, comparable worth could change our lives and incomes throughout the United States for years to come. However, it has been rejected by the United States Civil Rights Commission. Linda Chaves, as staff director of the Rights Commission, has called comparable worth the issue of the '80s. The theory calls not only for equal pay for equal work but equal pay for different work. In other words, a secretary and a truck driver working for the same company would receive equal pay in relation to their worth to the company. If I were the truck driver, I would certainly apply for the secretary's job. It is much easier to work inside in air-conditioned comfort with shorter hours. I wouldn't have to work and strain my back in the hot sun of summer or the cold of winter. What would happen to the secretary I wouldn't know, but if I could get the same pay, would I really care?

The company I would be working for would have to raise their prices to offset the rising costs. In the public sector it would mean higher taxes. It also would completely destroy our free enterprise system by giving the government the right to set wages instead of the market place.

I couldn't imagine anything worse than creating a brand new bureaucracy in Washington to check on all companies in our country to see if the truck driver is getting more pay than the office secretary. Just to maintain the new government office would cost hundreds of millions and I certainly wouldn't trust a guy from the government to decide which is worth more or less, the truck driver or the secretary!

August 7, 1985
DEMANDS OF PACKING FOR A TRIP

When it comes to packing for a trip, I think I'm about as good as they come.

Of course, I might mention here that it took me twenty-five years to learn the demands of packing.

Over the years, I have left more clothes in hotel rooms than an ordinary person wears in a lifetime. In that I traveled for a company out of New York for many years and was always on the road, I learned not to put clothes in drawers. My shirts and etcetera that needed washing always went into the nearest easy chair. There is always one in every motel or hotel room.

When I got married my new wife didn't think much of the way I stored my dirty linen, especially the socks. Things changed right then and there. I remember the first trip out with her. I left several of my shorts in a hotel room drawer in Midland, Texas. The way she corrected that was to have her mother make me a big cloth sack with a string around the top. I was to put those articles that needed soap and water in said sack.

The thing that always worried me in my travels was luggage getting to the right place on time. In those days, Greyhound bus was about the only way I could get around in Texas. I always made it a point to beat the little old grayhaired ladies on the bus. Two reasons for this were to get a seat in the middle of the bus so I would not be over the wheels for a rough ride and I could also watch the boy putting my luggage in the space under the bus. A warning signal in relation to luggage was when you saw a guy with your luggage in hand scratching his head and a big question on his face. In that instance you had better be on guard and very alert or your luggage would be on the wrong bus going in the opposite direction.

In later years, I have learned that one only needs about a quarter of what you take along on a trip. In fact, one of the last times we stayed in the Marriott in Bloomington, Minn., I was so sure of myself in relation to packing that I had to buy shaving equipment because I left the whole kit at home. So twenty-five years of traveling didn't help me a darn bit!

January 22, 1986
ON LONG WINTER DAYS

I can't think of anything more challenging than waking on a weekday morning in North Dakota in January. The idea of getting up in the dark and getting ready for work is plumb discouraging. I think the reason I dislike it so much is that in my Navy days the twelve-to-four watch always made me plenty grumpy. It must be that getting up at 5:45 in North Dakota has the same effect. Of course, our cat is always happy about 5:45 because I'm the one who takes her out of her room, combs her, feeds her, waters her (yes, long-furred cats have to be watered). Then it's my turn to face the day.

I should not be unhappy about all this because in the days when I grew up on the farm there were twenty cows to be milked before I went to school. I'll never know how I stood it. I guess mostly it's because that's the way it was on the farm in those days. Besides, if we didn't sell the cream, we really didn't eat very well. In any case, my dad used to tell me it was good experience. I can say this; I'm darn glad all that wonderful experience is long behind me.

However, I think the months of January and February are the toughest in North Dakota. It seems like the winter will never end. March isn't so bad because you know that you are on the down slope to spring. March really is the month one should go to a warm clime because you are a bit put out with winter and a couple of weeks in the sunshine gets you ready for April showers and May flowers.

Now that I have expounded at some length on the advantages of living in North Dakota, I shall get up tomorrow morning, feed that darn cat, and start the day all over again.

June 4, 1986
NOW THAT'S MORE LIKE IT

Three or four years ago when WDAY went off the air with their good FM music, I decided that I had come to the end of my rope as far as listening to radio. I did, however, tune my wake-up radio and car radio to KFGO. Country music is not exactly my cup of tea, but at least it doesn't drive me out of the car. I don't know what it is about the music today that the radio stations push, but it sure doesn't sell me. I really get stopped when I go into a restaurant to eat and visit with guests. It seems like the band is determined to kill everything in sight including the flies on the wall. My ears vibrate, my eyes water, and trying to carry on a conversation is completely impossible.

In any case, GOOD NEWS. KFGO has now gone FM and the music is pleasing to my ears. They call it easy listening and that's just what it is. Monday morning I was awakened to pleasant tunes of a bygone day. No guy singing about a boy named Sue or anything like that. Just very nice music to get me started for the day.

Those of you who would like to join me listening to *kind* music on the airwaves, you can turn your dial to 101.9, KFGO.

July 2, 1986
LET'S TALK ABOUT LIBERTY

We are hearing a lot about liberty nowadays and will hear a lot more by this weekend of July 4. Normally we don't talk very much about liberty or freedom in our country because we have so much of it. In fact, we have so much of that special thing called liberty that a great share of the time we misuse its privileges. In my opinion, a good example is the way our laws are misused and maneuvered to the advantage of those undeserving of any consideration at all.

I visited recently with a person who had occasion to talk to visitors from East Germany. I learned they don't talk about the state or someone might rap on their door at night. They can't even trust their personal friends or relatives. They can only bring fifteen dollars out of their country when they get permission to travel outside the East German borders. They have to go back because they have family there that would suffer if they didn't go back.

We take for granted that the policeman on the beat or in the patrol car is there to help us. If we travel to foreign lands, all we need is a passport. We are not asked why we are going, what we are going to do there, or how much money we are taking out of the country. Imagine if you travel across our country and you had to report to the police where you intended to go and how long you were to stay.

How about your attitude toward your job? In America you can quit. What do you think would happen to you in Poland? How would you like to stand in a food line in Russia for hours? We take as our privilege walking into a supermarket and buying anything we want. It's there for the taking. You can buy a car any place you wish. Your local bank is glad to loan you the money. You can do this today. In Russia you wait years, and I understand it is true in all Eastern Bloc countries. Keep in mind the wall in Berlin is not to keep you out; it is to keep their people in.

It seems strange to me that our news media are continually running our nation down. Everything we do is wrong and is done so much better in other countries. If our president comes out with a new idea (tax changes are a good example), the news media make a special point of picking it apart. In a nation like Russia they would last about three days. Reporting from Siberia isn't the easiest thing to do. If our country is so bad, why in heck are all these thousands flocking across our borders each year? I'm not convinced there are that many stupid people in the world. No, they see opportunity to do something on their own without big brother watching. They see good times, they see good clothes, they see lots of food, they see people with money who buy anything they want. They also see people who run down the government and call the president a dope and yet no one ends up in jail for it. It's a right they cannot understand. They want to learn all about this thing called FREEDOM! The people of our nation practically drown in it every day, yet take it as their right. Our forefathers told us two hundred years ago, "YOU NOW HAVE A REPUBLIC, IF YOU CAN KEEP IT!" ARE YOU DOING YOUR SHARE TO KEEP THIS NATION A REPUBLIC? If you should fail, listen closely. You may hear that knock on the door some night.

July 9, 1986
HOUSE ADDITION

This past year the wife and I have been thinking about an addition to the house. I might add here that thinking about an addition and really going ahead and doing it is an entirely different thing.

I think it all started when our friends, the Larsons, added on to their house. We made the mistake of asking who did the job, and it wasn't very long before a very enthusiastic young fellow appeared at our door. I think to shut him up, we made a down payment and that is the last we heard until this spring. Another fellow called and wanted to know when we wanted our addition. I told him I'm not sure we really wanted an addition. By the time he got through explaining that the guy who sold us the idea in the first place was no longer with the company and that he took his commission and left, I began to think maybe I do need a house addition. In any case, three workers are diligently putting on a new addition to our house. Now that the thing is really underway, the wife is making very big plans on what it is to look like when it is finished. I sort of go along with the ideas she comes up with, because, since 1950, I have found that to give on the little things can augur very well later when I want something for the car or office.

I have also been told that when it comes to planning furnishings in a house, my taste is all in my mouth. I am told that a blue stripe is going to be next to the ceiling, the ceiling will be painted, and white birch paneling will grace the walls. My background as a farmer seems to lean towards pressed board or whatever you call it. I don't mention my thoughts on this, and that, my friends, is a wise decision on my part.

I'm told that the building of the addition will be completed in a week. I have been down to the local bank and my friend, Arch Filley, has assured me the money will be forthcoming when I need it, and I'm sure I will be needing it very soon indeed.

I'm sure when all is completed, the cat will be pleased, for there are several windows for her to view the world. A word of caution for you fellows whose wives are planning an addition to your house: Prices have sure gone up since 1936 when I was on the farm!

September 24, 1986
OUR OFFICE KITTY

In that I wrote about the office cat, Dusty, a week or so ago, I thought it might be well to introduce you to our **daily** challenge in that regard.

She has everyone spotted, even the kids who come to the office. She takes one look and scoots away like a rabbit. However, when it comes to grown-ups, she takes right over. She sits on our desks and knocks papers to the floor. She climbs the dieffenbachia, and pulls the Kleenex out of the containers on the desks. She catches the flies on the windows, and falls asleep in the sunbeams on the floor. So far, she has managed to escape getting badly stepped on. One customer stepped on her tail and they both jumped about four feet. She eats everything in sight at her feed trough, and makes a great thing of her sandbox. One of the girls put a collar and tinkling bell on her this past week so we can hear her coming. When we have our weekly advertising meeting on Friday morning, she sits on Gary Hasse's shoulder. Maybe it's because she knows he's general manager and she wants to keep track of everything going on in the meeting.

Sometimes she checks the computer printer that puts out our paychecks, address labels, etc. When this occurs, we have to watch because she likes to swing on the paper coming out of the feed slot. All in all, I don't suppose she is much different than any other alley cat, but we all love her and think she's pretty cute.

February 25, 1987
SMOKING ADVERTISING BAN?

I ran across this excerpt from the Minnesota Newspaper Association news bulletin this past week and thought I might share it with readers of this column. It deals with smoking and restrictions involved in the past few years.

In that I have never smoked on a regular basis (outside of a cigar now and then in the summer and **I do mean outside**), I have never paid much attention to the restrictions I hear bleeding hearts yell out. My wife smokes about one pack a week and sometimes a pack in two weeks, so I really don't notice that she smokes at all. I know if I talked to the bleeding hearts, they could tell me almost to the day when she is going to die. In the meantime she is on the down side of sixty and has only spent one day in the hospital in her life to get her tonsils out. She doesn't have colds, works eight hours a day, five days a week and gives me a helping hand when I slow down. So that's the story of my smoking family.

THE FOLLOWING YOU MIGHT BE INTERESTED IN READING!

"An attempt to protect people from themselves," is the way John Edstrom, co-publisher of *Winona Shopper and Post* described the proposed ban on tobacco advertising. (We reported in past bulletins about the New York Bar Association joining the American Medical Association in calling for such a ban.)

"First Amendment Up in Smoke?' was the title of a Jan. 28 editorial by Edstrom which made some good points against the ban. He ends the editorial with this paragraph:

"This is, of course, not in the category of great evils that can befall one in a wicked world, but on the other hand, the prohibitionists of tobacco advertising have no evidence that such a ban will cut abusive tobacco use or save lives. A society such as ours, showing early signs of a weakness for Big Brother government, had best not experiment with First Amendment abuses even in the commercial area. That would well lead to a full scale addiction to totalitarian censorship of anything anyone might want to say that didn't jibe with government policy designed to create a brave new world, which nobody wants."

March 25, 1987
NORTH DAKOTA MUST BE BRAVE

This past week a hundred and twenty thousand North Dakotans went to the polls and voted a thirty-three percent income tax raise for the state. I would doubt if there is another state in the union that would even think in those terms. The people of North Dakota, I would say, are mighty brave. However, I'm sure they will wonder where their money is going when it comes to paying these taxes, that is IF THEY CAN PAY THEM. I talked with Jay Lindgren about this a few weeks ago and he explained that North Dakota is thirty-seventh in relation to taxes in the fifty states. He indicated to me that we, of course, will have to raise taxes. What I wonder is why it is a sin to be thirty-seventh on the list of the rest of the states. I certainly don't think we will take any honors by being twenty-seventh or –eighth.

What really interests me is a statement made last Thursday by Vernon Bennett, superintendent of the Fargo schools. When asked what he thought of the voting on raising taxes, he said, "The people had better get ready because taxes will have to be doubled next year." That means over sixty percent increase in the two-year period.

On the national scene we are in for a rude awakening as well. A liberal president will be elected in 1988. We will have a Democratic Congress, which I'm not going to throw up my hands about, but I can tell the American people that taxes on a national level will go up dramatically. The arrival of the 1990s will usher in a recession in the United States. In the meantime in the rest of the '80s, taxes on the state level and national level will cut across the board into personal and business incomes like has never happened in the last seventy-five years. A weakened economy will be the end result with hundreds of thousands of people out of work.

The wise will be saving now for the two years of leeway we have until 1990. This is not a pretty picture I am painting, but I don't look for many happy times ahead.

May 13, 1987
NO MORE SUMMER PROJECTS, PLEASE

I told my wife that from now on no more summer projects for me. Last summer we built an addition where our patio used to be on the back of our house. As we all say, we just wanted a small addition that doesn't cost a lot of money. I'm sure a lot of you have been over that road. And then, surprise, fifteen thousand dollars later and after a couple or three trips to the bank, the addition is completed.

However, when I looked out from our new, fancy addition, I noticed something missing. We didn't have a patio anymore. The more I looked the worse it looked without a patio! I contacted my friend Stan across our yard who said he could certainly put a nice slab for a patio right where I wanted it. I also talked to my friend Jim across the park from our house who said he would be glad to lay some nice brick and build a very, very nice step to our fancy addition. Now I have no idea what all this is going to cost, but I do know that I probably will have to make another trip to my friendly banker. I also know that my friendly banker may not be so friendly when I trip in to see him this year because I still owe him for last year. He could tell me we are in a recession and on the verge of a depression, but I owe him so much now he has to be nice to me. So recession and depression are out, and to say "no" to a guy who already owes you money is a bad approach, so he probably will tell me the bank is already loaned up. I could take a night job, but then I wouldn't have time to charcoal on my new patio.

In any case, full speed ahead with the patio project. I always say you might as well be hung for a sheep as a lamb, so we shall see where time and another loan (hopefully) take me.

Helen Hayes said, "The hardest years in life are those between ten and seventy. I'm inclined to agree!

September 2, 1987
A SEAMAN'S POEM

The following poem I received this past week. You will note it comes from one of the twenty-one minesweepers that the U.S. has in its fleet. These are old ships built shortly after World War II. The reason these ships are old is your Congress didn't think them necessary enough to order more, even in the face of two hundred minesweepers the Russian Navy boasts. Shades of Pearl Harbor!

I do not have the name of the young seaman who wrote this poem, and I cannot divulge the name of the ship. Minesweepers are very small and very vulnerable and carry little armament. The ships now heading for the Persian Gulf have a long, hard trip ahead of them. They will work in blistering heat, night and day. If attacked, in most instances, they will be sunk in less than a minute. Top speed for most of these ships is twelve to fourteen knots, so they cannot run out of harm's way.

* * *

A WORLD CLASS MINESWEEPER

Off we sail on the ocean blue,
A tiny ship and a top-notch crew.
With our colors up high, high in the sky
I look up in wonder, wondering why?
Why choose us, a ready reserve,
To go to the Gulf in danger to serve?
These questions arise, how often they do,
But I know the answers and I'll tell them to you.
We were the ones who were chosen to go
'Cause we're the best; just ask those who know.
Who would you send when trouble arises?
Surely the one without unpleasant surprises.
So we are the chosen, 'cause we are the best.
We lead the way in front of the rest.
Off we sail on the ocean blue,
A wooden ship and her iron crew.
To all who inquire, will we answer the test?
I confidently answer their humble request,
As ours is a mission important indeed,
One we'll accomplish; just bid us God's speed.

October 21, 1987
A VALUABLE GIFT . . .

I remember a day in the '30s. The school bus was just down the road and had turned the mile line to come to our farm. Reason, of course, was to pick me up for my first day of high school. But a thought in my mind was that I was fourteen and, after all, I had already passed through eight grades and in my thinking there was not much more to learn. I turned to my mother and in a rather knowing manner explained to her that I had completed eight grades of school. I could read and write and do a bit of arithmetic and it didn't take a lot of book learning to plow a field or cultivate corn or bring a pheasant down with my .22 rifle. My mother happened to be doing the dishes (in water she had heated over an oil burner, I might add). She handed me my lunch pail and informed me that the school bus was turning into our farmyard. "The word is – you are going to school," she informed me. I climbed aboard the bus and the subject never came up again.

I have often thought over the years, what if my mother had said something else, like "You really don't have to go unless you want to." Her one sentence started me down a road, started me on a life I never would have known. I sit here today typing out this column, just one small phase of a tool I learned in high school, because that is where I learned to type. A new world opened for me in high school. I met and enjoyed young people of my own age and learned to accept responsibility and teamwork on the basketball team.

When I joined the Navy in September of 1941, a deck mate of mine could not read or write. This I could not believe, and was more surprised to see him studying a first grade reader. It brought home to me again the value of education and how lost I would be without my abilities to communicate through reading and writing. The value of associating with people with a high school education was at that time a great lift to my morale. In those days a college education was not the usual end of schooling, but high school definitely was. Nowadays college is the norm and the foundation to many better things in life.

Over the years, since that day I stood in the doorway of the garage we were living in (our house had burned and we could not afford to build a home at that time) and looked at my mother and then at the school bus, I have often wondered how in the world a lady who went to only third grade in school in a dugout would know the valuable thing she was handing me!

January 13, 1988
CERTAINLY A TEAM TO RECKON WITH . . .

A couple weeks ago I wrote in this column a few disparaging remarks concerning the Minnesota Vikings. Frankly, I gave them no chance to win in New Orleans. I haven't read over what I said in the column because I hate to have to eat the feathers along with the "crow." In any case, I did receive a few telephone calls and offered to buy their *West Fargo Pioneers* back, but they all wanted more money than I could afford to pay.

I was smart enough not to write about what would happen to the Vikes in San Francisco. I did, however, say that they would probably get beat, but in that they won so decisively in New Orleans they certainly made their point and I would be back in the stands come next season. However, I sat for three hours and watched the Vikes run over the San Francisco Forty-niners, and that I couldn't believe. I will now say one thing: they are truly a team to be reckoned with. Looking back on their season, they had been a hard luck team all the way, and don't forget they could just as easily have beaten Chicago and Washington as not, and they certainly didn't do bad up to the strike. The Vikes have had the horses all along; all they had to do was get them to go in the right direction.

In relation to Washington, I shall again sit on the edge of my seat with the sweat running down my arms and yelling my head off every time a score for the Vikes shows on the board.

February 24, 1988
A REAL MEAL

It seems like someone at our house is either going on a diet Monday or saying she is going on a diet all week and then live it up on the weekend. I'm not going to mention her name, because I might get into a bit of trouble since I live in the same house. In that there are only two people plus our cat, Ossie, who live there, I'm going to let you guess who diets.

A few nights back, I was asked the question, "What are YOU going to eat tonight?" Someone was telling me that she was going to eat on the light side and I had better start deciding what I was going to eat. Pictures of glory came into my mind concerning the old days on the farm. Fat breakfasts were my special in those days gone by, so I tiptoed to the basement and picked out two big potatoes. I have always liked raw potatoes with a dash of salt, so while I'm slicing away I'm also nibbling on a piece of raw potato. Next comes the fry pan with a generous gob of butter melting in the center. If you are going to do it right, you have to fry those potatoes real slow. That way they become real crisp. When crisp, take them off the stove and put on a warm plate. Next come two very large eggs and, of course, don't forget the generous gob of butter. A little oil added will help you when the basting is needed. In the meantime sock two large slices of bread in the toaster and keep the butter plate handy.

That way when the toast is ready you can slap a very nice covering of butter on the toast before it begins to cool. In the meantime keep an eye on your eggs because you don't want them to burn. At the same time use a spoon to scoop oil and butter over the top of the eggs. This way you get them basted just right.

When all this is done, put eggs on the warm plate along with the fried spuds (that are almost burned but not quite) and then don't forget one of the most important acts of all concerning a royal meal like this! You must wash the whole she-bang down with a big, fat bottle of beer.

I know when Doctor Geston reads about this fine combination breakfast-lunch-dinner he will recommend it to all his patients. I have found when our gang goes out on the spring opening of fishing season, I'm a very popular guy when it comes to breakfast. I certainly don't mind being a hero every morning!

If any of you who read this need any extra suggestions in relation to a super breakfast, I will be glad to help.

April 13, 1988
CHANGING <u>ALL</u> THE CLOCKS

Every six months I have a rather challenging job when it comes to clock changing, which incidentally happened to me this past week. I had never counted the clocks in our house before, but I find we have twelve. Twelve turns out to be a lot of clocks and at least half of them are the computer kind. To say the least, I'm no computer guy. On the farm we wound the big clock on the shelf once a week and I wound the clock beside my bed every night. If I forgot to wind my clock my dad reminded me at five in the morning that it was time to milk the cows. Cows, I find, don't wait. They need feeding and everything else that goes along with a cow. I also found that if a guy sits down at the cow barn, the work seems to pile up. Those cows aren't putting it in one end to stay there.

In any case, nowadays with the music wake-up clock, I'm awake at six to hear the news before my feet strike the floor. I must say that darn wake-up clock really is a challenge when it comes to changing the time to an hour earlier or an hour later. For me it's a two day work out. The instruction book is part Japanese, part Italian, and two or three other languages, which leads to nothing but confusion for me. Not that I don't know English when I come on it, but with all those other strange languages in between I'm not sure what I'm reading.

The final embarrassment is I forget where all my clocks are. Some rooms have two clocks, others just one. This, of course, doesn't figure in the clocks on the cars and that's a real frustrating thing for me because they are all different. The other day I plumb gave up on the clock in the Sunbird. My wife got in the car, punched one button and the darn thing practically set itself. Take me back to the old tick-tock of farm days.

June 22, 1988
WE ALL NEED A GOOD CHUCKLE

There are some things in life that make living in this world challenging and at times downright funny. I happened to think of a few over the weekend and I couldn't resist sharing them with those of you who read this column.

A special feature in the Barnesville paper last week caught my eye. It seems that one fine night a few years back the alarm system at the Barnesville bank went into full swing and the police force, which consisted of a force of one, gathered at the front door to form a full scale investigation. Arriving at the bank, the chief pulled his trusty revolver and told the bank teller to go in first because the teller had the key!

* * *

During my traveling days with Columbia Artists Management, I traveled by car from city to city. In that I was always in a hurry to get to my destination, I felt it a real affront when stopping for gas if the attendant didn't get right on the job and fill my car tank. I remember once I stopped at a very small town some place in Kansas for a fill-up at a Standard station. The attendant was not on the ball. In fact, I sat about two minutes and drove away. As I was driving out of town, I noted another Standard station, so stopped there. A very cute girl came out to wait on me and in the process of filling my tank and cleaning the windshield, I was complaining about the poor service the other Standard station had given me.

"Yes," said the cute young lady, "my dad owns that station."

* * *

I remember my wife telling me about another story that involves Barnesville. She was working at the doctor's office, which happens to be across the street from the fire station. The whistle blew one day and the firemen came running from all directions. The next thing my wife noted was the firemen were pushing the fire engine to the fire which happened to be just down the block. It seems the fire truck had run out of gas! She made a note not to mention it to her dad, as he happened to be one of the firemen.

* * *

I remember a time when I was selling concert artists in Texarkana, Texas. I was in a meeting with local concert enthusiasts who were helping me set up a concert series. A couple days before, I had been in Camden, Ark., and stayed in their local hotel. During the meeting someone asked me the last city I had come from and I told them Camden, and as an afterthought asked if anyone had ever stayed in that stinky hotel in Camden. The fellow sitting next to me, who happened to be the publicity chairman for the concert series, smiled and informed me, yes, he had stayed there – in fact, he owned the hotel.

* * *

Father's Day was last Sunday. My wife informed me that she couldn't find anything to buy me for Father's Day so she worked up a strawberry shortcake. At my age I'll take anything I can get!

September 14, 1988
A BIT OF POLITICS

I must make some comments on the Yellowstone Park fires. In the first place it is a terrible shame to have a beautiful area like Yellowstone practically burn down. It is reported that at least a third of the park has burned. A hundred years is a long time to wait for replacement trees. However, I do not blame the Park Service. I understand they do let fires burn where lightning is concerned and let nature sort of take its course. In some cases designed burning is also used.

Down through the years I have always admired our Park Service and the way our parks have been taken care of and kept clean and neat. However, it seems a new voice has been added in the shape of some of our people in Congress. Right away they want to fire someone. They have all kinds of ideas of how the park fires should be fought and controlled, after the fact. It seems they have to find someone to blame for this major fire. Never mind that we have had the driest season since the '30s, and pay no attention to hot winds and no rain. Just get in there and play a bit of politics and cut someone down and then tell the nation what a good job they have done to run the culprits into the ground.

The parks in our nation have been around for many a year. It seems no one in Congress complained about fires until now. The blame lies where it should, on the shoulders of our United States Congress, the greatest sitters-on-hands the world has ever known.

September 28, 1988
OUT OF MY ELEMENT

When I was on the farm, a cultivator was something you hooked two horses in front of and drove to the cornfield and used to plow up the ground between long rows of corn. A couple weeks ago I determined that I had better go out to Big Iron at the fairgrounds and see what had been invented since I was on the farm. I looked for my little one-row cultivator and discovered they now plow up the ground like I used to, but do about six or eight rows at once. Not only that, but with tractors you have to climb up into. I used to take one hop to get aboard our little old Farmall, that is, after I had cranked it to get it started, making sure that I had tripped the magneto so the darn thing wouldn't kick me into the next county.

I took a short walk around the grounds and I saw machinery I had no idea what it was used for. Roy Larson, who was with me, said, "I'll bet half the farmers don't know what this machinery is for either."

I saw funny looking things with big teeth and a drill for planting seed that I could have put at least seven of our drills on the old farm alongside. When I got to the tractors, they looked like something so big they should be pulling a train.

Needless to say, I was completely out of my element, so I wandered over to the hospital barn and had my blood pressure taken. That gal wrapped a rig around my arm, pumped up the balloon and said I was good for another day or two. While there, I had my cholesterol count taken. Found I had to cut down on the cheddar cheese, etc. However, maybe next year I'll tackle Big Iron again or maybe I'll go to the old Threshers Reunion and find one of those old guys like me who can talk the same language.

January 11, 1989
STARTING THE NEW YEAR

Below you will read a short poem a friend of mine gave me some time ago. I know I have had this in my column before, but it deserves reviewing from time to time. We all are starting a new year. There will be many challenges which will frustrate us and in some cases turn us to despair. I remember another friend of mine, when a day seemed very dark to me in the business world, said one very important thing. "Look how far you have come." On that simple foundation, I picked up my panic and fear and traveled on.

The following was given to me some years ago by one Jack Lien, a friend of mine of Grand Forks, N.D.

* * *

DON'T QUIT

When things go wrong, as they sometimes will,
When the road you're trudging seems all uphill,
When the funds are low and the debts are high
And you want to smile, but you have to sigh,
When care is pressing you down a bit,
Rest, if you must – but never quit!

Life is queer, with its twists and turns,
As every one of us sometimes learns,
And many a failure turns about
When he might have won if he'd stuck it out.
Stick to your task, though the pace seems slow.
You may succeed with another blow.

Often the goal is nearer than
It seems to a faint and faltering man.
Often the struggler has given up
When he might have captured the victor's cup,

And he learned too late, when the night slipped down.
How close he was to the golden crown.

Success is failure turned inside out,
The silver tints of the clouds of doubt,
And you never can tell how close you are –
It may be near when it seems afar.
So stick to the fight when you're hardest hit.
It's when things seem worst that you mustn't quit.

February 22, 1989
DOUBLE-BREASTED SUITS BACK

A nice looking suit on a man does something special for his appearance. I have always tried to keep good suits on hand, even when I could only pay $10 a month on my suit bill. Most men's suits change very little in design, and if they do it is over an extended time. In relation to women's dresses, the designers have made so many length changes that now it really doesn't make any difference if they are so short it is challenging or so long they trip over the hem. They are always in style.

I now note the *Kiplinger Letter* tells me that double-breasted suits for men are the coming things, with wide lapels, big shoulders, trousers fuller and pleats deeper. Designers will also throw a vest in for a little extra profit. Also, three-button Ivy League suits will be pushed.

I don't mind these changes at all, and most men will not give it much extra thought. The reason is they certainly will not go right out and try to get into style. I shall keep right on wearing my single-breasted suits because I see no reason to spend a pile of money trying to keep up with a clothes horse. I also look better in single-breasted suits. Double-breasted suits make me look like I'm only three feet high. I have trouble enough trying to look five feet seven and a half.

To top it all off, I just had all my pants let out one inch, for reasons I don't have to explain in this column. At my age I'm not going to let a double-breasted suit style change the way I look in the world. The suit I am wearing as I type this column is over ten years old and I like it just fine. If I treat it right, I may get another five years out of it.

May 10, 1989

RUSSIAN ROULETTE SYNDROME

I'm not much of an advocate of secondhand cars. In fact, I have always tried to buy a new car during my lifetime when I needed a car. However, there is always a time when a secondhand car is the only thing you can afford. In that case, the Russian roulette syndrome comes into play. I have seen secondhand cars, last year's and others, not last a thousand miles. If that isn't Russian roulette, I don't know what is.

When I was traveling on the road for Columbia Artists Management in my early years, I bought a secondhand Chrysler from a dealer in Stevens Point, Wisc. It was a quick deal because I needed a car to make our next call down Missouri way. The dealer needed a quick deal because he had a fancy secondhand Chrysler he needed to get rid of right away. He informed me that he had just put in a new motor and I must not drive it over fifty miles an hour until the motor got broken in. This I took very seriously, loaded up my wife and luggage and headed for Missouri. All the way down there, every time I turned a corner I thought the car had developed Saint Vitus' dance. The car shook, the steering wheel shook, the front end shook, but I kept in mind the new motor and only drove fifty miles an hour. When I did arrive at our destination, I thought it prudent that I have a repairman look at the front end. He took one look and wanted to know how far I had driven and was amazed that I even got from downtown to his garage without ending up in all the wrong places.

I did end up back in Stevens Point the next year. In the meantime I had traded for another Chrysler, new incidentally. My wife and I were at a dance when, lo and behold, here comes my very special Chrysler dealer.

"Say, I said, "I bought a new Chrysler this year."

"Why didn't you buy it from me?" he said. I made no comment on that. However, later in the evening I recounted the fact that I had bought a car from the hotshot dealer to a friend who was out for the evening with us.

"You didn't really buy a car from him, did you? He belongs to our Elks club and we won't play cards with him because we can't keep him from dealing off the bottom of the deck."

He also wanted to know what car I bought, and I learned the car had been rolled and there was no such thing as a new motor. The hotshot dealer had told me fifty miles an hour because he didn't think the motor could stand sixty miles an hour.

I did trade the secondhand Chrysler for my new Chrysler, which I loved. However, a few days after trading, a friend of mine in Barnesville, Minn., told me he saw my car sitting on a street in Fargo with the motor running.

He said, "There it was with the pistons changing holes every time the motor turned over."

July 26, 1989
WHERE DID IT GO???

This past week I signed up for my Social Security. It didn't take long. Evidently my life has been relatively simple because I didn't have to do much mind-digging to come up with the answers to the questions.

As with most people my age, I keep asking where the time has gone. I still remember very vividly sitting on a one-row cultivator in a dusty cornfield trying to keep the dirt out of my eyes, dirt kicked up by the team pulling the rig. I also can well remember in the alfalfa field when I was on top of the hayrack arranging the alfalfa on the load on the hot summer days of 1936 in South Dakota. The trick was to keep the leaves from going down the inside of my shorts and sticking and itching on a very sweaty back. I cannot say those were the good ol' days because memory reminds me of when I had to skip out to the outhouse in twenty-five below weather. Those Montgomery Ward catalogs weren't anything to brag about, either. Couldn't afford toilet paper.

However, I find there are advantages in my age group. The gals smile when I walk past. They know I'm too old to make a pass. I don't have to worry about that special curl on my head. It disappeared long years ago. The young guys sort of let me go first on the fishing trips. They always run the boat motor while I do the fishing. When I speak up in a conversation, I note more listen than they used to. Sympathy, I guess. I attended a family reunion a few weeks ago. My relatives sure have gotten old!

This past week I had to renew my driver's license. The gal that checked me out said I just barely passed the eye test. Must have been something in my eye because I see plenty good. AND I'M STILL NOT TOO OLD TO LOOK AT A WELL-TURNED ANKLE.

September 6, 1989
GETTING TOUGH ONLY SOLUTION

In that I'm writing this before the President's speech on drugs, I thought I would make a couple of comments on my own. I may be dumb about drugs, but I do know when a country (Colombia) puts its so-called neck on the line to fight for its very life, everyone has a problem. Until the people of our nation start to realize that drugs can destroy the very fabric of our country, things will go on as per usual. There will be killings and threats of killings. Our young people will be constantly tempted with drugs because the pushers will make nothing but money. The bleeding hearts, of course, will wring their hands and tell us that we shouldn't be so hard on those that take drugs and those with drugs in their possession because they can't help their problem.

It has always been my thinking that those that take drugs, deal in drugs, push drugs, or in any fashion have anything to do with drugs should pay a very tough penalty. I know this will go against the grain of many people, but it is my opinion that people who sell drugs should pay the supreme penalty. Until the people of this nation start getting tough about what is going on in our nation, this problem will sit on our doorsteps morning, noon and night, AND WILL LAST FOREVER.

Always With'em

The 1990s

January 31, 1990

FIGHT COLDS... BUY A NEW TOOTHBRUSH

I was talking to my nephew from Oklahoma City recently, and for some reason we got to talking about toothbrushes. I didn't think it was the most exciting subject until he told me that I should change toothbrushes at least once a month, more so if in the meantime I had had a cold. I have never given my toothbrush much thought through life except that the paste I put on it left a nice taste in my mouth and also did wonders for morning breath. However, I was told that it is most important to follow a plan of changing toothbrushes. So here I am with an old toothbrush I have used for at least three years or more. I like it because it was all worn down and nice and soft. It took me a year to get it soft, so I thought I was real happy about brushing my teeth every morning.

After my phone conversation with my nephew, I did begin to worry about all those germs having a ball every morning in my mouth. So I ended up at our local drugstore and bought four toothbrushes. I was under the impression they would cost seven or eight dollars. The toothbrush I had been using, Dr. Callender gave me years ago, so how was I to know what toothbrushes really cost? You know, I found out toothbrushes really don't cost a heck of a lot. I think four came to around two dollars. I chose the nice, big, soft ones so my mouth wouldn't be real shocked with a brand new toothbrush.

If I never have a cold again, I can always say to everyone having a cold, "Buy a new toothbrush."

* * *

Special Note:

A lady in our city crossed over this past week. I use these words because my sister used those very words in a note she left for me. She died December 28. I thought the words used in her note made everything seem like an adventure.

Always With'em

Mrs. Esther Pyle did that same thing last Friday. I used the word LADY because she was certainly that and then some. Esther worked to bring in news each week for the *West Fargo Pioneer.* I cannot think of anyone more loyal to our paper. She started writing her column in 1968 until in past years her health kept her from her writing. We all miss her at the paper, but I know things are better in her cross over.

May 2, 1990
DORGAN'S REPLY

Recently I wrote Representative Byron Dorgan in relation to two important questions. One was concerning health care. Businesses in most cases pay a portion, and in some cases all of their employees' health insurance. This is an important growing problem for businesses in our nation. It is not uncommon for health care to go up 20 percent and more each year. Business in time will find ways around health care insurance and, in turn, government will see ways of tying business to the insurance problem. In the long haul, business, when hiring new workers, will take this problem into strong consideration to see if any new employee is really necessary.

I also wrote Mr. Dorgan concerning how much Americans save. I might add here they save very, very little. He answers this in his letter to me. In that these two subjects are important to all of us, I include his letter.

Dear Don:

Many thanks for getting in touch with me last month. Your letters are always insightful and to the point, and this one is no exception.

I did want to mention the Health Benefits for All Americans Act that is receiving increased attention. The Kennedy proposal is awaiting action by the full Senate, but the House bill is not nearly as far along. I am very concerned about the growing number of Americans who are without adequate health insurance coverage, but at the same time, I am concerned about the impact this proposal might have on businesses around the nation. It seems to me we ought to be considering getting to the root of the nature of rising health care costs before we put another expensive government program into place.

You also commented on the low rate of savings that continues to plague our country. Recent reports indicating that the rate of savings by the American public is plummeting even further has spurred enough interest here in Congress to examine why Americans continue to be so disinclined to save. Americans have always been a nation of spenders, but the continued decline in our country's savings habits is being viewed with considerable alarm.

Last year the Ways and Means Committee held hearings on the causes, effects, and possible cures for the country's low personal savings rate, and we will be examining the tax code as we search for ways to boost the national rate of savings. This is an extremely complex issue, and certainly one which exceeds the reach of the tax code. I anticipate further examination of the issue by a variety of congressional committees. I'll certainly be pushing for this.

Thanks again, Don. Keep in touch!

June 13, 1990
WHAT ARE WE GOING TO DO?

I am not against guns for sport. I was raised with guns in our home and learned very early in life what they were all about. Also, I was trained in several types of guns in the service. I also am not against the National Rifle Association in its interest of sporting guns. I am against what a large share of guns is being used for today. For the life of me, I don't understand the need for fast-firing guns just to shoot a deer, pheasant or turkey or any other birds or animals. If a guy can't get them on the first or second shot, he shouldn't be hunting anyway.

What I'm really talking about here are machine pistols, automatic rifles and machine guns. They are used to kill people every day in our nation. I'm also not proud that our nation's capital is known as the crime capital of the world. This stems from narcotics, and that leads to guns and, no matter what you say, guns kill people, and anyone is going to have a hell of a time convincing me otherwise.

Before the Senate and House at this time is a bill that will enlarge the application of the death penalty, and many of its facets are designed to curb crime and stop this killing of our people. YET OUR CONGRESS HESITATES AND DILLY-DALLIES AND DISCUSSES, MANY EVEN VOTING AGAINST YOUR AND MY SAFETY IN OUR EVERYDAY LIVES. What kind of people have we sent to our nation's capital? Are they "nuts"? A lot of this stems from the National Rifle Association influence, a group that is even protecting the production of plastic coated bullets which will penetrate the protective vests of policemen.

WE ARE LIVING IN ONE OF THE MOST DANGEROUS PLACES IN THE WORLD RIGHT HERE IN OUR OWN COUNTRY. NOW WHAT **ARE WE** GOING TO DO ABOUT IT?

July 2, 1990
WE'RE GOING TO PAY

I know everyone at some time or other has talked about the Savings & Loan debacle. It seems everyone is talking about it, but nothing seems to happen. As I see it, there is a very good reason for not much action. It all started several years back, even before the Reagan administration. This is why you hear a lot of accusations on both sides in relation to Democrats and Republicans, but, of course, that is not the problem because it doesn't solve the problem. The problem is trying to get some of the money back. This can only be done by selling the properties that exist that can be sold. Keep in mind the money that was stolen or just plain confiscated and spent cannot be collected and brought back where it came from.

That is long gone. You can toss these guys in jail, but you still don't have the money.

Of course, politics is well woven into the whole mess. I see Pat Schroeder, senator from Colorado, is doing her best to plaster Neil Bush (the President's son) with all kinds of accusations, but this is just plain politics. If Schroeder looks around she will find some of the plaster probably on her feet, stuff she doesn't even know about. The reason for all the silence on the S&L mess is the Congress is basically responsible for the plight and THEY JUST DON'T WANT TO TALK BECAUSE PEOPLE WILL FIND OUT MORE THAN CONGRESS WANTS THEM TO KNOW. When it comes right down to the nitty-gritty, the Justice Department will pursue only the most flagrant offenders, so don't get your hopes up that hundreds of savings and loan people are going to jail.

It will all take 20 or 30 years to work out, and you and I will be paying the bill, probably in more taxes on just about everything you buy.

November 28, 1990
WORRY OF WAR

I know most Americans have filed away in their minds a very important item. However, the little drawer in the file is kept open. In this case, it is a worry note, a worry of war. Basically, Americans have never wanted to go to war. In both World Wars, the United States was the last to shoot back. The so-called wars since World War II into which we were drawn in one way or another, we never wanted to be there, but circumstances of world leadership demanded we be there. We can stand aside and let things go as they will, but that is not the way things work on the globe we all live on.

We are again faced with a world problem. For the first time, most nations of the world are with us in our decision to enter the Persian Gulf affair. Again we are on the horns of a dilemma. The rest of the world, with the exception of Britain, is telling us to do the big fight. However, they also say we must wait and let time do the fighting for us. Japan, of all countries, should be in the forefront with our servicemen and women. She needs oil like no other country in the world.

There are points here that demand our nation's attention in the very near future. President Bush moved to the Gulf to protect our oil. No doubt about it, with no oil we all would be in real straits in a hurry. Oil is a very important factor in our everyday living; we had better face up to this. Oil on an international scale is very, very important. Keep in mind the Arabs sit on top of 70 percent of the oil in the world. If Saddam Hussein were to take over this oil, certain things could and will happen. It would be like turning off the water tap to the whole world. He could control what you got and how much you would pay. Europe would be at his mercy. He could dictate to Japan how and where they spend their money. Keep in mind, if Japan were to take their money out of our country, our nation would be in dire need in a hurry. This would be followed by a depression across our country, and in turn the whole world. If you think going to war in the Persian Gulf is big, give a thought to what would and will happen if we let Hussein call the shots to the Arab world.

"The world as we know it will change forever. Maybe, just maybe, Saddam can be scared out of Kuwait by the threat of a war that would destroy his military machine and/or his life. But that would require something like an ultimatum, backed by a genuine readiness to fight, and Saddam might not believe it even then. So the U.S. has to prepare for war. Anyone with a shred of human feeling can say that only with a suppressed scream of fear and pain. The U.S. confronts a bitter, tragic, even ghastly necessity. But, this time, it is a necessity that there is no honorable way to avoid." (The last paragraph was taken from *Time* , November 26, 1990, magazine, under the heading "The Case for War.")

February 6, 1991
KUDOS TO WEST FARGO POLICE

Not many people mention or talk about our police department until they need them. I for one have always been of the opinion that our police department in West Fargo is one of the best in North Dakota, or elsewhere, for that matter. Over the years, the department has been no end of help to me and our company, at times calling me in the middle of the night concerning something that had happened to our trucks or a regular check on our office doors. When any door has been open, they made sure someone was notified.

Now that Riverside is a part of West Fargo, I feel safer because I know a quick call to our police will be answered immediately. Last week I noted a small truck cruising through the north park across the river from our house. In that it was dark and early in the morning, I called our police. They told me to wait by my phone and they would call back. In four minutes they were back to me and informed me the truck was a city truck that was cleaning out our dead elm trees. This instills confidence in the department, and I also at the same time know they are there for the home folks of West Fargo.

To add to all this takes organization. I know about organization because our business depends on confident people to make deadlines and do a good job. Most important, it takes people in charge who know what they are doing and know how to get a job done without irritating their own people and people outside of the department at the same time.

I wish to take this opportunity to congratulate one man who I'm sure does not get the credit he deserves. Ken Hansen has been our police chief for several years. He is a quiet man, who instills confidence and gets the job done with no ill feelings. I hope Ken is with our city as police chief for many years to come. CONGRATULATIONS, KEN HANSEN, FOR A JOB WELL DONE!

March 20, 1991
DENTAL REFLECTIONS

I have no idea how many times over the years I have been to my dentist. In any case, it is one heck of a lot. I remember one time during the war (the big one, that is) when one Navy dentist was mad as heck at me for letting a front tooth decay. I didn't tell him I had been at sea for five months and couldn't get back.

If you are anything like me, the mere fact you need your teeth cleaned is somewhat of a trauma. I was at Doc Callender's last week with my mouth wide open, waiting for the young lady with that little pick to not find anything challenging. However, it wasn't long before she struck a nerve. I gritted my so-called teeth and hoped she wouldn't notice. Doc Callender found that it was a tooth I don't use, and I could pull it, fill it or ignore it, so I chose the latter.

I'm intrigued by the gal cleaning my teeth. Usually I close my eyes and dream of my Aunt Ethel's strawberry shortcake with real whipped cream, liberal gobs of butter, hot shortcake piled high with strawberries inside and out. I'm always rudely awakened by a whirling brush on my teeth or a poke in a tender place. Last week when I awoke from my dream, I asked my cute tooth cleaner if people ever kept their eyes open and looked at her. I was surprised to learn lots of people do. She said it is sort of disconcerting. She added a note to this by telling me some people who watched her while she was cleaning their teeth, she discovered, were really not looking at her but were watching the reflection from her glasses to see what she was doing in their mouth.

In any case, I shall keep the faith and try to keep the teeth.

May 8, 1991
MINORITIES RULE . . .

If you think you can advertise almost anything in your newspaper, or any paper for that matter, you have another guess coming. You can be sued because of the Federal Fair Housing Act if you have a preference for or discriminate by: age, ancestry, color, familial status, handicap, lawful source of income, marital status, national origin, race, religion, sex, or sexual orientation. The newspaper can be sued. Keep in mind, any reader can file a complaint.

Always With'em

Ads that ask for an "older man" or apartment ads that say "perfect for a young couple" can get a newspaper in trouble. Ads can say "no smokers" or "no pets" because those are not legally protected categories.

If you don't want Norwegians to rent your apartment, of course you can't put in your ad, "No Norwegians need apply," but you could put an ad in saying, "Apartment to rent. Incidentally, I hate Norwegians."

I don't know if this has anything to do with what we call FREEDOM in our nation, but I do have the strange feeling that a few people are making us all jump to a tune we don't like.

All this makes me want to go back to the farm. At least all this crap I'm hearing will be the real thing when I get there, and I'll know how to recognize it when I step in it.

June 5, 1991
MOTHER NATURE HINTING

I have always wondered what goes on at the YMCA, so this past November I joined the organization. I wasn't sure that I wanted to go by myself, so I waited for my friend, Hank Newgard, to retire from his years of work and go with me.

When the day came for me to take the step into building my muscles and wind with exercise and twenty-nine times around the exercise track, I approached the whole procedure with a bit of trepidation. Twenty-nine times around the track means I have walked one mile. After that comes all the lifting of weights and the grunting and groaning that goes along with that sort of thing. In my day, I loved to play basketball and, of course, Hank did a lot of that in his day, also. I will say right here, after three minutes the both of us on the basketball floor found that they must have lifted the basket rim since we played because that rim seemed a lot higher than when we used to play. I'm sure someone made the floor a lot larger, because about two times across the floor had us both almost flat on the floor. I also learned that throwing the ball over my head to make a basket is a little different than when I used to play in our gym in Amherst, S.D. For some reason, I not only missed the basket, but the whole backboard. To top all this off, I encouraged a bad case of bursitis and ended up on the hotpad for two days. I'm not giving up the YMCA, but I think Mother Nature is trying to tell me something!

July 3, 1991
FREEDOM, LET'S KEEP IT

Shortly it will be the Fourth of July. When I was a young fellow, the fourth of this month meant firecrackers, picnics and generally a day of fun or, better yet, a trip into town from our farm to a ballgame where they sold more firecrackers for which I could con my dad out of a few nickels to buy that extra pack of crackers. I didn't realize what the 4th really meant in those days, except a day of fun running with the other kids and watching the red, white and blue flutter in the breeze. I had heard my dad talk about the First World War and thought that really must have been something. He wasn't in it, of course. Guess he had to stay home and raise grain for the troops. Yet, I never really connected what freedom, honor and country were all about. I was just a little guy filing memories away about that big war.

When things began to come apart in the late '30s, I paid little heed, because there was farming to do and school to attend and passing grades to worry about. I remember going to the theater in Britton, S.D. *The Path News* showed London being bombed. The great fires filled the screen, but of course that was what we called "over there." I used to sing a song, think I still have the sheet music in our piano bench today. "Just stay on this side of the pond," were the words. I now wonder what our world would be like today if our nation had done just that! I was a proud, young guy in those days. I remember the days of 1940 when our country began to draft our nation's youth. I told my dad that I guess I would be drafted and that I would probably have to go to the Army. Farming is important, I was told, and I could stay home, but that didn't seem to impress me much because I well knew what farming was all about. I figured I had eaten at least a half acre of Dad's farm in my lifetime already.

The sequel to all this is I ended up in the Navy because I couldn't find the Army office. Just a farm boy, you know, following the call of "Now is the time for all good men to come to the aid of their country." Four years, one month and 11 days later, all this aid didn't impress me so much that I thought I should "ship over," as we called it in the Navy.

In any case, I did learn a bit about freedom and what it must mean for those who don't have it and have never experienced it. The years have taught me some of its values: the privilege of saying what I think, the opportunity of changing my work world, the advantage of getting into my car and going where I please, and most of all learning when you work hard, be honest, things in most cases give you what you want out of life. This does not happen in a great share of our world of today. There is a stirring of the world's great masses. Most see and hear what happens in a country that gives its people a choice. They hear what can be done, all in the name of one word, FREEDOM. There seems to be a great stampede over the world toward a light that offers all these things we in our nation take for granted. At one time at the beginning of our nation, the word went out, "YOU NOW HAVE A REPUBLIC, IF YOU CAN KEEP IT." Let us hope there will always be those men and women, strong in mind, kind in thought, generous to all, in our countrymen, who in the end will say, "THIS IS OUR REPUBLIC AND WE ARE GOING TO KEEP IT."

August 21, 1991
NEVER TOO YOUNG, AND NEVER TOO OLD

The following has been hanging on my wall at the office for some time. I look at it when I feel a little low and need to kick myself in the pants. You will note one is never too young or too old. I, of course, fit better in the old part, but there are times when I feel like a young sprout again. When that happens, I usually take a trip. I think everyone should take a trip, if it is only to the Galaxie in Barnesville, Minn. When I arrive at the Galaxie, they bring me my favorite cigar just to get things started for the evening. Yep, there's nothing like feeling young, even though you are not twenty-five.

The following is from the *Express Press* in Fargo:

"Quality of living is not a chronological affair. Before deciding we are too young or too old to try a new adventure, or to make our mark in history, or to face new challenges, it might be wise to consider the lives of people who didn't let age interfere.

"George Burns won his first Oscar at 80.

"Golda Meir was 71 when she became prime minister of Israel.

"William Pitt was only 24 when Great Britain called on him to become prime minister.

"George Bernard Shaw was 94 when one of his plays was first produced. At 96, he broke his leg when he fell out of a tree he was trimming in his backyard.

"Mozart published his first composition at 7 years old.

"Ted Williams ended his baseball career with a home run in his last time at bat. Williams was 42.

"Grandma Moses didn't start painting until she was 80 years old. She completed over 1,500 paintings in the remainder of her life, with 25 percent of those produced after she was 100.

"Benjamin Franklin published his first newspaper column when he was 16, and had the honor of framing the U.S. Constitution when he was 81.

"Michelangelo was 71 when he painted the Sistine Chapel.

"Albert Schweitzer was still performing operations in his African hospital at 81.

"Neither Henry Ford nor Abraham Lincoln realized any success until after they were 40 years old.

"Gordie Howe remained a top competitor in professional hockey into his early fifties.

"Winston Churchill assumed the role of Great Britain's prime minister at 65. At 70, he addressed the crowds on V-E Day, standing on top of his car to speak.

"Casey Stengel didn't retire from the rigorous schedule of managing the New York Yankees until he was 75."

And Everett Paulsen of 1444 River Street, West Fargo, is making major structural changes and additions to his house, including roof work, at age 82.

October 16, 1991
TIME LIMIT

At this time we are printing a book for a fellow in Phoenix, Ariz., in relation to limited terms for our elected officials in Washington. I can relate to this, because I have advocated limited service in office for our congressmen for years. I not only am referring to age and service in office, but we don't have the worries of trying to get someone out of office who is doing a job we don't like. Why the people of Massachusetts have made a habit of electing Teddy Kennedy back each term is one on me. If the people want a congressman in office bad enough, they can re-elect him after an elapse of time.

In my opinion, I don't under any circumstances think congressmen should make a lifelong ambition of service in Washington. New people in congressional service mean new ideas and a new approach to the challenging things that go on in our government.

To add to all this, I must say it is sickening to watch what has gone on in the Judge Thomas trials, and I do mean trials. To come up with the decision that they are both right blows my mind. Also to pass judgment on someone without a guilty verdict is not the American way. I always am of the opinion, innocent until proven guilty. To really make a travesty of justice, there sits Ted Kennedy right in the front row.

January 8, 1992
1992... LOOK OUT, HERE I COME

I could ask a few simple questions like how does Senator Kennedy plan to cover everyone in this nation with a medical plan? Who pays the bill? Congress has worked it out so an IRA plan does no one any good in relation to a guy trying to save for old age. They have lowered the interest rates so far that what little money is left in the country is being taken out of the banks and put into other savings, that is if anyone has any savings. They can't lower taxes because there would be much less money sent to Washington. They can't raise taxes because they might get voted out of office.

After thinking all this over, I decided I couldn't do much about it anyway, so New Year's Eve I took off for Barnesville, Minn., and had a ball at the Galaxie. I didn't spend much money because I didn't have to. Twenty dollars bought an excellent prime rib dinner and midnight breakfast. Now if I had been in New York, the twenty wouldn't have paid the cover charge. I might have bought breakfast with tip extra.

I danced until one o'clock in the morning and talked some Barnesville friends of ours into letting us stay overnight. That way, when we awoke, my wife and I were just in time for breakfast, and we didn't have to drive anyplace. Now that's what I call working a good thing all the way. I had it planned so well that I ended up in front of the TV at home in time to catch all the football games.

If this is the way 1992 is going to be for me, I can't knock it.

February 19, 1992
CANADIANS COME TO U.S. FOR MEDICAL TREATMENT

Most of you who read newspapers, listen to radio, or view TV have not missed the fact that there is lots of talk about a medical plan for our nation. I myself am all for a medical plan, but what I want to know is how it will work and who pays. When I think about the thirty-five million people without a medical plan, I think it would be nice if Congress would give us some answers as to just who is going to pay and how this plan will be paid. I also want to know if the hundreds of thousands of illegals will be covered by this plan, and does this also include the people who carry green cards?

The following is information from Canadians Dan and Elaine Johnston, who live in Winnipeg, Manitoba, Canada. I thought it might be interesting to give a short rundown of how things happen in Canada when you need medical assistance.

Canada is, to a great degree, socialist in nature.

The Canadian health care system is not well understood by many Americans. The rich cannot buy better health care than the poor. To this point, this probably sounds good to you.

In Canada, a patient's ability to access a specialist is restricted, and lengthy waits occur. The wait to get into a pain clinic in Winnipeg can take anywhere from two to ten months, AND no guarantee with respect to the service one will receive once that person arrives at the appointment.

If you are unfortunate enough to require surgery, you go into yet another waiting queue that can now take years.

The Canadian system is seen as FREE... but what they pay in taxes to support the system is far in excess of the current tax burden in the U.S.

The reality is that in order to receive timely, sufficient and adequate care, one must, in many instances, go to the U.S.

The Johnstons say, as Canadians who out of necessity have had extensive experience with both the Canadian and American medical systems, they would encourage each and every American to be very skeptical when your presidential candidates start extolling the virtues of the Canadian medical system.

The Johnstons travel to the U.S. four times a year for Mrs. Johnston's medical treatment.

I want to include a comment or two in addition. First off, keep in mind there are only about thirty million people in Canada. We have more people without medical insurance than live in all of Canada. All I hear from Washington is we must have medical insurance for all people. Again, I say I'm all for it, but no one has stepped forward with a plan that will make economic sense. Of course, Teddy Kennedy has a plan, one that would break everyone except him. It's nice when you have a daddy who left lots of money for you when he took the trip.

March 25, 1992
TIME TO CARRY THE "CLICKER"

As per usual, the national TV news media are having a ball with all of the big race for the presidency. I might add that, again as per usual, they are trying their best to guide people's thinking right up to election time. I get a big kick out of the way they are pushing Clinton now that the rest have fallen out of the horse race, with the exception of Governor Brown. I note they have Clinton running neck and neck with President Bush. I also note they are trying as hard as they can not to use the President's name, but that of course is hard to ignore.

In any case, with all the slanted news time they are doing the best they can, which I know the American people will take with a large grain of salt. One would think the way they talk about the candidates that we Americans just got off the boat concerning what they are trying to tell us. As the saying goes, "same old crap," or what is better known as just plain "bull."

At least I'm getting smart in my old age. I carry my TV clicker around in my pocket. Before one of our esteemed politicians can finish the first word, I promptly cut to "Evening Shade," which I think is a super good TV show. That way, at least something pleasant will enter my ears in the place of someone trying to save the whole damn country for me.

April 1, 1992
JUST GOING FOR A DRIVE

Last Wednesday afternoon I suggested to Mrs. Witham that we go for a ride in my shiny black car. She thought that was mighty nice, so off we went for a ride around Pelican Lake. I zipped my shiny black car up to sixty-seven miles per hour and headed down I-94 to Barnesville, where I came to the turn-off to the lake region. A couple miles down the road I noticed a definite red, glaring light in my rear view mirror. I looked down and noted I had forgotten speed limits, and had again punched the cruise when I came onto the lake road.

In past years I have found when a red light appears in my rear view mirror, you might as well throw yourself on the mercy of the court, so to speak, of which I did the very same thing again Wednesday.

"I was traveling too fast," I said to a tan-suited officer as he approached my car. I did have the common sense to get out and meet him halfway to his car.

"Yes, you were traveling sixty-seven in a fifty-five mile an hour zone," he said.

The next question I was not prepared for when he asked, "Did you have your seat belt on?" However, I assured him I sure did, and that was no lie. He informed me that he was going to give me a warning ticket. I, of course, thought that was just fine and thanked him. When he approached my side of the car after I got back in, he smiled and handed me my warning ticket. My wife said, "My garsh, we should give him two *Midweek* papers next week." In that I didn't think that would impress him very much, I sort of passed that one by.

The point I do want to make is I rarely travel much over fifty-five on a road that shows signs of fifty-five miles per hour. I also want to compliment the State of Minnesota Highway Commission. This young officer conducted himself in the best manner, very polite, very neat, and if he is an example of the Minnesota highway patrolmen in the state, the state of Minnesota can be well proud. The only other thing I could say about the encounter is when the officer saw an old duffer with a red checkered cap climb out of a black shiny car, he decided he would do his good deed for the day and give me only a warning ticket.

April 22, 1992
STILL CLICKING MY HEELS

There are times in life when you begin to notice a bit of a change. By that, I mean you don't get out of a chair as fast as you used to. However, I find when I hit a nice, soft chair, I appreciate it a lot more than I used to. So goes life in general. I have found that I don't require as much sleep. That's because I know I can sleep longer if I want to. Now that I can sleep longer, I wake up at six o'clock like I always used to. Don't ask me why. I just do and I can't help it. In fact, sometimes I get right disgusted when habit forces my feet to the floor. The other day I said to my wife, "Maybe I should retire. After all, I'm almost seventy-three." She in turn asked what I thought was a very important question. "What are you planning to do when you don't have anything to do for the rest of your life?" I will say one thing. It doesn't cost as much to feed me. Seems like I get along on less food. Maybe that's because I'm always searching out that nice, soft chair!

You know what? I think my feet are getting smaller! For some unknown reason they slide around in my shoes a lot more than they used to. Now that I'm on Social Security, I don't reach down and pick up that penny that I discover along my path. I think there are two reasons for this. It's always so darn far down there to pick it up, and besides, if it's around the last of the month, my Social Security check I know is on the way. That makes me a little more independent. I was talking to a friend of mine last week and told him about the penny episode. He agreed with me because he's a couple of years older than I. "However," he said, "if it's a nickel I might just lie down beside it and pick it up that way."

I can add here that I used to have hair like all the rest of the guys. Being thin on top isn't always bad. My hair never gets mussed up, it's easy to wash, and besides, I see a lot of guys on TV with less hair than I carry around on top. Of course, they make a thousand dollars to my one, but who cares about that. I can still jump up and click my heels, still have all my teeth, and am not too old to view a well-turned ankle that walks by.

July 15, 1992
"MAKE YOUR HEAD SAVE YOUR HEELS"

I remember my mother saying to me many years ago, "Make your head save your heels." Of course at the age she told me that, it really didn't sink in like it should have. Remember, I was just a kid, and a dumb one at that. In any case, through the years I have found if one applies a little common sense when traveling around in relation to saving the heels, it pays off in many ways. However, I still go into our backshop printing area and stand there, forgetting what I really went back there for. A little thought before going would have saved the puzzled look on my face after my arrival.

I am getting a little smarter about my travels from place to place. In relation to my glasses, I make sure I have a pair waiting for me in the rec room, one on the porch, another next to the phone, and of course a pair in each car. Now I didn't buy these glasses all at once. I just keep saving the old ones from years past. I haven't talked to Greg Dye, my eye doctor, about this, but I'm sure he wouldn't be pleased. Incidentally, I always carry a pair with me – but not always, so my wife carries a pair in her purse just for me. Now that's what I call service.

I have learned over the years when I think about something I want or should do to get right up and do it while thinking about the need. I don't want you to think that I have done this all my life. Far from it. Just keep in mind I'm well over seventy. I won't tell you about the first sixty years of making my head save my heels. I must admit I'm somewhat pleased with myself at this point in life, so I must tell you about when my brother-in-law visited me last week. He headed up his 50th high school graduation reunion. He was supposed to bring printing of their graduation class day, and he was supposed to bring his golf clubs and golf shoes for an outing. He forgot all those things. He isn't seventy yet, so I'll forgive him.

December 9, 1992
CLINTON DEAL: TAKE FROM THE RICH, GIVE TO THE POOR

I'm rather amused at the media reports in relation to how much improved the economy is in the past few weeks since Clinton was elected to be our next President. Of course, before the second week of November the reports from ALL the news media were that the whole country was about to go down the drain. Now all of a sudden things have taken a complete turn around. Isn't it amazing what can happen in a couple of weeks? Now the news media will have to say many nice things about Clinton almost forever. After all, they were the ones who put him in there. Those dozens of promises Clinton has made to the bleeding hearts across the country, they will have to back up one hundred percent. Too bad, all we must hear from now on is how wonderful and how super the new era of our nation will materialize. Just think, all the poor people will now have homes and a warm place to live. And FREEDOM will ring all across the country. Everyone will have a job. The rich people will be taxed and all people will be happy because now we will be living in the Garden of Eden. We will take from the rich and give to the poor. How can we lose on a deal like that?

* * *

I don't look for many good things to happen by our entry into Somalia with the idea of feeding starving people. If the nations who back this have an idea everything will be fine in a few weeks, they will have to give some more thought to the situation. I do not think there will be much bloodshed, although if we have one man killed, in my opinion it is too high a price to pay. On top of everything, I understand this country is one of the most disease-ridden places in the world. All we need is another new disease brought back to our nation.

In my opinion, I don't think there will be any fighting of any degree. What I do think is the people who steal the food and kill people will wait out the whole challenge. When things quiet down and we and other nations leave, they will return and kill everyone who helped distribute food and essentials.

* * *

If you wish to see a good movie, without violence and porn, go see "A RIVER RUNS THROUGH IT."

February 24, 1993
I LIKE NORTH DAKOTA

As I go about our city of West Fargo I'm asked quite often why I don't take off for a warm clime for the winter. My stock answer is I like it right here in North Dakota. Oh, I don't mind a week or two where the sun shines around seventy-six or eighty degrees, but after that things get kind of boring. In other words, I do like a book or two to read, saddled in with long walks and maybe following the wife around shopping for things she seldom buys. But in the long run, after a few days I ask myself, "What in heck can I do now?" I do hang around the office in our business and get in people's way. My wife tells me, "Now don't go into the backshop, because you get things all mixed up." I grant that most of the time she is right, but I don't see anything wrong with telling them a risqué joke or telling them about the days of 1936. For some reason, my wife doesn't think the gals in the backshop really want to stand around and listen to me tell about the old days. I do enjoy going out to our press. I don't go out there every day, so I guess I couldn't foul things up much out there. Besides, I don't know what is going on out there most of the time at the press, so I'm a bit reluctant to ask questions.

However, I still feel good and can still click my heels when I want to show off. I can still take three meals a day without Mylanta, my clothes still fit almost as good as they used to, a little baggy in the rear end, but I don't think anyone pays much attention to that. I still like a good joke; even the bad ones are sometimes good in my thinking. My wife tells me that I have a bad habit of visiting friends when she is waiting for me in the car, but I don't worry too much about that anymore, either. I think getting older has many advantages. You can always say, "I'll think about that tomorrow."

April 7, 1993
RUSSIA HAS ONE OVER ON US

I have a question. How come Russia can have prayer in schools but in the land of freedom and free speech it is firmly restricted in our schools?

Now I know all about that crap about church and state, but the people had better watch out because the future of religion in our nation might come home to roost.

* * *

Last Saturday, as some of you know, I put in time at the annual Lions pancake feed. I'm pretty good for the first six hours and I do hand out pancakes and sausage with a flourish and a smile, but for some reason there occurs wear and tear on feet and other places. I made the excuse I had to feed the cat at our office, which I did. After that, I took a nap and dreamed of the toddy I was going to have when I woke up.

May 19, 1993
MY TRAVEL AFFINITY GOES ON

In that I have an affinity to tell my experiences concerning travels, I am about to let you who read this column in on a couple.

Two weeks ago our general manager, Gary Hasse, and I traveled to New York to attend to a printing account we have in the Big Apple. No one should go to New York without attending at least one musical. In our case, we attended two musicals. One was *Guys and Dolls,* which was a rerun from years ago. Our second musical was *Will Rogers Follies.* The music, dancing, lighting and history of the life of Will Rogers combine to make this one outstanding production. In the middle of the music and dancing, everything stopped. Of all things, a dog trotted nonchalantly across the stage and took the steps leading down into the audience. Needless to say, the gal talking and singing had to turn her face from the crowd and giggle like mad. She then turned and said to the crowd, "I have lost my place." She then checked with one of the team, who refreshed her memory. It all was taken in good humor, and the musical proceeded.

New York in May is about the perfect time. The city seems fresh from the winter doldrums. It was cleaner than I remembered in the past. I felt safer than in past visits. I might add here that I was rather impressed when a young, attractive blonde, who just happened to be on the same sidewalk as Gary and I, made a point of saying "hello." Of course, we said hello right back, but a voice out of the past said right back to us, "Keep on walking." Looking back, I noticed we weren't the only ones she was saying hello to, and here I thought it was just our good looks!

Last Saturday night my wife and I attended the Royal Winnipeg Ballet in – Winnipeg. Henry and Joyce Newgard were in the next seats. Henry, of course, is not so sure he likes ballet, but he and I, as the saying goes, "just put on our tutus and joined the crowd."

May 26, 1993
THE POWER OF A CELL PHONE

This past week I bought a cellular phone. I have had one for some time, but the kind I had was rather big and it also took some time to charge up. The number of times I use a cellular phone is very limited indeed. I think the reason I didn't use it more was that punching all those buttons and hoping for the best sort of scared me. When the guy sold it to me in the first place, he took about three minutes to explain the buttons to punch, and away he went to the next guy whom he would probably confuse just as much as me. I remember he mentioned something about access code, roaming, also SND and END and STO and RCL, and other stuff which still confused me after four years. Well, last week I put my phone up for sale, and naturally I put the ad in the *Midweek* and *Midweek Plus*. My phone has been ringing off the hook ever since. One guy who wouldn't give up even though he could not find me ended up with Gary Hasse, our general manager. The poor guy who had tried to get me for two days informed Gary that I must own the paper. Gary said, "Yes, he does." The guy remarked, "I thought so, because he's never there." He just didn't know I'm an old duffer. I could have told him at one time I ran the hundred yards in twelve seconds. 'Course, now it would take me all day. As the saying goes, "Time does everything." In any case, I guess that's the reason I'm not around a lot of the time. It's because I'm always on the way to the office, and about the time I get there it's almost time to go home.

Getting back to the cellular phone, I have reinvested, not that I intended to, but a neat-looking little gal came to the office a while back who knows how to sell cellular phones. I now have a cellular phone I can carry around in my vest pocket. It's amazing what new inventions like these little phones can do! I asked her if I could call London on that little gadget. "Yep," she says, "any place in the world." Not that I want to call London, but just to know I can if I want to gives me a great sense of power.

Next week I'm off to see my brother-in-law. I shall take my little vest pocket phone along and call him before I arrive. There is a reason for that. I want him to have plenty of refreshments ready when I enter his door.

August 25, 1993
THE Y TRACK SHUFFLE

A couple years ago I began to get the idea that maybe I should do like some old guys do and show up at the YMCA and wiggle some muscles that haven't been wiggled in many a year. About this time, a friend of mine, Henry Newgard, retired. I thought I might find a friend with the same feelings regarding my view of keeping fit. With a little help from Henry's wife, Joyce, Henry joined my sojourn twice a week to the Y.

Always With'em

I might add here that old boys still have thoughts of the great days of basketball, when we both earned letters and paraded around with years of stripes on our right arms. Only, time changes everything. Henry and I checked out a basketball and enthusiastically proceeded to the gym. I tried my over-the-head shot I used to be such a hero at, and not only missed the basket, but didn't come within five feet of the backboard. I didn't feel so bad when Henry followed my lead with about the same results. We did dribble the ball around a little, tried another shot or two. Then we stood and wondered why each of us were huffing and puffing. I think we went to the gym one more time.

Now in regards to the Y, we have found a few other old guys shuffling around the track with hopes of making it all the way to a mile marker. Once in awhile a couple of young gals shows up and we old guys perk up the best we can. After all, we're not too old to look at a well-turned ankle. I always practice with ten-pound dumbbells. I'm pretty good with those because all I have to do is point them towards the ceiling a few times. One day I saw a young thing looking over the barbells, I guess you call them, and being the nice, ol' guy I am, I offered to show her where the five-pounders were. She gave me a smile and said she was looking for the fifteen- or twenty-pounders. It's a new world out there, and sure as heck it has passed me by.

December 1, 1993
THE BEDMAKER

When my wife went to work for the *Pioneer* in 1967, I made her a promise which I'm glad to say I still keep. I told her I would make the bed as long as she worked on the paper. I must say, she is still working and I'll be darned if she is ever going to quit. I have, to say the least, become an expert at making a bed. Not that I object to any great degree, but I certainly didn't think I would be around this long making a bed. I do some other things around the house, like washing dishes and cleaning the cat's sandbox, charcoaling a steak when asked, and carrying drinks to company. Now that I think of it, I think I'm really quite handy around the house. I'll bet there are a heck of a lot of husbands who read this column who DO NOT MAKE THE BED EVERY DAY. I know I'm going to get some comment on this, but that's alright. At my age, who gives a darn?

* * *

DOES THIS MATCH?

Last week I hopped out of bed and made a decision of what I was to wear to the office. Usually I don't work that fast, but in that I had already seen the light as to what to wear for the day, I was way ahead of myself. Over the years I have been asked more than once ,"Are you going to wear that tie?" Not that I let my wife pick out what I am to wear for the day, but in that I'm not too smart about colors, I take off my tie and find one that matches. However, last week my wife didn't catch me before I arrived at the office with brown socks, blue pants, black coat and brown shoes.

It isn't so bad in the summer in relation to matching colors. The sun is peeking through the shadows and I do a better job in the matching world. I would bet my brown socks, any guy who gets up at six in the morning would have a hard time telling blue from brown. I take my pants to the window to check color, but black looks blue and blue looks black. My ties are so many colors that I put on my selection for the day and hope for the best.

January 5, 1994
"HAPPILY EVER AFTER"

I note our news media are telling us everything is super special in the economic world, and from now on for the next year nothing but good is going to happen to our pocketbooks. However, I note they haven't mentioned anything about the nice tax hike coming our way when we pay our taxes just before April 15, 1994. Therefore, we are surrounded by an area of green which is supposed to end up in our pockets and we all will be happy ever after.

HOWEVER, I DO WANT TO POINT OUT ONE IMPORTANT ATTENTION GETTER. It's called:

Taking from Peter to pay Paul.

Politicians can't give us anything without depriving us of something else. Government is not a god. Every dime they spend must first be taken from someone else. Unfortunately, stealing money from Peter to give to Paul really makes Peter a "Paul-bearer." The last Republican administration signed off on nearly $300 billion in increased taxes and regulatory costs during its four years. The current Democratic administration wants to at least match that with its very first round of tax hikes.

No wonder Washington, D.C., is so often described as 67 square miles surrounded by reality, an influence-peddling pleasure palace, a whorehouse where every four years we get to elect a new piano player. Politicians just don't seem to understand that taxes are a disincentive to people who work, save, and invest. High taxes actually reduce tax revenues from the rich, as they motivate individuals to reduce their taxable income and economic activity. And the problem is compounded by the fact that politicians spend at least $1.90 for every dollar collected in taxes. Tax rates have gone up and down over the years, but spending continues to rise.

February 16, 1994
PHOENIX AREA IS GROWING

It has been my habit during the winter to take a few days off from the snowdrifts and, more so, the thirty-below temperatures. So last week I spent a few days in Mesa and Chandler, Ariz. I don't have to tell you I was a little off balance after arriving on the plane, mainly because I was so used to constantly trying to keep from falling on my butt in the North Dakota ice and snow. In any case, I was happy to see sun. We did run into a bit of rain, which in my book at this time of winter is a very welcome sight.

I must say there is always good and bad when it comes to traveling to other places in our country. The Phoenix airport is one rush, rush place. You have to be on your toes or you really don't get to where you want to go. I was definitely impressed with what I saw as we traveled from the airport to Mesa. Whole tracts of land staked out for homes and hundreds of homes going up everywhere you look. These towns, Phoenix and surrounding area, are going to be one big city and it won't be long in the future. The car traffic is very, very challenging. Indeed, you have to drive for yourself and three other guys. The city is in the throes of building a beltline, which of course is some time away. In the meantime, the battle of car traffic goes on.

I want to add here that I didn't hide from the world. The area contains many swimming pools where an old guy like me can sit in a sunchair and sip vodka tonics. I also kept a watch out for those well-turned ankles. I'm not too old, you know.

As for night life, four gals took me to a very neat ballroom. I'm not really up on the music of the day, but, not to be outdone, I was on the dance floor showing the young whippersnappers how we used to do it in Amherst, S.D. I do want to add here that my wife, Betty, was not just along for the ride to the ballroom. We trucked out like all the young ones.

March 9, 1994
<u>WHO</u> WILL PAY FOR THIS TAX?

I have been keeping in touch for some time now with activities of the West Fargo Home Rule Commission. They are talking HOME RULE. I will not mince words on their meetings. WE ARE TALKING ABOUT TAXES. Those of you who work and pay taxes to our state might take note of the following comments from my side of the street.

The city is proposing an added sales tax on things you buy in the City of West Fargo. The commission tells us not to worry because a share of the tax will come from out-of-city residents. Of this I'm not sure. As I see it, the major part of the tax will come from you and me. There might be some tax from outside from a company like Dakotah Truck, but limited to twenty-five dollars on a purchase. That will mean nothing compared to taxing people to $380,000 or more. That is the income estimate as to what this additional one cent sales tax would raise. It's going to come on gas bills, local telephone service bills, taxes at liquor stores, restaurants and all of dozens of companies in West Fargo where we West Fargoans buy.

What is the city going to do with your new tax? We talk of economic development. However, it will be called "Jobs Creation and Retention." It does sound better, but there's an old saying that a duck is a duck when the sounds match. What I want to know is, "IS OUR CITY REALLY HURTING FINANCIALLY?" It seems to me we have done mighty well since I came here in 1967. I have talked with former mayor and state senator, Clayton Lodoen, about this tax. He said this has been brought before the commission many times in past years and was looked at with a jaundiced eye.

What is called PACE Funds is suggested. The city has already found $200,000 in funds for PACE to use for this concept, without the city tax. PACE Funds are designed to go to strong companies within the city and area when they show they are creating new jobs. These funds go to companies to buy down interest rates that you or I cannot get.

We have strong companies in our city; they do not need these extra benefits. Don't forget you and I will be paying the bill for low interest rates they would receive. It is important to remember we already have a state sales tax, which in turn is to provide for economic development.

As I see these whole proceedings, it turns into a double tax. I cannot go along with this approach because THE MACHINE IS NOT BROKEN. Of you who read this column I ask: If you don't mind paying this tax and want HOME RULE, this is still a free country. YOUR VOTE WILL TELL THE TALE.

March 23, 1994
REMEMBER WHEN DUTY, HONOR AND COUNTRY CAME FIRST

The following paragraph is from a speech given in 1962. **General Douglas MacArthur** was 82 years old at the time he gave it. This is a small paragraph from the speech given upon his acceptance of the Sylvanus Thayer Award for service to his nation. He spoke without text or even notes. The speech covered over a half page in the *Denver Post,* published on Sunday, June 24, 1962. In that there were no notes or text, the paper had real difficulty finding someone who had recorded the speech, which was delivered in his farewell to the cadets of West Point. To me, this speech, which I have in full page, points up a day when **"duty, honor, country"** came first. I now sit back and wonder. There seem to be so few who look on our nation with these three ringing words which mean so much to the nation's greatness and security.

"They teach you to be proud and unbending in honest failure, but humble and gentle in success; not to substitute words for actions, nor to seek the path of comfort, but to face the stress and spur of difficulty and challenge; to learn to stand up in the storm, but to have compassion on those who fall; to master yourself before you seek to master others; to have a heart that is clean, a goal that is high; to learn to laugh, yet never forget how to weep; to reach into the future, yet never neglect the past; to be serious, yet never to take yourself too seriously; to be modest so that you will remember the simplicity of true greatness, the open mind of true wisdom, the meekness of true strength.

"They give you a temperate will, a quality of imagination, a vigor

*of the emotions, a freshness of the deep springs of life, a tempera-
mental predominance of courage over timidity, an appetite for adventure over love of ease."*

May 4, 1994
WE WILL MISS OSSIE

Ossie has lived in the Witham household for some nine years. Ossie in her early years with us was a challenge. Being a highbred cat, she had her own plan of life in our house. This, of course, caused her sojourn with us to come to some crossroads at which the wife and I were somewhat perplexed. Ossie knew what she wanted but, in that her language didn't fit our language at all, we learned the hard way to follow her direction. In the first place, she showed us where she wanted her sandbox. We also found she was a combination cat, the combination being sandbox and paper (newspaper preferred, of course). Ossie came with national awards, so I could understand her being a bit "hoity toity," as the saying goes. She was not one to ignore you like some cats. Ossie looked you right in the eye, whether standing on the floor or sitting on a table. I might say she preferred the table. In that way, she could keep an eye on you, and also she didn't have to duck any feet passing by.

As the years passed, she gradually taught the wife and me how she wanted things done. Ossie liked toys and insisted they be placed in handy places, like the porch where she sunned herself and watched birds on my feeder. She, of course, had her own room with toys, dry feed, water and the things she liked, like my old, green lounge chair which she delighted in clawing until the stuffing came out on the floor. She also liked to irritate the neighbors' dog by sitting in the window by the hours and watching Alex turn flip-flops trying to bark his way into scaring Ossie.

I might add here Ossie was also a loving cat; however, it was in her own way. You picked her up and she immediately objected by leaping out of your arms. You sat her on the couch and she jumped down. In relation to her own way, if you happened to be reclining on the couch she carefully and softly would nestle on your chest, look you in the eye and purr like mad, her big eyes watching you with nothing but love. How in heck could a guy not melt a bit with all that long fur covering half your chest?

In any case, the nicest things in life come to an end. Last week with no little pain, I took Ossie to Valley Vet, where Dr. Christian informed me Ossie had cancer of the mouth and I must not let her suffer. Ossie is now reposing at Sundown with a lot of other kitties, and I'm sure she is already holding school on just how to bring up all the adults they might find in heaven.

May 18, 1994
WITHAM NAMED FRIEND OF THE MILITARY

(The following is not an "Always With'em" column, but a news release to the *West Fargo Pioneer*.)

Don Witham, Davon Press, Inc., and publisher of the *West Fargo Pioneer*, was recently named 1993-94 Friend of the Military by the Joint Military Affairs Committee of the Fargo, Moorhead and West Fargo chambers of commerce.

The award distinguishes an individual who has utilized professional expertise or personal talents to further the understanding and awareness of the military in the community by creating opportunities to advocate the interest of military personnel.

Witham grew up in South Dakota and following high school studied music. He enlisted in the U.S. Navy prior to World War II, serving more than four years. He spent most of that time with the armed guard on merchant ships. He participated in allied invasions of North Africa, Sicily, Okinawa and Iwo Jima.

When the ammunition ship "Santa Catalina" was torpedoed by a German submarine in the Atlantic between Florida and Bermuda, Witham was one of the survivors.

He spent 20 years with a New York-based organization setting up pre-subscribed classical concert series in cities throughout the United States.

Witham and his wife, Betty, started the *West Fargo Pioneer* in 1967. In 1970 they branched out to establish the *Midweek Eagle* and later added the *Midweek Plus*.

They established their own printing company, Davon Press, in 1974 and added the *FM Greeter* to the company in 1992.

Through his publishing career, Witham has provided publicity for events sponsored by Friends of the Military Committee of the Tri-Chamber of Commerce, including all four major military service bands that have performed in the Fargo-Moorhead area in the past 3½ years. He has provided financial resources, advertising space and coordinated the donation and printing of the performance programs.

June 8, 1994
YOUR VOTE WILL DETERMINE THE FUTURE OF WEST FARGO

This column ran last week, and I am repeating it this week. These are my opinions only. If the people who live in West Fargo want Home Rule, the people will vote in Home Rule. I'm not a person to waste a lot of words. It's just that I feel people who work and pay taxes have and are getting TAXED TO DEATH.

* * *

I have commented about Home Rule before. However, I am reminded that those who live in West Fargo will be going to the polls Tuesday, June 14. It is imperative that a very good showing at the polls becomes a fact. Home Rule, if passed, will bring a change to our city. This change I am very, very concerned about, because it means, in the end, control and advantage of assessing taxes, which I am not so sure would be to your and my benefit. I know the charter provides authority to levy taxes, both sales tax and mill levy taxes, subject to voter approval, after Home Rule is voted in. However, a tax is a tax. You all know if it sounds like a duck what happens. I am concerned that the "quack" will become louder as time goes by, and I am also very concerned about where the "quack" stops. In other words, like our government, more and more taxes are raised when the commission thinks they need money. I am reminded about a machine working very well that some people now think is in bad repair and needs fixing. If Home Rule is so great, why do only 27 cities have it in the State of North Dakota? I am told this action on Home Rule will reduce your property taxes. What percentage? West Fargo property taxes are not out of line as it is. The motor of city operation has been purring very nicely since I came here in 1967.

To anyone who talks taxes to me, I listen very closely, MORE SO WHEN THEY TELL ME TAXES ARE GOING TO DO ME A LOT OF GOOD AND SAVE ME REAL MONEY.

To get down to the nitty-gritty, Home Rule gives too much authority to the commission to spend tax dollars raised by mill levies wherever and for whatever a commission majority chooses. The Home Rule Charter was printed as a public notice last week in the *Pioneer*. Right there it states that the governing body shall be permitted to spend the city budget "without regard to the specific dedications of mill levies." I'm not sure people in West Fargo want to give this freedom to alter what we have now.

I'm going to vote NO on Home Rule.

August 24, 1994
MALL OF AMERICA, ANYONE?

Our daughter met us in Minneapolis last week. Kathy, for some reason, could not get enough visits in to the Mall of America. I'm one of those people who have been there in the past (once only), and I didn't relish going again. So I spent three trips to the Mall during my stay. I held up pretty good the first day, but from then on I looked for a seat every time Mrs. W. and daughter Kathy entered one of the hundreds of stores. I one time sat beside a heavyset lady whose feet were killing her. Needless to say, we discussed feet until she had the courage to get up on hers and go on. I was very tired in one spot that was killing me, but we didn't discuss that.

September 14, 1994
EVERYBODY NEEDS A GOOD CHUCKLE

Last week I was in Oklahoma City visiting Bonnie and Alan Witham, very special relatives. At a party they threw last Sunday before Labor Day, I met an old friend of mine, former governor of Oklahoma George Nigh, whom I like very much even though he is a Democrat. I couldn't say much about the Democrats because he and Donna, his wife, had recently visited Clinton at the White House. In any case, he told me a story I thought you who read this column might get a kick out of.

In 1959, he was lieutenant governor and was called on by the governor to travel to Alaska for the admission of Alaska to the union. When he got there, he found he was the only one sent as a representative from the Lower 48. No one thought the event worth sending anyone up there, so George Nigh found himself as the top executive from all the states in the United States. He did, however, come in contact with Edward D. Keller, who was the great developer of the atomic bomb, who happened to also think the trip worthwhile. After the celebration of a new state joining the union, he was invited to have lunch the next day with Mr. Keller. George explained that the great man of the atomic bomb showed up, but no one else did, so George was highly complimented that he alone could sit with such a man and listen to stories of past atomic bomb days. During the lunch, the hotel restaurant began to shake and the lights on electrical cords from the ceiling began to sway. The great man with the bushy eyebrows and stern demeanor began to rub his right knee and planted his foot solidly on the floor. He explained that the tremor was about 6.5 to 7 points in strength and was 50 miles west of the city. This, of course, impressed George greatly. The next day before he took a plane back home, Bill Egen, the new governor of Alaska, invited George to breakfast. The same thing happened at the hotel the next morning, so George, to show he was "in the know," rubbed his knee and explained the tremor was about a 6.5 and was 50 miles west of the city.

The new governor then explained to George the tremors happened every time a bunch of trucks went by, and some day a new hotel would be planned that didn't tremble every time big trucks went by.

In any case, George Nigh came home the hero because he was the only executive there from the Lower 48 of the United States of America.

October 5, 1994
SCARE TACTICS, OR REAL THREATS?

I have been standing on the sidelines watching information pass down from many directions regarding our health. Most of this comes from our own government and other sources just as confused about ordinary down-to-earth common sense about life in the United States and how we should live. You see, there are persons in many different fancy offices in Washington who have nothing to do but find ways to screw up our daily attempt to make a living. They work very hard to make their jobs seem important. Otherwise they wouldn't have a job and the country would save a few billion dollars.

I shall point to a few of the stupid laws and scare tactics these people use on us poor citizens. I remember split toilet seats. The guy who thought that one up definitely had a split personality, one in the nuthouse and the other on Cloud Nine. Do you remember the big fuss over alar, a chemical used as a growth enhancer on apples? Meryl Streep got in on that one and, of course, the situation was fanned by the press. No proof to this day if alar is good or bad. Radon in homes seems to be big stuff. Call in the handy helpers to tell you a small investment of hundreds of dollars will take care of the situation. I have lived many a year in my house and I feel just fine. Asbestos is one of my pet peeves. After schools and businesses across the nation have spent millions upon millions, I am told it is now best if there is a problem to seal all places where asbestos might be challenging. In other words, asbestos is best if not disturbed. The next wild hair comes from environmentalists who claim dioxin is a threat to fertility. Again, no conclusive evidence, just someone who must keep his job, and this is one way to do it.

Greenpeace demands a phase-out of chlorine. This seems simple. However, the guy who thought this up did not realize or care that chlorine is involved in practically every part of our everyday lives.

I know I'm not being politically correct, which I make a point of not being, but I must say 90 percent of what we hear about dangers in our everyday lives is just a bunch of crap.

December 7, 1994
SAYING GOODBYE TO ELDA HASN'T BEEN EASY

I have come to the end of an era. Yep, I must say my shirts will no longer be pressed and taken care of by Elda. Elda came to our house when she was 29, and has been looking after house and home for the Withams ever since. I'm not going to tell you how old Elda is now, but I will say she is over the spring chicken slot in life. I have always liked the way she doubles over my socks and folds them back so they are in a neat ball. I like the way she never disturbs my gadgets in the rec room. I can always find them where I left them. She keeps tab on the sump pumps so they always work. If I forget to put out the trash can for the garbage collector, Elda is the one who takes care of the situation. I always tell whoever is coming to the house to fix the furnace, deliver Culligan salt, change the batteries in the smoke detectors, do any painting or anything else that needs checking, "Come on Wednesday; Elda's there."

I must say, Elda was never at a loss for words. Repairmen, fix-up guys or anyone else were informed just how things should be done at our house. As far as Elda was concerned, our house was her house, and I must admit it ran that way. All our cats liked Elda, but Elda has a high voice and I can see Ossie yet strolling through the house with her ears back to prevent too many high sounds crossing those ears.

Whenever a disaster occurred, Elda was there to help out or, in many cases, take care of everything when we were away. When our sump pump didn't work in the basement, Elda brought help from the neighbors. All in a day's work for Elda. Elda has now moved away, and I'm learning how to operate a new sweeper the wife bought just for me. However, I know time will take care of the empty spot on Wednesday at our house, but Elda will always, always have a special spot in my heart, and I know our cat will miss her for sure.

January 18, 1995
THINKING AHEAD IS THE KEY

I find most people are either working for a business or own a business. Of course, business is what makes our nation go. Too bad more people in Congress don't understand this fact. However, I would like to relate a story Tom Gould told me some years ago in relation to Henry Ford. The Model T Ford, as history will tell us, went through the early days of the car world in fine fashion. This, in those days, included nothing but muddy roads, snow, sleet and anything the weather conjured up. No matter what, the Model T Ford came through. Henry Ford in all matters was a businessman. An example, as I remember, involved Ford car floorboards, which were made of wood. Henry directed his buyers of tools and parts to have these items come in wooden boxes in specified measurements. These wooden boxes came as Henry Ford directed. They, incidentally, when broke down, fit perfectly into all Model T floorboards. A small matter of thinking ahead, which in this case meant millions of dollars in savings to his company. Thinking ahead to our futures can mean the same thing to each and every one of us.

February 1, 1995
AN INVESTMENT TO GO

I'm sure most of you have talked to those who say, "I think I'll take it with me when I go," meaning, of course, the final trip in life. Well, I was reminded this past week about how I might do just that. This past

June, I got the idea about having two implants. Little did I know what teeth implants are all about. All I knew was that having a plate to fill in for a couple of teeth was not my idea of living. I also found out you don't get implants in a couple days, two weeks or two months. I know this because I just got those two super-special teeth last week. I might add here they are just fine, in fact like the two I lost or better. I also might add here, they don't come for nothing. If you are planning anything like an implant, I would suggest you take a night job on top of your day job. Gary Hasse, our general manager, said to me, "You said you always wanted to take it with you. With your investment, now you can!"

March 15, 1995
DROPPED OPPORTUNITIES

I know that most of us through our lifetimes have missed opportunities, and also have regretted later those opportunities that cruised along out of our lives. I regret to say, many came my way in past years, of which I didn't take advantage. I remember during the war, I was invited to John Kraft's home. He happened to own a large part of Kraft Cheese, and invited me to check with him after the war, as he thought I might work into the business. I never checked with him. After the war, I had an appointment with the largest advertising agency in Chicago. A special executive was assigned to arrange entry into advertising. I didn't show. A very good job (and also very lucrative) was offered by the Baldwin Piano Company. Another good job with excellent pay was offered by a friend in Barnesville, Minn., working with schools in relation to school supplies. A friend of mine and I were going to start a Dairy Queen. I don't really know whatever happened to that. I know neither one of us got "on the ball" on that deal. I do know the guy who did start that Dairy Queen when we dropped the ball spent his winters soaking up the sun in Florida for years.

All of the above I let pass. It means I did not recognize an opportunity even when it kicked me in the butt. The last position I turned down was with the *St. Paul Pioneer Press*. They had me take a test that cost them $50. I passed the test and was hired. I didn't show for that work date either. Instead, I was offered the small city of West Fargo in March of 1967 as a place to start a newspaper business. Three papers had already failed in West Fargo. However, there was an advantage to not knowing anything about the newspaper business. I didn't know I could fail. With the help of my wife who worked until the work was done (and newspaper work never gets done), and an almost empty pocketbook, the long days seemed to get a bit shorter as the years passed.

I know there are lots of you who have gone through the same trials and have come out the other end making life worth the challenges of the past. I just want to add here, WHEN OPPORTUNITY BITES YOU IN THE REAR END, HANG ON AND WORK LIKE HELL!

Incidentally, I did pay back the *Pioneer Press* about 20 years later for their investment of $50. They smiled.

April 5, 1995
A GOOD BEGINNING ON A LONG ROAD

In this column is a paragraph from the April 2 *U.S. News & World Report*. I felt it so important that I should pass it along. The paragraph, written by Mortimer B. Zuckerman, whom I have read for years, in most cases hits many important facts. I urge you to read the following.

"The change in our political vocabulary is instructive. Duties and responsibilities have given way to rights and entitlements. Juvenile crime becomes juvenile delinquency, illegitimacy becomes alternative parenting, crime becomes victimization. Meanwhile, middle-class Americans, themselves under economic siege, have watched with dismay as their tax dollars have subsidized what they see as irresponsible behavior – teenagers having children they cannot support – as race and gender preferences have zapped their sense of fair play. As Democrats learned in November 1994, it is they who bear the burden of this popular anger. In the minds of many Americans, the so-called party of the people, led by an elite that is sheltered from the effects of its policies, has governed on behalf of a minority rather than on behalf of everyone."

I cannot resist including the final few sentences:

"And for all our difficulties, perhaps we are on the verge of a new era in which leadership will genuinely seek to inspire change in the culture. Gingrich and his Republican colleagues have shown an ability to touch what the country deep down is thinking, and they have demonstrated great courage in responding, in moral terms, on such issues as welfare reform and balancing the budget."

April 12, 1995
SOMETHING ABOUT A COWBOY

I have always admired cowboys. When I was on the farm, I loved to ride, but on our farm, about as near as I ever got to being a cowboy was herding 30 cows home from the pasture so I could milk them at six o'clock. I never did learn how to rope, and I never was a real good rider. I remember a frisky filly who loved to toss me in the ditch on the way home. In any case, as a boy on the farm, the cowboy in my mind was the romantic figure riding the range singing, "Git along, little dogie."

I think the part that intrigued me was the hat. I always wanted a cowboy hat, but the best I could do was a beat-up straw I wore from year to year. Never did have a real cowboy felt hat. Nowadays I see a lot of guys wearing cowboy hats. I guess being a non-cowboy has nothing to do with the hat. For some reason, they never seem to take them off, and I'm sure they have hair underneath. I keep wondering when they are eating if their hat might drop off in their soup. I also wonder what they do in a high wind. In a wind, I have to pull my cap down tight on my head or it won't be there when I get home.

Do cowboys sleep with their hats on?

July 5, 1995
SIGHTSEEING IN BANFF

A few days back I had the opportunity to visit Banff and Lake Louise, Alberta, Canada. We entered Canada after an overnight stay at Glacier Park, Mont. Traveling through Montana, which, incidentally, is one of my favorite states, I was disappointed in the way the buildings and ranch homes were kept up. I must say in most cases shabby indeed. I did not pay much attention to this until we entered Canada. I was very, very impressed by the way the farms and ranches were kept in appearance. It seemed they had made a special effort to make Canada look special. Even on the ranches, I noted white picket fences surrounding the buildings.

I was very impressed with the circle road around Vancouver. A very clean, neat-looking city. I did not, however, figure out why large, beautiful homes were built so close together. After all, Canada has unlimited land to spare. Maybe someone can give me a rundown on this. People I met in Canada didn't see to know.

We stayed at Banff Springs Hotel, which had excellent accommodations. However, I mention the lodge because, from morning to night, I was practically stepping over Japanese. They came in four great buses with tons of luggage. I might add here, they were polite and, from what the bellboys told me, were very well-stocked with the do-re-mi! The lodge catered to their tastes in food. I asked at breakfast time if I should get in line for the buffet. I was informed that I really didn't want to get in line. I sat down and ordered eggs and bacon. I still don't know what I missed in the Japanese line.

Visiting with the lodge crew, they informed me German clientele when visiting from Germany were the toughest to wait on– very gruff and no thank yous.

August 16, 1995
THE PLANE RIDE THAT WASN'T

In my last column, I was most enthusiastic about an invitation from Maj. Dennis Aune to take a ride in one of the biggest Air Force tankers in the nation, the KC-10. As you all know, the air show this past week was one huge event. In fact, I have never seen so many cars in my life in one area in Fargo. They stretched for miles in all directions, all heading for the air show. I might add here, Betty and I did attend the air show, but lining up with all those cars to get to the show made me wonder if the show wouldn't be over before we arrived.

Now I must tell you about my adventure in relation to the KC-10 tanker plane. I had scheduled our arrival at the airfield for 8 a.m. The part I was most happy about was Mrs. W. would be going along. I did not expect her to want to go, but when asked she was most happy and really enthusiastic about the whole plan. To make sure there would be no slip-ups, I was up at 5 in the morning, fed the cat, did my exercises, made sure I had my sunglasses in pocket and my passes to the big event. We took off for the airfield 45 minutes early to make all the proper connections. We arrived 15 or 20 minutes early and sat in the operations room waiting for the major. No one seemed to know where the major was, so I checked with people in the room as to what happened. To one young officer I said, "Look, here in his letter it says I have to be here at 8 a.m. Right here in the letter it says 'Saturday.'" I looked again at the letter. In plain typing with black letters, it said "Friday." The officer said, "Say, you're a day late and a dollar short." The only thing I could think of to say was, "Well, I do have the dollar."

October 4, 1995
MANY HOURS AND MILES FOR THOSE FIRST PIONEERS

We started the *West Fargo Pioneer* in the middle of March, 1967. It seems only yesterday and often I wonder where all the years have gone. It will soon be 29 years your paper has served the city of West Fargo. I do remember very well my arrival one cold March day when we were to settle into 500 square feet of space on Main Street with a steep walk up to the second floor. I had about $300 in my pocket and a Texaco credit card. Many businesses have started on more shaky ground but I'm sure they didn't sweat or worry more than I.

It comes to me brightly that the citizens of West Fargo did all they could to keep a very weak fledgling from falling into the abyss. The schools pitched in and sold subscriptions to get us off the ground. The advertisers stuck with us. Few of you know this, but the paper traveled a demanding route each week before it entered the mail. The ads were sold by yours truly, then taken along with what news we could gather to Barnesville, Minn. In that the ads had to be put together, I could not do this all by myself, so I drove over 200 miles each week to Windom, Minn., to meet my wife, Betty, where she was employed at the Windom paper. We worked Saturday and Sunday on the ads and I drove with completed copy back to Barnesville so they could be put in the paper. To accomplish this and take time to help with the rest of the paper, I lived with my father-in-law in Barnesville. When the paper was ready for press, I drove the paste-ups, the pages as you would know it, to Wahpeton, N.D., which was another 25 miles. After three hours of press time, I was on my way to West Fargo, another 40 or so miles. By the time I got the paper into the mail and on the newsstands it was time to start selling advertising all over again.

One last sequel: I had no one to write a local column. I am no writer but someone had to put something in a local column. I tried my hand and no one seemed to object, so I did it the next week and also the next. First thing I knew I had created a habit. I still can't write a column worth a darn, but until someone tells me to please stop you will just have to put up with the adventures of this ol' duffer.

* * *

A FRIENDLY PHRASE

I was coming out of Dakota Hospital after a checkup. There was a couple leaving at the same time. The man had a special van to load his wheelchair. The lady following was watching her step. I figured as long as I was there I would at least open the door for her. I also followed her to a large van and opened the door for her to climb in. When seated, she turned to me and said, "It's always nice to have a *young* gentleman help an old lady." I couldn't think of anything to say, in that I'm well past the three-quarter century mark, except

"Ma'am, you're saying all the right things."

December 6, 1995
HOW TIME HAS CHANGED.

My dad in 1936 brought home a brand new top-of-the-line V8 Ford car.

"How much, Dad?"

"Seven hundred dollars," came the reply.

I remember Mother buying me a new pair of Crosby Square shoes, $5. Best shoes you could buy at that time. Of course, you had to work five days for the shoes, if you were lucky enough to earn a dollar a day. In 1941 I worked for Montgomery Ward in St. Paul. That was before I joined the Navy. The pay was not too bad — 16¢ an hour.

On the farm in the '30s I remember taking eggs to town and collecting six cents a dozen. My dad at one time owned a gas station in Britton, S.D. Gas went for 10 to 12 cents a gallon. I can say in those days when you went out back to the little house it was hoped the Sears catalog would have an easy page to work with.

I do well remember my first days in the Navy at Great Lakes Naval Training Station. In those days you paid for your uniform. Maybe they still do. In any case, my pay was 16 dollars a month. By the time I paid for my uniform and other items I was issued, my pay was taken up for the next two months and then some.

Oh for the good ol' days.

December 27, 1995
HELP WANTED

There is always concern about those who are looking for work in our nation. Several times a year I visit Minneapolis. I make it a point to check through the *Minneapolis Tribune*. Three weeks ago I ran across the Help Wanted section. Not that I was looking for work, for no one would want an old duffer like me mixing up things anyway, but the Help Wanted section caught my eye. There were so many companies needing help that they seemed to be competing with each other for those people looking for work. I started to count the pages of those ads. WHEN FINISHED, I HAD COUNTED 50 pages! Some of those ads looked so good I almost applied myself.

* * *

SPECIAL NOTE

I have said this before and I say it again. People who talk to me about being "politically correct" are talking to the wrong guy. I say it's just a bunch of crap. As an ordinary guy facing life's problems, I'm shocked that ordinary people give it a second thought. Most likely they don't, if they are ordinary people.

January 3, 1996

Ever wonder why illegals flock to our nation and come in risking life and limb to get here? It's easy. The ambitious ones work and make money. The rest who don't work will be taken care of by our government whether they really need it or not. Wednesday, Dec. 27, on C-Span, there was a bleeding heart informing the audience that whoever sets foot on U.S. soil should have the privilege to vote. Of course, he doesn't have to worry; we all pay the bill.

Most PEOPLE WHO WORK do not understand what SSI means. It's called Supplemental Security Income. What it really means is the government begs anyone who has a good line to come and feed at the trough that the PEOPLE WHO WORK TRY TO KEEP FULL. One day I shall write information in this column just what SSI is all about.

It doesn't take a large brain to figure out why everyone and his dog who doesn't live in the U.S.A. wants to come to our shores. It's called FREEDOM, freedom to do most anything you want. You can become a millionaire or live off the fat of the land. No place else in the world can make this happen. Keep in mind there are 263 million people living in the U.S. today. By the year 2020 there will be, through immigration, 326 million people, and that is legal immigration. What about all those thousands coming in each week and month illegally? Are you ready for a TAX RAISE?

January 10, 1996
NOTHING NEW

I have decided everything must be perfect in my life, because I can't think of one New Year's resolution I must make. I don't have to quit smoking because I never learned to smoke. I don't drive fast so accidents in my life have been rare. I go to the YMCA twice a week so I must still have a heartbeat. Doc Geston tells me I'm healthier than I deserve, so I'm planning no New Year's resolutions. I'm also too old to get into trouble, so 1996 should be a good year for this ol' feller.

February 7, 1996
OH, OH

The wife and I attend all the Vikings games in Minneapolis every year. There are times when I wonder why, but we never seem to give up, always saying to ourselves, "Just wait 'til next year." In any case, we (out of habit) stay at the Marriott.

I remember a couple years ago coming down the semi-crowded elevator with my relatives when the door opened, and there stood a long-bearded guy ready to step in.

I said, "Whoop, you can't come in here."

I was asked, "How come you wouldn't let that guy on?"

"I don't like long-bearded, suspicious-looking guys along on the elevator I'm on," I said.

I was informed I should have let him on because the Vikings game wouldn't start until he showed up. It seems he was part of the Oak Ridge Boys singing group. They had to sing the national anthem before the game started.

March 13, 1996
READ THIS IF YOU PAY TAXES

The following information I thought might capture your interest, especially those of you who pay taxes, and I'm of the impression most everyone and his dog pays taxes. In that you hear from most politicians (except Forbes) that the flat tax will not fly, you might review information I have received from The Heritage Foundation in Washington, D.C. I put this in my column because I have not heard so much prevarication from politicians in many a day as regards the FLAT TAX.

"THE FLAT TAX: SIMPLE, FAIR AND A TAX CUT, TOO"

"Few Americans like the current tax system. It's complex, unfair and forces taxpayers to send too much money to Washington. Which is why the flat tax – a proposal to scrap the tax code and replace it with one low tax rate that applies to everybody – is seen by many as a winner.

"Don't like spending weeks filling out tax forms? The flat tax is so simple you could fill out your return on a postcard.

"Think the tax code should treat everyone equally? A flat tax plan would impose the same low rate on all Americans. Wealthy Americans would still pay more, just not a higher percentage.

"Taxes too high? The flat tax would give every income group in America a tax cut, studies show. This is true even though most flat tax plans would eliminate the popular home mortgage interest deduction. But this deduction is popular precisely because it reduces Americans' tax bills.

"Skeptical? Just fill out the postcard below, provided by the Washington think tank, The Heritage Foundation, and you'll see how a flat tax would affect you. The rate is computed at 17 percent, as proposed in several flat tax plans now under consideration."

April 3, 1996
OLD-TIME REPUBLICAN *AMERICAN*

A bill is sponsored by Sen. Byron Dorgan. I happen to be an old-time Republican, but when a Democrat comes up with a bill that makes this much sense, that's when I become an American.

"DORGAN BILL WOULD END CASH PAYMENTS TO DRUG ADDICTS AND PROVIDE TREATMENT INSTEAD

"U.S. Sen. Byron Dorgan introduced legislation that would end cash

Supplemental Security Income (SSI) and Social Security Disability Insurance (SSDI) payments to alcoholics and other drug addicts, and would instead provide treatment for their addictions.

" 'The current policy is simply wrong-headed,' Dorgan said. 'Substance abusers need treatment, not cash hand-outs.' Dorgan noted 'The number of people receiving monthly SSI payments because of an addiction to drugs or alcohol quadrupled in the last four years, with an annual cost to taxpayers of about $630 million.' He said there is little effort to direct or limit how the cash is actually used by the addicts once they receive the payments.

"SSI was established in 1972 to provide cash benefits to people who are disabled and poor. 'Most Americans would be surprised to learn that drug addiction can qualify a person for monthly cash payments under the program,' Dorgan said.

"Under the current system, Dorgan said that many recipients receive the cash without enrolling in a treatment program. They are required to participate in treatment programs only if they are available. In many locations, however, they are not available or are not easily accessible to SSI and SSDI recipients. 'To make matters worse,' Dorgan said, 'The Inspector General of the Department of Health and Human Services reports that even where treatment is available, the Social Security Administration, which oversees the program, does not know the treatment status of most SSI recipients and does not monitor the program.

" 'Treatment for drug addicts and other chemically dependent persons not only helps them, it is also cost-effective for the taxpayer,' Dorgan said. 'Experts estimate that every dollar invested in treatment saves between $3 and $7 in health and criminal justice-related costs.

" 'Cash payments don't help alcoholics and drug addicts overcome their diseases, but quality treatment and medical care will,' Dorgan said."

June 5, 1996
RETRACING STEPS

Once a month I try to remember that State Bank, across the street from the office, has cookies for their customers. This occurs on the first of each month, so, if memory serves me, I'm at the front of the line when the door opens. I'm a bit disturbed this time because I found I have been living up when I should be living down. The scale at the YMCA tells me

I'm five pounds overweight. So, the one time I do look forward to a couple of cookies at State Bank shall have to wait till the first of July.

Speaking of trying to remember things, I'm at a point I have to write everything down, even to a haircut. It has to be my age. I think that's a darn good excuse, and I have been playing it to the hilt for some time now. However, it is a little embarrassing when I pay the bill at the cleaners and walk out without taking the cleaning with me. Now glasses are another very challenging situation for me. I have no idea how many pairs of glasses I own, but it seems every time I need them I don't have one on me. I keep two pairs at the office, one pair in each car, a pair in the rec room, a pair in the sunroom, one pair beside the phone in the livingroom. My wife used to keep a pair in her pocketbook for me when we were out at a restaurant. I don't have to tell you, one day she shut down that service.

The part that really gets me irritated (talking about forgetting things) is when we are home having a drink, I invariably set my drink down to do something and I never can find it again. I swear there must be a little guy living with us who moves my drink every time I set it down. I plan on getting one of those gadgets that whistles back when you clap your hands. I'll hook the darn thing on all my drinks and live happily ever after.

* * *

On Memorial Day the wife and I traveled to Barnesville, Minn., to watch the parade. As the red, white and blue fluttered by, I removed my cap and placed it over my heart. No one else on that street corner indicated in any fashion that they were watching our nation's flag go by. Am I missing something?

August 21, 1996
WHAT'S HAPPENED TO THE AMERICAN WORK ETHIC?

I was watching C-Span Thursday morning when a young caller called in. He wanted to know what Dole was going to do for the young college people between 20 and 24 years old in relation to schooling. The comment struck me that maybe more than he in our nation today are asking what Dole can do for them. It's time those living in the United

States started thinking about our nation, where it is going and what is going to happen if everyone gets what he wants from our government. It is rare indeed when someone in our country cannot find a job. It won't be anything fancy and probably not high-paying, but it is work and that is where we all start. Too many sit back and wait for something to happen. If our nation is to grow in the right direction, people have got to stop asking, "Who's going to help me?" Those who help themselves manage to get what they are after in life. The past 20 years or so this "I deserve what I get because this is a free country" has been a road taken by a share of people in our nation.

Special Note:

As I have said before in this column, only one in ten in our news media of today is conservative. Therefore, you will be cognizant of a definite trend maybe not noted before: A MUST STOP DOLE CAMPAIGN THROUGHOUT ABC, NBC AND CBS. What I am saying is the news media today call the trend; that trend is liberalism. In other words, let's make the people who work and sweat pay the way for everybody.

Special Note:

I was reminiscing recently about our trip to Hong Kong a few years back. One remembrance included mentioning to our driver one day that there were no panhandlers on the streets.

"That's easy to answer," she said. "Here, if you don't work, you don't eat!"

September 25, 1996
ADVENTURES ON THE HIGH SEAS

I was cogitating about things that happen in our lives that make changes in the road we take in life's challenges. I remember one day in 1942, I listened to the crack of the four-inch 50 gun I was setting sights on, and watched as the shell from the gun cracked into a flag pole five miles away on the horizon. A sight-setter's job is to properly set range of the gun to fire horizontally or vertically. This has to be done in split seconds. A mistake causes a miss. A miss could mean disaster, because the enemy ship might be setting sights that don't miss. As we finished practice-firing, I turned to face the young lieutenant who had just been assigned to our gun. He, being impressed with my part of the gun, asked if I would like to come aboard his ship's gun crew. I was complimented no end. I had practiced sight-setting until I could set the gun sights on the darkest night with no light.

Little did I know from that hour on my life was already on a new path. I plan to continue my ocean experiences in following columns. I did serve three and a half years on the high seas, and hope some of my travels might be of interest. All these things I will be talking about are dark ages compared to what the Navy does in fire control today. I will continue my story, my part in World War II.

October 16, 1996
DOES A CAT REALLY NEED HELP GETTING DOWN A LADDER?

I heard a mournful sound from the garage a couple days ago. On investigation, there sat that damned cat on the very top of the ladder. I let her sit, but another sound caught my attention. Mrs. W. wanted to know when I was going to rescue the cat. As far as I was concerned, she could stay right there. After all, I didn't put her there and I figured she could get down the way she got up. To further the discussion, I informed my wife that my brother-in-law discovered his cat had climbed to the top of a tree in his yard. I do remember he called the fire department to get the cat down, and was promptly rebuffed with words to the effect that they had never seen a dead cat in a tree yet, so the cat could come down by itself.

I don't have to tell you who won between me and my wife. I climbed the ladder, grabbed the cat by the scruff of the neck and dropped her into my wife's arms.

"Don't be so mean to Kitty," she retorted.

December 4, 1996
WHAT A MONSTROSITY!

Have you thought what a monstrosity our Federal Tax Code is? Talk about a flat tax, the sooner it comes, the better! The Gettysburg Address runs about 200 words. The Declaration of Independence runs about 1,300 words. The Holy Bible runs about 773,000 words. But our federal income tax code runs about seven million (that is, 7,000,000) words and is growing longer every year.

January 20, 1997
DON'T BE SAD

I noted a week or so ago new letters have been coined in relation to these long winter days with nothing but wind and lots of snow. It's called SAD and I can't remember what those letters mean except people really get out of sorts and just plain unhappy. They can't go anywhere because the roads are closed. If they get on a road that is halfway open, the wind blows snow so you can't see. But have heart, on the farm in the '30s you sat home until the first spring thaw. You had a radio, if the battery hadn't run down, but you didn't worry too much because you had things to demand all your attention, like milking the cows, feeding them, feeding the pigs, chickens, horses and any other animals demanding your attention. Cleaning out the barn after the cows will keep you occupied for three hours, maybe four or five. By the time you get all those things done, it will be time to go to bed and start all over again at five the next morning.

Now that's what I call Winter Blues.

Nowadays, there's TV, roads get plowed out the next day, there's always electric lights and heat, your car starts because it has been hooked up to the heater. The movie houses are going strong, the restaurants are open, and most always with nothing else to do you can go shopping.

So, don't be SAD. The winter blues could be a lot worse, like in 1936.

March 26, 1997
TIDBITS FOR THE DAY

I was at my typewriter last week, and a child by the name of Breanna Rubertus was looking over my shoulder. In that she reads very well, I typed a few words out for her. I then explained the advantages of the typewriter. First, it always works, no motors to conk out, no switches to turn on, no electric plug-ins to get shocks from, and it gets cleaned only every 10 years. Then I explained that my typewriter was many years older than both she and I. When I sent for a new ribbon a couple weeks ago, I learned that my Underwood was made around the turn of the century. I didn't think anything around here was older than I.

* * *

Last Friday I was having some work done in our basement. Stan Dreckman, one of my favorite people, is doing some work for me there. He inadvertently turned off the switch to the water heater. Betty and I awoke to cold water in our showers. I got out the washcloth for my part of the day. Soon I heard the water running in my wife's shower. I asked how she could do that. Just hold your breath and jump in, I learned. I have been told by Betty not to mention an age in relation to her, but I do have to say, at our ages she sure is tougher than I am.

May 7, 1997
DONATIONS FOR FLOOD VICTIMS OVERWHELMING

I have had many concerns about our people in West Fargo, Fargo, and most of all, Grand Forks, because they have suffered plenty and will continue to do so for many months to come. I am impressed with what is being offered for our flood victims. In fact, Friday I took a trip through the disaster relief building set aside for receiving materials for people in need of assistance caused by the flood. I cannot tell you here what is stacked up in the buildings, but what I saw overwhelmed me.

I know it will all be used, but I keep wondering how in heck it is going to get to the people who will need it right now. I talked with one lady who was loading stuff into the trunk of her car. (I want to add I am very impressed with The Salvation Army and what they are doing at the disaster relief site – the old Builders Square.) She was from Grand Forks and, I must say, the things she was taking I know for sure were really needed. A great share were cleaning materials, very little food, but lots of things I know will mean many hours of work for her.

I wrote a check for another friend of mine who has lost his home and most everything he couldn't put in his upstairs — piano, etc., things he couldn't get upstairs or move as the flood came before he could make any plans. His wife said, "We will swallow our pride and accept your check." People are having to do that! I would, too. I'm informed his house will be torn down and the area made into a park. I will add here I received $100 from a relative of mine in Weslaco, Texas, for me to pass on for flood relief. I know she doesn't have money to toss around, and $100 means something to her. We know lots of people have given money these past weeks they could well use, but it does show something special when it comes to the American Way.

Most of you who read this column know that West Fargo years back constructed a diversion channel around the city. I must say this saved our city many heartaches. I well remember fighting floods every year in West Fargo. The thing that really is discouraging is you have water in your basement and at your back door for weeks. *The Pioneer* is in the process of a special issue called "West Fargo 2000" which will come out around May 21. In that issue will be a special section in regard to those people who went to bat for a diversion. I know we pay plenty in taxes for it and some were not happy, but I do know they are happy today.

June 4, 1997
ENOUGH TO FILL A BOOK!

Last week I happened to be in the Indianapolis area, not to attend the races, but just for a visit with relatives. I did find out that when you hit that town at Memorial Day, you must plan to pay right up front for a hotel room. I checked the Marriott and decided I could apply $300 a night to better use. We ended up at what is called Signature Motels. Even they had tacked on some extra. What I'm talking about is the Indianapolis 500 mile race. It rained for two days, people stood around in the mud, drank beer, and waited for the sun that never came out. After three days it cleared enough to run about half the race. I understand there were accidents because of the wet track. A sad year for the 500.

* * *

Over the years I have been watching the TV show, *This Old House*. When I see that, I'm always interested. Why, I don't know, because most of the time I'm not sure what is being talked about. However, it always looks very neat the way they eventually put things together. However, I would like to add a few things about adding to a house.

When I moved into our house in 1968, I thought, "Gee, this is mighty nice. I won't have to do much to this house and, besides, I don't have the time to do anything even if I wanted to." As the saying goes, "famous last words." The rec room was half finished. You don't look at things like that when you're anxious to get into a home. It had a shower stall but no shower, windows that fogged up in winter, and an attic that needed circulating air because heat from below in the house came smack against cold air from the attic, condensation took over and we had water to spare from on high.

Time passed and the years passed, but our house was still there and then, of course, I decided to add a patio. The thought was to screen in, but what really happened cost several thousand dollars before I got the darn thing up. Next I decided to add another patio on another part of the house. Then I added a bay window. By this time I needed a new garage walk. Two new roofs on the main house followed and three roofs on one patio that wanted to leak no matter what.

I finally decided to put in the shower that wasn't there when I moved in. When you do that, you might as well fix up the bathroom. Also, about this time, Betty, my wife, decided with all the fixing going on she should have her bath fixed up, new carpeting in the living room, redesign of the fireplace, and a new patio, glassed-in and winterized, of all things.

When I sold the house last fall, my heart skipped a beat. Now I know where in heck all my savings went.

Now that I am putting all these things down, I don't know why in hell I'm not writing a book.

June 11, 1997
DEVASTATING SIGHT

Last Sunday I traveled to Grand Forks to see for myself what transpired in relation to the flood. In my opinion, this city, at this time, is a dead city. Row after row of empty homes, windows out, trash on the street side and also everywhere in yards. Driving around I could not help a lump in my throat that developed the more I saw of what has gone on in Grand Forks. I hope it won't be years before the city will begin to live like it used to. Everyone who can must help if only in small ways. I noted the Salvation Army people were there, but the situation is so overwhelming I don't see how they can face the devastation. I noted the only things with much life are dandelions in every yard growing nearly two feet tall. The downtown, what I saw of it, is at a standstill, boarded up, closed up, and at this time out of business.

July 9, 1997
HORSE SENSE AND KID SENSE

I have to admire you who put up with this column each week. There is always a time when I sit here in front of this old Underwood type-writer and wonder what is to come next. I don't claim to be a real writer. Never have. In fact, I just peck away, and let you in on adventures present and past as my life proceeds from day to day.

This week I happened to think of one of my adventures in the past, in fact way past, in the 1930s. I don't mind getting along in years like I used to when I was a young "whippersnapper." However, I do remember a day when I must have been 12 or maybe 13. I had convinced my dad and mother that it would be nice if I could ride my horse to my Uncle John's farm just outside of Britton, S.D. The ride would be 16 miles, so it took some convincing of Mom and Dad to let me go. Kids most times get their way, so the next day I was well on my way to Uncle John's.

Riding across fields and down dusty roads, with limited fences in those times, I came upon what we called the Big Ditch, which drained water from the hills east of Britton. I couldn't ride across the ditch as it was too deep, so I rode on until I came to the railroad track, which of course spanned the ditch with a rail trestle. As any kid knows, this is a real break; just ride the horse across and cut off a few miles to Britton. The horse, of course, had horse sense and the kid had no sense, so the horse hesitated. The kid, of course, as per usual, convinced the horse that all he had to do was walk across. So there I was up in the saddle as the horse was walking across the trestle. Halfway, the horse, having four legs, couldn't keep track of all four at once. The next thing I knew, my trusty horse had one leg between the ties and I was almost dumped into the Big Ditch. Now panic set in and the kid found out he was not the big brain he thought he was. However, wherever I went in those days, I always carried my Remington octagon barrel .22-short rifle. I mention the bore and type of rifle because I want to tell you a little of this rifle later.

I pulled the rifle out of its scabbard, put it under the horse's leg and pried it out from between the ties. The horse then rose to his feet and walked the rest of the way by himself. I'm sure he was saying to himself, "What a damn stupid kid,"

When I arrived at Uncle John's farm, he asked me a question about which I have nightmares to this day, "What if all four legs had gone through the trestle and a train came along?"

Always With'em

I saved that little gun for many years. Will always remember how it saved me from what could have been a terrible time in my life. I have now learned the gun is worth lots of money, because they don't make that type anymore. It is still in the Witham family. My nephew in Oklahoma has it in his gun collection and shows it with great pride.

August 6, 1997
FIFTY BUCKS WAS A LOT BACK THEN

I was visiting last week with someone about how much money they had in the bank when they got married. In that I was married some time ago, money seemed to be more valuable in 1950. When Betty and I got married in 1950, I know that I certainly wasn't rich; in fact, I had $200 in the bank, and that didn't go far even in those days. However, we took off for Colorado as if we had a thousand dollars in the bank. I do remember on the way out of Barnesville on our honeymoon, Betty asked me to stop at the local store. She came out and I asked her what she had bought.

"Cigarettes," she said, "and I have something to tell you. That was my last 20 cents. From now on I'm depending on you to pay all the bills."

I also remember we were in Greeley, Colo., where I was working for Columbia Artists Management. I had just bought a new Chrysler, one of those with the big tail fins and, of all things, yellow in color. We had to go into Denver to meet with another representative from the company. While on the way, Betty asked me how much money we had in the bank. I thought for a second and said, "Fifty dollars," How we got by in those days I'll never know. The one thing we did do was pay our bills. Outside of that, we "had a ball."

* * *

Arland Rasmussen, our police chief, stopped in last week for a visit. He told me Wednesday morning Smokey's was broken into. However, before they completed their job the police picked them up.

It seems they were out of Minneapolis and thought West Fargo (just a hick town) was easy pickings. However, they didn't know we have one of the best police departments in the state headed by the best police chief in the state. Arland told me they measured one's rap sheet, and it was longer than their police car. The guy had been into everything you could think of that wasn't loose. I asked Arland what will happen to him. Arland didn't say, but I know he knew the guy in a few weeks will be breaking into someone else's store or restaurant. It's nice to live in the land of the **free.**

September 10, 1997
CAN'T RESIST A TURN IN A 1929 MODEL A FORD

Bob Alin called me last week, and I was surprised to learn he wanted to take me for a ride. I was busy, but Bob is a special friend of mine so I took time out for a short run. He drove up in front of the *Pioneer* building in a 1929 Model A Ford Tudor. In that we had Fords on the farm, I couldn't resist stepping in for a trip around our city of West Fargo. I know we talk about the lack of room in our cars today, but when you get into a 1929 Ford, compact is the word; no room to wiggle. I might add, at least I don't bump my head like I do in my own car. If I don't bump my head, I knock my hat off. Just modern times, I guess. It seems Bob and I have something in common. He is 67, he completed the car in 1967, and I am of all things 77. Sevens must be a good number.

I couldn't resist a copy of an ad Bob gave me. This brand new car cost the grand sum of $525. Maybe you could buy a set of tires and a running board for that today. However, I do remember if you had car trouble, with a crescent wrench, a screwdriver and a pair of pliers, in ten minutes you were on your way again. Have you looked under the hood of your car lately? I did. I slammed the hood down and walked away.

November 12, 1997
RESORTING TO SELF-SERVICE

Reading the help wanted ads recently, I find most every business can use some help. In fact, I find most will hire almost anyone who is warm and breathing. Keeping this in mind, I filled my car at Dan's Oil in West Fargo a couple days ago. They had announced that from now on due to a shortage of available help, people would have to fill their own cars with gas. I found they really meant what they said in relation to no help available, so I pumped my own gas, went to their office, and asked for a job.

I could still hear the laughter as I got into my car and drove away. I guess I should have told them that in 1933 I used to pump gas at a filling station in Britton, S.D. But they probably wouldn't have hired me because when I pumped gas it was done with a handle that pumped gas into a glassed-in tank that held only 10 gallons. After that, I collected for the gas at eight or nine cents a gallon.

December 3, 1997
ONE VERY SPECIAL CAT

In that I have always been somewhat of a cat enthusiast, I have to expound on one special cat called Sandy. Before I tell you about Sandy, my introduction to cats was on the farm in South Dakota in the '30s. We fed them milk, which I have learned is not good for cats. However, there were always plenty of mice around, so I suppose that helped out on the food end. I do remember after milking the cows we poured generous portions of milk into a large pan. I could call the cats and 25 came every day.

In relation to Sandy, some folks had too many cats in Council Bluffs, Iowa, where I was working at the time. I ended up with a very loving, little tan kitty that I took home to Barnesville, which was my home where my daughter Kathleen and my wife Betty lived when I was on the road.

In that the kitty was tan, naturally she acquired the name Sandy. Sandy turned out to be the perfect cat. She never clawed the furniture, she never missed the sandbox, and wherever we placed her with neighbors when we were gone, that's where she stayed until we came home. Sometimes we would take her and her sandbox with us when we traveled from city to city. She always stayed in the room, very contented and loved to get under the bed covers whenever she could.

Sandy put up with the traveling Withams and finally settled with us in West Fargo. Mr. and Mrs. Jack Sinner lived next door and, of course, became good friends with Sandy. I had talked with Jack one day about what would happen because Sandy was near 20 years. Several days later Jack called me to his workshop where he had, of all things, made a perfect oak casket. Not only that, but he had the carry handles on the sides. I opened the casket and there inside he had lined it completely with pink silk. A year later Sandy began to fail. She really had trouble making it to her sandbox in the basement.

Overall it reached a point where I couldn't face her pain and trouble. I called Valley Veterinary Hospital and talked to Dr. Christian as to what should be done. In that he had always taken good care of Sandy, I asked him if he would perform the final trip home for our very special kitty. He went above and beyond. He came to our home and brought an assistant. I directed him to our recreation room where Sandy was sleeping. I couldn't face the situation, so I brought out the casket for Dr. Christian. He said he would take care of Sandy after she went to sleep. I gave him a screwdriver. He sealed Sandy inside and I took her to our neighbor, Jack. A while later, Jack dug a deep place in our backyard. That is where Sandy rests today. I planted a Ponderosa pine where she lies. Today that pine is 30 or 40 feet tall.

January 28, 1998
A GRACIOUS WELCOME IN OKLAHOMA

This past week I had the opportunity to bask in a bit of warm weather. It wasn't real warm, but at least warmer than good ol' North Dakota. Yep, I took a trip to visit relatives in Oklahoma City where the temps were holding around 45 to 60 degrees.

Reason for the trip was my wife Betty's birthday. Of course, a good time was had by all. However, I had received a card from the First Lady of Oklahoma, Cathy Keating. She had invited us to lunch, in that I had been in contact with her since the bombing of the federal building in the city. I will add here I had not met her before, had only seen her when she appeared on TV when Robert Schuler had her and the Governor on the *Hour of Power* at the Crystal Cathedral in Garden Grove, Calif., after the bombing. I will say she is one super lady and very, very pretty. She explained in quite some detail plans for the future of Oklahoma. We were escorted through the state mansion and through the state house.

I was very impressed with one room in the state house dedicated to the bombing. There was one full patch blanket with all the names of those killed, their ages, etc. It will bring a tear to your eyes when you, of course, know what happened. First, you have to see the devastation left by the bomb to really appreciate that special room at the state house.

I might mention here there are still many buildings that suffered great damage and still stand without anything being done to repair them. I had thought there would be great changes, but little really has been changed since the bomb. Of course, the spot of the federal building is now nothing but a bare area as if there never had been a building.

March 18, 1998
WE HAVE ENOUGH STARS

I wish someone would explain to me what statehood for Puerto Rico is all about. I'm not really excited about adding another star to our flag. In the first place, Puerto Rico has been getting along mighty fine on the ten billion a year our nation hands them anyway, or rather our Congress, which I'm beginning to think is enamored with adding another star to our flag, whether the people of our country like it or not. I do note that H.R. 856 gives Puerto Rico the right to demand statehood. I hope against hope Puerto Rico backs off on this demand. It will be good for them and us to let everything stay as it is. Otherwise, it will mean billions of dollars in new welfare handouts.

1. Almost 20 percent of Puerto Ricans are unemployed.

2. Over 50 percent of Puerto Ricans will be eligible for food stamps.

3. The entire island speaks Spanish. Tax dollars needed for bilingual education will amount to billions each year.

4. Drug addiction and alcoholism are rampant. This makes the crime rate very high.

5. Puerto Rico wants statehood but language is not negotiable. If someone from the state of Puerto Rico sues someone in Iowa, the lawsuit and the trial will be in Spanish. Imagine being in court, and depending on an interpreter to translate what the judge is saying to you.

6. What happens to Social Security?

7. In fact, Puerto Rico will have more congressmen than Rhode Island, Montana and Alaska combined.

There is a lot more that I won't go into now. I don't get into politics very often, but I think people should know what goes here.

Last but not least, how come the people of our nation can't say YES or NO to Puerto Rican statehood?

May 27, 1998
TEACHERS ARE A SUPER CLASS OF PEOPLE

I had intended writing my column on this before, but some things in life get by me and then I have to run to catch up. However, at my age I tell people that's my privilege.

A statement about teachers and mainly teachers in our own school system deserves attention. In my years in school I never gave much thought about the pressures teachers must go through each day, not only to keep guys like me in line, but at the same time get my attention long enough to get me through school. This part of school life came home to me several years ago when I was asked to give a half hour presentation to members in our high school of West Fargo. I was asked to give them information about life in the newspaper business. In that I had never done anything like that before, I was of the opinion talking to these kids would be a breeze. I must say after 15 minutes I came to the conclusion that this is damn hard work. Since that day, respect for teachers has increased dramatically to the point where I view them as a super class of people.

I know Mike Drew, as principal of West Fargo High School, is a very special guy. I have known him for several years. Jim Bjorklund as a counselor is also a very special guy. Counseling kids is a real responsibility, for a few words at the right time and in the right place could in many cases map new paths for young men and women, and change lives with a new light to follow. I know not what Mike and Jim plan in retirement, but I'll bet one point... they will not sit down.

June 24, 1998
BAILING NIAGARA FALLS

Yesterday I wasn't sure what I was going to write about in my column. In that this is Friday, I usually write this column for Wednesday's *Pioneer* for next week. However, I darn well know what I'm going to write about after Thursday's four inches of rain.

I'm used to fighting flood waters from years past because most every year West Fargo flooded for five or six weeks. In that my house was on the river, I kept five sump pumps handy during flood season. Now I'm in a new second-hand house. What happens with four inches of rain? Thursday night I was again invaded by water in my basement.

Early in the evening I checked my sump pump. Everything was fine; the pump was cruising along with no problems. Then my lights went out, so I thought I might as well check my pump. Lo and behold, water was at the top level of the sump. In a panic, I rushed for a pail to bail the pump hole out. Can't you just see a 78 year old guy filling a pail, then running up a flight of steps to empty it? By the time he got back down to the pump hole, the water was already running over the floor. About the sixth trip the lights came back on. What a super feeling to see the water being pumped out! When the pump was under control, the lights went out again, so back to the pail trips. The lights were off for 15 minutes. By this time, this ol' guy was huffing and puffing. I didn't even have enough time to swear.

Stan Dreckman and his daughter, Susie, came to the door and pitched right in cleaning up water and hooking up all the right things and squeegeeing down the floor. When that was complete they left. As Stan was leaving, he mentioned if the lights kept going off and on it would be very challenging for the West Fargo pump system that controls the sewer. I gave that little thought until 20 minutes later. I heard Niagara Falls take off in my basement.

I hit the basement in a couple grand leaps. What I found was really Niagara Falls coming up out of the stool and joined by the bathtub in no uncertain terms. Even the wash sink was filling. I might add no clear water this, by any means, but it did have an intriguing brown color with little bits of white paper floating by into the rest of the basement. Betty, my wife, said all she could hear was me and my boots sloshing around. So back came my neighbor, Stan. He put my extra sump pump into the bathtub. We both would have knelt in praise, but the nice brown water was too deep. Stan said, "I think we are holding our own. It isn't going up or down." With that statement he went home and I went upstairs to bed saying words like, "If she floods now, the hell with it!"

July 15, 1998
SPECIAL WORKMAN

I looked out our front window a week ago Monday morning and noted our garbage pick-up emptying our garbage barrels. When he had completed emptying, he noted three small pieces of paper had floated to the ground from the barrel. He very carefully bent over and picked up all three and placed them in the garbage truck.

I have no idea who the fellow was, but if he comes by the *Pioneer* office he will receive a ten dollar bill from me.

August 5, 1998
WHO DEFINES DISCRIMINATION?

I do know from time to time over the years, most people will use a classified ad in their local newspaper. However, most of you who want to advertise the need for something in your lifestyle do not realize the restrictions of what you can say in your ad. This being a new world we live in today, the word DISCRIMINATION takes front place in what you say. Fair Housing's job is to keep an eye on what you want in your ad. In that the *Midweek* and *West Fargo Pioneer* take in hundreds of ads each week, a share of calls we get have to be changed or those that come in the mail have to be rewritten. You will find some examples following. At times we in the office are confused as to what discrimination entails in an ad. Fair Housing may look at an ad and tell us we are discriminating when we don't think so at all. Two different viewpoints and basically who's to know. However, I don't have to tell you who wins.

Classifieds you can't use:
Students, walk to MSU, nice 2 bedroom, heat paid, off street parking, plug-in, laundry. School year lease.
For rent to woman.
Sleeping room for working man.
Senior citizens' condo for sale.
1 bedroom, quiet non-smoker.
North Fargo male efficiency.
Students welcome.
Sleeping room, men only.
Senior citizens welcome.
Furnished apartment, one person.
Females only... large one-bedroom apt.

There are at least 71 words you can't use in an ad.

November 25, 1998
IF SHE DIETS, I DIET

My wife and I are on a new diet. When I tell people about it, they say they have been on it, too. However, I don't hear any wonderful comments about how it goes down in the tummy.

I have been on this diet of two eggs, two slices of bacon, and a grapefruit for four hours (breakfast). Now I have just finished a chicken salad with a dressing that I don't like, thousand island. I have never liked thousand island, but I had it this noon. You know, I already think I have lost a pound. Tonight, the wife tells me I'll have a hamburger. That doesn't sound bad, but she didn't tell me what I'll have with it. She mentioned something about a salad. I might be the guy who didn't come to dinner. I shall let you know how all this turns out in days to come.

December 23, 1998
THOUGHTS FOR THE DAY

I read an article of 10 points pasted to my niece's refrigerator in Indianapolis. I felt if those who read this would place these thoughts in their life from day to day, I'm sure most of the rough spots would become smooth.

  I. *Thou shalt be happy.*

 II. *Thou shalt use thy talents to make others glad.*

III. *Thou shalt rise above defeat and trouble.*

IV. *Thou shalt look upon each day as a new day.*

 V. *Thou shalt always do your best and leave the rest to God.*

VI. *Thou shalt not waste thy time and energy in useless worry.*

VII. *Thou shalt look only on the bright side of life.*

VIII. *Thou shalt not be afraid of tomorrow.*

IX. *Thou shalt have a kind word and a kind deed for everyone.*

 X. *Thou shalt say every morning – I am a child of God and nothing can hurt me.*

February 3, 1999
MEMORIES ABOARD SHIP STILL VIVID

I remember in late 1942 when the invasion of North Africa was going on, our ship was tied up at Oran, North Africa, to deliver arms and other equipment. I might add here it didn't take the natives long to figure the Americans had money. Oranges jumped from 10 cents a bushel in the three days we were there to a dollar a bushel. I have no idea what the troops paid after we left. In any case, it was interesting to discover habits of the Arabs. To our dismay, when they were unloading the ship they would eat soap from anywhere on the ship they could find it. The only way we could stop them was to pass information that the soap was made of pork. They, of course, avoided pork at all costs so that was the end of soap as food.

At this time the battle of Caserine Pass was at its height. One of the troops just back from that battlefield was talking to me about what was happening at the front. We got into a conversation about battles from the foxhole. He said all night long pals of his were getting killed in hand-to-hand action. He could still hear them screaming in his mind as he told it to me. He said many times they would jump into their foxhole, pull out a Bible and start reading. There are no atheists in foxholes, he told me.

I remember we later took aboard German prisoners. I asked one through a friend of mine who spoke German how come they fought for Hitler. He said, "When we were hungry Hitler fed us; when we needed shoes Hitler gave us shoes." They hadn't had butter since the war began or white bread. They couldn't imagine they could have butter aboard our ship. As I told a young lady a few weeks back who didn't know what Dec. 7 meant or was all about, "Good men died on that day that you and I might live to walk free."

April 7, 1999
IT'S A SMALL WORLD

How many times have you remarked, "Small world, isn't it?" This past month the wife (Betty) and I have coasted. Yep, we've been spending time in the sun in Palm Desert, Calif. In fact, we spent four weeks there, the most time away from the office ever in our lives.

Getting back to the small world, we started for home at seven in the morning of March 25. We drove close to 500 miles to Gallup, N.M., where we stopped for the night at the Holiday Inn. We were unloading our car when another car pulled into the next parking spot to our car.

I called my wife from our room to show her the beautiful Persian cat in the car that had just pulled up next to us. As the people prepared to leave their car, I remarked about the cat and told them we were also cat people and explained our Persian had died. The conversation continued and I noted they were going on to North Carolina and I mentioned the cold northland of North Dakota. The man's wife said her husband was from Marion, N.D. We said we used to have a young lady who worked for us who came from Marion. The wife asked what her name was. We said "Shirley," but since she is married we had some thinking to do in relation to her former name. Finally Betty remembered it started with a Bo-something. The wife said, "It wasn't Boom, was it?" Of course, the name made real sense. The wife then said, (her husband was putting clothes away in their room), "My husband's name is Boom." Of course, then things began in earnest. We talked at length about Shirley, in fact learned about the whole darn family, many things Shirley had not told us. The people's names, we learned, were Mr. and Mrs. Loren Boom. They said to be sure to call Shirley and tell her Uncle Ole said a big hello. How the name of Loren turned into Uncle Ole I never learned.

In relation to the wording, "small world," the Booms started from Rancho Margate, Calif., at seven in the morning of March 25, drove 500 miles, parked at the same Holiday Inn, and had lived in California eight or nine blocks from where Betty and I stayed for a month. We ended up three feet from each other in the parking lot and wouldn't have said a word to each other if not for a beautiful Persian cat.

April 28, 1999
WE MUST BE LATE BLOOMERS

I know I'm starting out being a grandpa for the first time a little late in life. I'm this side of 80, so when something new like this comes along this ol' guy stops in the middle of a beer and asks, "Who and what is this?"

Yep, we have a new one in our family by the name of Morgan. My wife, Betty, and I have not seen her since last August 20 when she was born in Medford, Ore. However, Morgan now lives in Billings, Mont., so we old folks will be heading that way in the near future.

I might add here that Grandma Witham thinks that the kid just doesn't have any clothes. So the two of us take off for every store in town that might have something that fits a nine month old little smiling girl. (Our daughter tells us Morgan smiles all the time.) As I have said before, I HATE SHOPPING. However, seeing pictures of Morgan, even Grandpa is taking notice. I must admit that I follow Grandma around suggesting nightwear with feet in them.

"She doesn't need nightwear with feet," I'm told by Mrs. W. I thought all kids liked feet in their night clothes. Next item is a fluffy dress that I think is very neat.

"She wouldn't look good in that," I'm told. "She's a girl. You picked out brown; pink is for girls." I found really nice shoes.

"She can't wear those clodhoppers; remember she's only nine months old."

I have found as a shopper, I'm a miserable failure. Maybe some day she will grow up to play football and then I can buy her shoulder pads and a helmet and whatever else goes with football gear.

May 5, 1999
MY FAITHFUL UNDERWOOD STILL GETS THE JOB DONE

At my age I have not paid much attention to computers. In fact, I guess I have avoided them more than anything. I know all the guys and gals that work at the *Midweek, West Fargo Pioneer* and Davon Press know where to turn them on. The only thing I know how to turn on is my 1918 typewriter. However, in that our office and press is overrun with those strange boxes that tell about all kinds of things, this past week I took courage by the hand and asked about websites or whatever you call them. In that, from what I'm told, we are on a website, I wanted to know what shows up on that screen I see in several places in our office.

I found the darndest thing. Pictures of the *Midweek* come up on the screen and, I might add, in real color. This pepped up my curiosity to no end. I asked what all is on there. I find all our *Midweek* ads appear and people can read them and find out who wants to sell something and who wants to buy something. I ran across Nelson Ford in Fergus Falls. Of all things, you can see just what they have to sell; you can copy information on the car you like right from the screen. When I got my bifocals working, I could see the ad better than reading from a newspaper. What really knocked me over is I could read information from any newspaper in the country.

I next asked, "How far does this darn thing go?" I was told any place in the world.

"You mean they can read these ads in the *Midweek* in England?" Yep, any place in the world.

"Wow!" I say.

Right now I'm typing this super information on my 1918 Underwood and I'm thinking this whole darn world is passing me by. I can say one thing: I can still jump up and click my heels! So there, too.

August 4, 1999
LONGFELLOW'S POEMS MADE SENSE

I well remember Henry Wadsworth Longfellow poems when in school. What I want to know is why in heck these guys who write poems nowadays can't write poems like his that make sense. In the first place, they make neither rhyme nor reason. They go on for pages and are just plain boring, boring, boring.

I may be old-fashioned, but what is wrong with *The Children's Hour?* It makes sense, it rhymes and it has a story to tell. I hope I will be forgiven if I conjure up memories of what my kind of poetry is all about.

> *Between the dark and the daylight, when the night is beginning to*
> *   lower,*
> *Comes a pause in the day's occupations that is known as The*
> *   Children's Hour.*
>
> *I hear in the chamber above me the patter of little feet,*
> *The sound of a door that is opened, and voices soft and sweet.*
>
> *From my study I see in the lamplight, descending the broad hall*
> *   stair,*
> *Grave Alice, and laughing Allegra, and Edith with golden hair.*
>
> *A whisper, and then a silence; yet I know by their merry eyes*
> *They are plotting and planning together to take me by surprise.*
> *A sudden rush from the stairway, a sudden raid from the hall!*
> *By three doors left unguarded they enter my castle wall!*
>
> *They climb up into my turret o'er the arms and back of my chair.*
> *If I try to escape, they surround me; they seem to be everywhere.*
>
> *They almost devour me with kisses; their arms about me entwine...*

There is more, of course, but there is a story here of family life and love that only comes around once. It's too bad in our travels through the world we can't keep things a bit more in rhyme. It might make the bumps a little smaller and rivers easier to cross.

August 25, 1999
A LITTLE ONE IN THE HOUSE AGAIN

By the time this paper comes out I will have faced a very small challenge for three days. I cannot tell you what happened because she hasn't arrived yet. Her name is Morgan and she will celebrate her first birthday at the Witham household. Morgan is our first grandchild and, from what I'm told, there will be no more. However, at Betty's and my ages, it is a very new experience to have a little dynamo traveling on all fours across the floors of our home.

To get ready for this invasion, I have hidden the key to my grandfather clock, put away my handy TV schedule that I know would be gone with the first chubby grab. I have taken down the cat's swing, lifted all those little knick-knacks that I'm sure would catch her eye. Betty said she will sweep the floor because all those little crumbs and hairs will be found and will end up in the mouth. I'm sure the pots and pans from the kitchen will take a good going over. We are standing by to see how Dusty, the cat, takes all this commotion. After all, she has the run of the house so we shall see what table Dusty will land on when she takes a look at Morgan.

Anyway, Grandpa and Grandma will be all smiles and taking pictures because that is the thing to do.

* * *

A while back a neighbor called, said his wife was away and could he come over for a visit. He did come. He brought fish with him he had just caught. He also brought his own frying pan, ingredients for the fish and proceeded to cook my wife and me dinner. I might add that he also brought along his own refreshments. Who could ask for more?

November 3, 1999
I'M SAD AT DEPARTURES

I'm sad this week. Geri Walz, who has put up with me in the advertising layout department going into 28 years, and Joyce Newgard, who is in her 33rd year, the last ones as executive vice president, will not be here next week. They both gave me the sad news a month or two ago, but of course it will really "come home" Monday morning when they aren't at the office. I'll get over it, but it is like losing part of our family and that leaves me with a heavy heart.

* * *

I was talking with a friend of mine and she explained something to me I never thought of.

"Do you know lots of kids nowadays cannot read time on a clock?" Not believing a word she said, I wanted an explanation. I was told that the kids don't have to worry about telling clock time because it's all on digital clocks, so it isn't necessary to learn how to tell time on a regular clock.

* * *

I know you who read this column are not surprised to pick a catalog out of your mailbox most every day. They also cross my desk each morning. In fact, so many that this past week I began to count them. At last count it was 26. I also note (being in the paper business) that the catalogs are on coated paper (slick, shiny paper) and that means nothing but big money. To add to this, all pictures are four-color; this is also lots of bucks. I'm of the opinion people buy from these catalogs or they wouldn't be coming in our mailboxes. What happens to our local merchants?

The 2000s

January 19, 2000
BE SURE TO THINK BEFORE YOU ACT!

I know I could be writing about politics and I could be writing about the times, good or bad, about West Fargo. However, we have an excellent editor to do that. I'm not very good about athletics; we have a very, very good writer to do that. So what does that leave me? It leaves some space to visit with those of you who read my thoughts in my column each week.

I'm intrigued with people who don't think before they act. One instance is a couple fellows last week who blew up a mailbox in Fargo. They forgot it was snowing. Police were called, followed the tire tracks to the culprits' doorstep. I was visiting with Dave Braton about the robber who held up a liquor store. When he had all the money in hand, he told the clerk to give him a bottle of vodka to take with him. The clerk said, "You don't look 18 to me. I want to see some identification." The guy produced his identification. After leaving the store, the clerk, of course, called the cops.

February 23, 2000
THE LADIES MAKE IT GO

It has always been important to me that women are running a liberal share of the operation of Pioneer Enterprises. In all cases, they are dependable and like what they do.

I learned this years ago when I saw them work late into the night to get the paper ready for press the next day. So over the years I have found women are special human beings when it comes to work.

I often wonder how in the world they managed to exist in the early days of our nation when they rode the covered wagons out to California. I have the impression they wore those long dresses in hot and cold weather because that is what those days demanded of women. I remember my mother out working with cattle and horses in hot summer or cold winter, always with a dress, its length well below her knees.

A few years ago at our Lions Club, someone brought up the idea of including women in our organization. I will add here there were some men who were a little shocked to think that a lady would consider joining a Lions Club. I also must insert here a note that some few, a very few, fellows wondered if they should be let in at all. Of course, you will have read the first paragraph of this column so you know what I had to say about the gals joining our West Fargo Lions Club.

Several neat gals have joined the club. They not only have added a dash of glamour, common sense, vitality to our club, but they downright get in and work. In a lot of cases, they are the first to volunteer for jobs that require a generous dash of work AND I MIGHT SAY THEY GET THE JOB DONE.

Now we Lions, the men that is, make every effort to bring these neat ladies into our club because they make it sort of extra special. The gals nowadays have been liberated, and for me that's just fine. They wear what they want, be it slacks, shorts, dresses, etc., or a fetching gown. It all comes down to the fact women are special in our nation and I'm damn glad to have them around.

March 1, 2000
A TURN UP ONE BLOCK

Four years ago the wife and I bought a house. I'm not quite sure why, but that is what we did. Coming home from church one day, Mrs. W. said, "Turn here." As we passed the first house, she said, "Don, look at that nice home and it's for sale."

I have often wondered just how we happened to turn up that one block when there are so many other blocks in West Fargo. When we looked in the front door, I made a fatal mistake and said, "Betty, this looks like it might be a good investment for someone." As the saying goes, those were famous last words. I like the house, but I really didn't know I was the guy slated to live there.

I was at the YMCA one day and one of the fellows down there wanted to know "how come you two oldies bought that big house?" I couldn't think of an answer so I told him at our age we needed the exercise. As an afterthought, I asked him how come he knew we lived there. He said, "I'm your mailman."

April 19, 2000
WHAT NEXT?

I learned something last week that stopped me. My car battery failed to do what it was supposed to do so I ran for the battery charger. Lifting the hood I could not see the battery. I said to myself, "I know darn well cars don't have a carburetor anymore, but I'm sure they still need a battery." I got out the flashlight and looked in all the dark corners, but NO BATTERY. As I always do, I rushed right down to Dan's Oil.

"Don't tell me they have done away with the battery in cars now." They all smiled and informed me if I would look under the back seat I would find they still put a battery in cars.

April 26, 2000
DOIN' IT RIGHT

Three weeks ago I was sitting in California under a nice warm sun. I also was a bit upset that North Dakota was having somewhere near the same temperature. I came to the conclusion if I'm going to pay money to sit in the sun, maybe next March I had better stay home; it's the same sun in North Dakota.

In any case, while I was sitting in the sun outside at our condo, I watched the gals play golf for almost four weeks. I know I'm not worth a darn when it comes to golf, but I do know I could do just as well as they. I noted some also cheated a bit, not much, but just enough to get by.

However, during the four weeks the gals put about 432 golf balls in the little pond outside our condo. I got used to the plop, plop, plop of golf balls going into our pond.

Then came an old duffer with a youngster and a long pole with a cup on the end. He salvaged about eight balls and drove away in his golf cart. I can still see the smile of satisfaction on his face.

But during the last day of our stay the real golfer came along. He pulled up in his golf cart, walked around back and with one pull a small motor came to life. He then brought out snorkel gear, pulled on a rubber suit, grabbed a wire basket and disappeared into our little lake. I have no idea how long he was under the water, but I'm sure he made a haul and a half of golf balls. The old saying applies: If you're going to do it, you might as well do it right.

June 21, 2000

"Without'em"... Don's *Always With'em* gives place to guest writer, his daughter, Kathy Chaffee.

DEPRESSION ERA TAUGHT MORE THAN HARD WORK

Since I moved to Montana one year ago, I have met some interesting people. One in particular is my friend and neighbor, Mildred Dunlap.

Millie, as she is known to her friends and family, was born Dec. 4, 1908. In visiting with her from time to time, I find myself lost in the past with her stories. She tells of the Depression in the 1930s and how people had to get by with little or nothing. But, in particular, she tells of the feeling, the attitude of the nation at that time, the work ethic and the kindness of the people toward one another that seems to be somewhat lacking in the world these days.

One story Millie recently related to me showed me very directly the meaning of hard work. During the late 1950s, Millie's husband, Bill Dunlap, became ill and could no longer work driving his logging Caterpillar in the woods of Butte Falls, Ore. Millie decided to supplement their income by raising chickens, not just a few chickens, but 1,200 White Leghorns. This enterprise turned out to be hands-on hard work for Millie, as every day the eggs had to be collected and then checked for blood spots by using a candle. They then had to be crated and delivered to her egg customers in her black '55 Ford two-door or '31 Model A. Millie also had to clean, feed and water these 1,200 chickens every day, summer and winter. In a word, life in these times was nothing but work. But the times as they were in those days seem to bring a quality to life, an understanding of making do and getting by and of being able to grasp a feeling of a slower time, of helping each other and growing from the experience.

Millie recently suffered a broken hip resulting from an accident in a local store. She spent two weeks in a hospital here in Billings. She was then released to finish recovering at the home she shares with her son, Don.

Millie recovered from this accident in record time for a person 91 years old. Perhaps the wonderful spirit she has developed from all her years of hard work and getting by is still paying off.

December 20, 2000
GETTING USED TO STEPPING OVER LEGOS AND PLASTIC TOYS

A small challenging whirlwind entered our home last Tuesday at 5 in the afternoon. Her name is Morgan. She comes with a smile that will melt you into a puddle. She doesn't say anything much; however, she has named me "Baba." I didn't realize I was named until she took my middle finger and said the fateful word, "Baba."

I also know she can travel, short legs and all. I know this because she is always 18 inches behind me wherever I go and I do mean wherever I go. Each morning she tries to help me dress. I thought I could do that myself after 80 years, but to no avail. She helps with my shoes and assists when I pull on my pants. I have never had a lady do that before so at this time in life I am a bit shy.

Grandma Witham early in the morning placed Santa Clauses all over the house. When Morgan wakes, we find it takes about 45 minutes to collect those big white Santas and put them all in a pile on the livingroom floor. I must say we do have a well-behaved little lady. Morgan gives a close ear when Baba says NO. I guess she finds a note in Baba's voice that tells her NO is NO.

In any case, I have found I can't run as fast as I used to when I was 35. I have found a short nap in my easy chair is not accepted either; dozing is not accepted. A pat on the hand or a poke in the cheek brings me back into the real world.

However, after the week Morgan has been in our household, Grandpa and Grandma are getting used to stepping over Santa bears and lego toys and plastic horses and wiping sticky fingers. After all, a smile from a beautiful little girl just plain heads the list.

January 31, 2001
PLAN AHEAD FOR YOUR FINANCIAL SECURITY

From what I read and hear, I note that we are on the edge of a recession. I'm not so sure what they mean by a recession. However, I sure do know what a depression is all about. I'm reminded how I used to save as best I could in the Depression and the years that followed. I do remember that after working in the farm fields all week, my dad would give me 50 cents. I could fill our Ford car with tractor gas and head out

Always With'em

for Claremont, which was six miles away. My girlfriend and I could go to a movie or even a dance. Fifty cents went a long way in those days. I did find, if I were careful and saved 10 cents, that would come in as a bonus later.

Through those years, I learned what money was all about. It was the difference between staying home or going someplace on Saturday night.

At 18, I did leave the farm and ended up in St. Paul, Minn. Friends of our family took me in, fed me and charged me nothing to live with them until I found a job at Montgomery Ward, where I pulled down a salary of 16 cents an hour.

I write this because in our time there are so many opportunities to save for the rainy day of the future. For some reason, a large share of people don't realize that Social Security is not designed to keep life comfortable in old age. It is only to supplement what you have put aside for retirement. When I was traveling on the road in the concert world, I found if I saved only dimes, it counted into savings that surprised me when I opened the little flat box of dimes I carried in my suitcase. I had other savings in an insurance policy which was for later years, but I was always amazed how those dimes counted up.

If we are in a recession, as we keep hearing, a dollar reserved now might calm your nerves in the months and years to come. Keep in mind the story about the grasshopper and the ant. If you plan like the ant, you're going to be happy all your life.

* * *

Will Rogers said something to remember. *"Even if you're on the right track, you'll get run over if you just sit there."*

* * *

Tips for exercise buffs: It is well documented that for every mile that you jog, you add one minute to your life. This enables you at 85 years old to spend an additional five months in a nursing home at $5,000 a month.

February 14, 2001
QUICK POLICE WORK

I was talking to Arland Rasmussen, our West Fargo Chief of Police, last week in regard to a stolen pickup truck. Seems that Jason Anderson, a West Fargo patrolman, was listening to his radio. A call came through that a pickup truck was stolen in Fargo. Patrolman Anderson noted the color and type of vehicle at the Kum & Go store. He pulled his patrol car next to the truck. When a fellow came out to get into the truck, Anderson arrested him and took him to jail. What is intriguing about this is the whole proceeding from theft of the truck to arrest took just 90 minutes.

When you next pass our West Fargo patrolmen, smile and wave. We need these guys. They all come from a first class police department.

* * *

As with most people when they get home from their days at work, the TV is the first button pushed. I am one of those people. It has been a habit of mine in the evening to check for a movie. I prefer the older movies for mostly one reason – the "F" word. I'm not really a prude about this, but I sure get tired of actors trying to express themselves by liberal use of the "F" word. As an old Navy bos'n who has heard most every risqué word invented, I resent the use of this word. There are over 50 people working at Pioneer Enterprises. To this day after many years, I have not heard the "F" work used. In our business, we seem to get along nicely without it.

February 21, 2001

"Without'em"... Don's *Always With'em* gives place to guest writer, his daughter, Kathy Chaffee. (You will note that my daughter, Kathy Chaffee, will be writing some six or seven columns in the *Pioneer*. In that she lives somewhat in the wilderness of Montana, where she has had the necessity of shooting a rattlesnake off her back step, she should have some things to tell about life in what I call "The Outback." ...DCW)

RATTLED, BUT NOT SHAKEN

Since moving to Montana several years ago, I've been confronted by several wild creatures. However, in Shepherd, MT, where I currently live, these creatures are something you don't want to step on.

Yes, I have snakes.

My first assumption was that all snakes were bad, and I had to begin an elimination routine that would rival a similar routine I had for mice in my house.

I began my research by visiting with a man who was drilling my water well, and at the same time watching a five-foot snake go by. After I swallowed about four times, and found I could still speak, I asked about getting a gun to shoot the snake, to which my well driller replied, "Absolutely not."

At the point I was beginning to question my intelligence in hiring him to drill my well, he explained the difference between a bull snake and a rattlesnake. He said bull snakes were *helpful* because they eat rodents and don't harm people or other animals at all.

My next question was how to tell the difference without close examination. I was told it isn't easy because they're practically identical, with the exception that the rattler will "rattle."

Armed with this information, I went to the house and loaded my rifle. At this time, we have killed four snakes, all rattlers.

I just shoot and ask questions later.

April 4, 2001
READING AT ARM'S LENGTH...
By guest writer, Kathy Chaffee

As I was writing a check the other day at the grocery store, the woman at the counter asked me why I was standing back so far from the checkbook register. I replied that in the last few months I have had to get further back from the printed work in order to see it. She then asked me what's going to happen when I'm at the end of my arms and the subject at hand is still blurry.

I left with the question stuck in my mind and only one answer. I am faced with getting reading glasses. Now this issue itself is no big deal. My problem is actually going to begin when the new reading glasses and I have to work together. You see, I am genetically predisposed to what is termed the "where are my glasses now" syndrome.

As far back as I can remember, my father has been searching for his glasses. I can recall several times at restaurants he had to borrow my mother's glasses, only to be brought up short by the look on her face as she dug through her purse, and at the same time she asked him what he did with his. He never had an answer to that question, and at my tender age I had already learned when to say nothing at all.

He seemed to have corrected the problem to some extent a few years ago when he bought several pairs of glasses and installed them in his cars and many rooms of the house. However, when I was back there to visit at Christmas, the glasses always seemed to be in another room when he decided he needed them. And so life goes. My father has had glasses since he was 40, and has been searching for one pair or another all these years, and I'm reading out at the end of my arm.

April 11, 2001
I'M BACK

I'm taking my column back from my daughter. The reason for this is I'm getting too many nice comments liking her column. After all, you have been putting up with my upside-down and backwards stuff since 1967 and I don't want to lose you completely.

To tell the truth, I have been in sunny California for over a month. Old guys like me need more sun than you who stay here all winter. However, since I came back last week, I'm beginning to think I should have stayed another week or two in the sun.

Next week I will introduce you to Fred and Mable, two wonderful young folks I met in California. They were nice to me while there, so I will have a picture of them next week.

I used to think Macular Degeneration was something you purchased at the drugstore. However, I find it's not that at all. It involves the eyes. I found that I have such a challenging situation and have also learned not much can be done about it. To explain it some, when you read, things get all squiggly. I thought I was the only one in the world that had such a thing. Over the past months I have learned thousands of people have it and live with it every day. Now I have an excuse when I run into a telephone pole. I now know lots of other people have the squiggles so I'm thinking of forming a club.

In any case, I'm glad to be back at work. The company gang seemed not to be disappointed that I'm back, so I guess I'll hang around awhile. Besides if I stayed home I would just stumble over the cat and I know

Betty, that gal I live with, wouldn't appreciate my being underfoot every day. So I'll just come to the office and sit around and hope people think I'm important. I do say it is very nice to be home where my friends are. Friends are special, you know, and they can be sorely missed.

May 16, 2001
ON SMOKING

I don't smoke yet today for reasons that came home to me in my early days as a kid. I remember I first tried wrapping cornsilk in newspaper. That seemed to work okay, but it wasn't like the rolled paper cigarettes I used to watch our hired man smoke. I did find an old Bull Durham sack one time with about one smoke left. That, of course, made my head whirl around. I progressed from there to Pay Day Chew and that made my stomach turn flip-flops. I did find cigarettes that seemed to work for me; cost was 10 cents a pack, and they were called Wings. However, my mother would have brought the razor strap out for sure if she had caught me, so I really didn't smoke Wings very long.

I really don't know why I didn't smoke after I was old enough to pay my own way. I guess I still had the taste of that Pay Day chaw in my mouth.

September 6, 2001
A LITTLE BIT OF DISCIPLINE GOES A LONG WAY

I have empathy for teachers. I know it isn't easy for them to show up for school every day to face the charging mob of kids. I know most kids are there to learn... but there are always some who come just to put in their time.

Discipline problems on a national basis for young students are a challenging thing for our teachers. Basically, in relation to discipline, their hands are tied. They know what should be done and they also know that there is always a parent who shows up at the school and blames the teacher. Either because their kid isn't learning or he's just there to have fun. And the parents are happy just to get him, or her, out of the house.

I remember once in grade school the teacher caught me throwing a sandwich at another kid. Down to the superintendent's office I went. Of course, the super explained to me that throwing food wasn't to happen.

The next thing I knew, he had me over his knee and there was a whack, whack, whack. And I decided right then and there that there was somebody around there that would kick butt if I didn't behave.

I found out in the early days at home that I lived under the same circumstances. I remember my mother always kept a razor strap on a nail under the clock shelf. If I got out of line, I knew what was going to happen.

I got the bright idea one time to hide the strap. And by golly, I guess Mother was pretty sharp after all, because the next morning the strap was hanging under the shelf.

Discipline, in my way of thinking, is what youngsters need and understand. Sometimes they don't really understand this until they go into the Army or Navy or the Marines, especially the Marines. Discipline is taught there in no uncertain manner.

I'm still of the old adage that a whack on the butt tells the one who gets it that there's a better road to travel.

May 29, 2002
THERE'S A STORY BEHIND MY RED CAP

Sitting here looking out the window in the office on a beautiful Friday afternoon, I'm reminding myself that I have to change my cap.

Now, usually I wear a bight red cap and it's made of wool and that's, of course, to keep those few hairs up there warm and so that they don't blow away in the snowstorms.

People have mentioned my red cap through the winter and I tell them that I wear the red cap so that people will see me coming so that they can sort of step aside and they won't step on me. So that's why I've worn my red cap most of the winter.

But now with the beautiful sunshiny day, I've been a little perplexed about what I should be wearing. So without a lot of further thought, I hunted around in my summer caps and found a bright yellow one. As I started out of the house, my wife mentioned that, after all, it wasn't quite summer yet. But that's alright, I don't do everything she tells me to do so I'm wearing my bright yellow cap in the hopes that when people see me coming down the street they'll know I'm there and they won't step on me.

* * *

Always With'em

Dave Samson is our photographer here at our corporation, and over the years he's won many, many firsts with his photography. He always figures he should turn his selections into the North Dakota Newspaper Association competition every year to see what happens. He did so this year. Prior to this, he had turned a picture into the Publisher's Auxiliary, which is a national magazine, and he won first place for his picture taken of baseball. However, he turned the same picture into the North Dakota Newspaper Association contest. Whoever looked at it didn't look very closely. They just gave him an Honorable Mention, no First, no Second, no Third — just Honorable Mention, way down the line.

So it proves that two different people looking at the same picture make two different decisions. Needless to say, it didn't make David Samson real happy, but that's all right; he'll keep shooting pictures no matter what.

July 24, 2002
POST OFFICE LACKS BUSINESS ACUMEN

For years Davon Press has been buying postal delivery trucks from the United State Postal Service. They're neat little trucks and they travel from *Midweek* mailbox to mailbox all around the town. We bought them when the USPS decided they were no longer good for their service. We have always been glad to buy them, fix them up and use them for our delivery to boxes and other delivery drops in West Fargo, Fargo and Moorhead.

Awhile back I checked with the local postal people to see if we could buy two or three more of their post office delivery trucks. I checked through the authorities and found out, much to my disappointment and chagrin, that they do not sell these trucks to the public any longer. On further investigation I asked what happens to them, because they just couldn't drop them in the river or something. I found that the trucks are taken to the scrap yard and crushed. It seems to me that the post office doesn't understand that these vehicles are still worth money to the post office. Sell them to the public where they are still useful.

I do note that the post office is raising their rates. I question this vehicle destruction when the postal authorities are saying more money is so badly needed.

August 21, 2002
RENOVATION PROJECT AT VFW RESTAURANT NICE IMPROVEMENT

Just recently we went to the VFW here in West Fargo to have dinner in their renovated restaurant. Personally, I was very, very surprised to find that they have almost turned the restaurant into a glamour place with all the decorations and pictures. We were most pleased to spend an hour or so there for dinner. The service was excellent, the food absolutely superb. It was well served, perfectly cooked and everything that you'd want in relation to a fine restaurant. I just want to repeat again that I was most pleased and I urge everyone to make a point to have a lunch or dinner there at the VFW.

* * *

In May Betty and I received the West Fargo Chamber Civic Excellence Award, which we feel very highly honored to accept.

We both wish to extend our appreciation to the community of West Fargo, and we wish the city much good fortune in the future. Thirty-five years ago we came to West Fargo on more or less a wing and a prayer and hoped for the best. West Fargo supported us through all these years. We've had a happy life and that, we know, will continue for years to come.

September 18, 2002
SOMETIMES YOU JUST HAVE TO SHUT THE TV OFF

In that I don't see too well, I do very little reading, so naturally I end up getting my news and the basics of what's going on in the world from our TV. There are some things I like about TV because I am interested in the news and somewhat in politics.

I note that it's often interrupted to quite some extent by advertising. Now, naturally, being in the newspaper and shopper business, I'm interested in advertising. So I end up watching advertising that I'm not particularly enthusiastic about. I know there's one clip that really turns me upside down and that's for a Listerine ad. I cannot stand watching that guy or gal rinsing Listerine around in their mouth and it doesn't just stop after a few seconds, but it continues for minutes, which just drives me up the wall. I am a Listerine enthusiast and always have a bottle handy, but that ad really turns me off.

Always With'em

Last Thursday night I was cruising the channels to find something of interest. After you've covered 20 channels, it gets a little boring when there's really nothing on of great interest. Once in awhile there is a very old film production that I'm interested in, but most of the other stuff is "catch as catch can" and it bores me to death.

Whatever happened to super special shows like Archie Bunker and Jackie Gleason? Ninety percent of shows on TV today just don't have much to say.

In any case, I am glad that we have TV and I neglected to say that anything I don't like I can switch to the next station or I can turn it off.

December 18, 2002
A CHALLENGE... OOPS!

You who have read this column over the past few months know that I have macular degeneration. And along with it come little challenges of life. They intrigue me because I've always been able to see very well.

I bring up the fact here that last September we were on our way to Indianapolis with relatives to visit some more relatives. In our travels I was using my lack of eyesight to much advantage because checking into a motel I really didn't have to sign much. I just let Betty do that. But on the way, we stopped off to get fuel at a filling station and naturally you don't always stop at a filling station just to get fuel; there are other demands to be taken care of.

I headed for the men's room, and I was just a bit embarrassed when I heard a familiar voice behind me saying, "What are you doing in here?" And I said, "Well, what does it look like I'm doing in here." And the lady spoke up, who in this case was my wife, and said, "Well get your rear end out of here because you're in the ladies' room." I said, "Well, it sure looked like the men's room to me when I walked in." So I just sort of crept out of the place and found one that said M-E-N. From there on I proceeded in safety.

January 22, 2003
WE NEED TO STAND BY OUR PRESIDENT

Over the past few weeks I've listened to dire things emanating from the news media in relation to our question of attacking Iraq. In most cases, they don't really predict a disaster but they do emanate clouds of doom. There must be a different cloud somewhere on the horizon.

When President Bush took office I said in my column, "We have a new and different president." And I'm sure that, in the picture that appears before the public today when people view his ideas and his determination, they understand what I was talking about. For once we have a highly determined president who understands what's happening, not only in our nation but around the world. Our president is telling us that in the future and the not-too-distant future we will have to face the issue of not only Iraq but the challenges that come across the world from Al-Queda. If we do not face now the imminent dangers on the horizon appearing from Iraq and Al-Queda we are taking a dangerous step.

People are gathering from some large cities across our nation crying "peace, peace." But there will be no peace unless the people of our nation face up to their responsibilities. For without this, we are facing challenges to our own livelihood. We can sit in the name of "peace" and wait for these monsters of evil to come to our front door. Or we can face them now. President Bush knows what can happen to our future. That is why with great determination and steadfastness he faces those who cry "peace." Because he knows that without facing the challenges across the world, there will never be peace. In these hours, weeks and months ahead we must stand by our president.

April 30, 2003
LIFE ISN'T ALWAYS EQUAL OR FAIR

In a recent column of mine, I mentioned that we had spent three weeks in Sarasota, FL. However, I didn't mention the trip down isn't the easiest when you're riding by car, because from West Fargo it took a little over three days. I think an airplane would serve very well.

However, on our trip down, we stopped at a Holiday Inn in Paducah, Ky. As we were unloading to go into the motel for overnight, we came across a family that caught our interest. I shall remember the look on the wife's face as she passed to go into the motel. I noticed that she and the kids and the husband were all tan. So naturally, I stopped the husband and asked him where he'd come from.

He said, "Sarasota. It's a wonderful place to go." He couldn't say enough nice things about it. But, as I mentioned before, the poor gal, who was relatively plump, proceeded past with four bouncy kids behind her just raring to go. You'd think that at eight or nine o'clock at night they'd be all worn out, but there were no worn out kids here. So she was carrying clothes and proceeding on her way and I noticed that she looked very, very worn down. I asked her husband how long they'd been down there. He said, "Oh, we've been there a month and, as I said before, we had a lot of fun." But as the lady went on into the motel I could notice that a month in Sarasota for her wasn't quite the lovable, wonderful vacation she had anticipated.

With four bouncy kids behind her, she went on into the motel and we visited with the husband. He was a very talkative guy and told us all about Sarasota and how much fun he had there. While he was talking I began to wonder, "I'll bet he sat by the beach with a beer in his hand while the poor, little plump wife rushed around trying to keep all the kids from drowning themselves."

As we were talking to him, he said he went down to Sarasota with the intention of buying some property or a house down there. After visiting several houses, he reluctantly found out that the best thing he could do in relation to a house was, with luck, buy a mailbox. "So I've given up trying to buy a house in Sarasota, Florida," he said.

Later that evening, we ran into the dad at the swimming pool and the kids were all hopping around like mad, diving in and running around the pool and having a ball. There sat old Dad with a beer in his hand, and he said, "Well, a couple of beers always cheer me up and that's what I'm participating in, and I don't think I'll be going back to Florida to buy a house."

October 1, 2003
CELEBRATING MY BIRTHDAY IN GRAND STYLE AT WEST FEST

I must say, last week I had a ball. The 20th, which was West Fest Days, landed just about right for me to capitalize on having a lot of fun on my birthday. Betty, my wife, and I turned out to be grand marshals of the event. I don't know what made them decide that the two of us old folks should be in on this fancy parade, but we showed up anyway.

I had the duty of being at the park by 9:00 so I could fire the gun for the big race that kicked off at 9:30. I did that. Later, we ended up at the Chamber office where things really began to happen. I want to say here that Andy Buckley and his nice wife picked us up at the house in time for us to get to the Chamber office at 12:00. It was nice of them. We rode in their quite old Fairlane, which had the top down and it was pretty classy and very shiny. Our little five-year-old granddaughter, Morgan, hopped into the car to ride with us in the parade.

We proceeded from there to where the parade started down on Main. We sat there for a while and when things got ready to go, everything headed toward Sheyenne Street. We proceeded to go up Sheyenne a couple of blocks before we were to stop and get on the viewing stand in front of State Bank and Trust to watch the parade go by.

We watched the rest of the parade from the platform, and tried as best we could to duck all the candy that was flying through the air. Of course, our little granddaughter Morgan enjoyed that very much because she was busy picking up the candy and putting it in a sack to take home.

I must tell you that a good friend of ours from Casselton came by with balloons and three small bottles of VO, which naturally I appreciated very much. The VO was attached to the balloons so I thought that was mighty neat. All came from Carol Rademacher who works at this bank. Those three things I appreciated very much.

Well, of course, life didn't end there because I was handed a beautiful cake from the Chamber of Commerce. It was so pretty I couldn't resist shooting a couple of pictures of it.

I might add here that that was just one birthday cake. The next Monday the gang at our office presented another cake for my birthday and, of course, we all gathered around and sang *Happy Birthday* and I jumped up and clicked my heels twice, if you want to know. We sat around and had a wonderful potluck.

Now, a potluck at the *Midweek* is something special because all of our gals seem to outdo themselves in bringing food, and naturally my tummy was poking out by the end of the meal. In that we had lots of desserts, I proclaimed the next day, Tuesday, would be my birthday again. So we reserved my birthday cake until Tuesday noon, so that made three birthdays for me.

Now what 84-year-old could complain about three birthdays all in a few days? So I'm living so high now that I'm already looking forward to next year when I'm 85.

November 12, 2003
THANK GOODNESS FOR MY MOTHER'S DETERMINATION

I guess in most instances in our lifetime when we think back and give a little thought to our mothers, we recall how they guided our early lives. I remember my mother who dictated a line of life to me without saying a word.

As a youngster graduating from the eighth grade, I figured I knew most of the things necessary for me to make it along the challenging path that I would be traveling.

So, without any great amount of fuss, I informed my mother that now that I graduated from the eighth grade I really didn't need any more schooling because I could work on the farm and help out there and do most of the things necessary to keep body and soul together.

I very well remember my mother just looking at me and walking away. As the grasshopper and the ant lived the life of the future, I became the grasshopper and to some point my mother became the ant.

She just kept along her life's path and I, like the grasshopper, fiddled away the whole summer. I didn't give school much thought because I had capped that part of my life.

I remember the first day of school though, because I knew it was coming. And I was quite determined to sit this one out. I well remember the school bus pulling up at our front door and the door opened and the bus driver looked out. Mother still didn't say anything. She handed me my lunchpail and pushed me out the door.

I didn't know what to do so I climbed onto the school bus and went to school. And four years later I graduated from high school.

Now, how do I go back and thank her for silent determination.

January 31, 2004
REMEMBER... DON'T EVER GIVE UP

In March of 1967 our company was formed and eventually evolved into what is known today as Davon Press, Inc. In that I'm president of the organization, every day in one way or the other I'm talking to our sales people.

In that I've always made an attempt to be pleasant to everyone, when I meet our sales people I always say, "Well, how you doing?" "How're you getting along?" And as I leave after our conversation I say, "Don't give up."

The reason I say this is down through the years in my experience in the sales world, I've learned that the words "don't give up" mean most everything in life.

It all started after World War II when I was working for Sears Roebuck in Aberdeen, S.D. After I had worked there for a year or so I had an offer to go to work for Columbia Artists Management out of New York. So I told my boss that I was going to be leaving. His question was, "What are you going to do?" I said, "I'll be selling and working with concert artists in the selling field." His reply was, "You'll never make it." I said, "Why?" He said, "You're a poor salesman."

I ended up selling in the concert field for 20 years.

My next experience was in the publishing business in Windom, Minn. My wife Betty and I worked there for about a year and a half and an opportunity presented itself in West Fargo, N.D. I informed my boss of this, and he didn't object too much but said, "Well, I don't know about West Fargo. It's a pretty small place." I said, "Well, I think that I can make it." He said, "No, you'll never make it in West Fargo as a publisher." And added, "I don't think you'll make it at all."

I went to work selling advertising and Betty hurried morning, noon and night to keep our new paper going in the right direction.

At that time I had a partner, and after a little over a year I thought maybe I could scrape up some money and buy his half of the paper. I approached him (Barry Pritchard) and said, "Listen, I'd like to buy the paper." So after much negotiation and conversation he said he would sell his share to me. I immediately cashed in my years old insurance policy and wrote him a check. As he was leaving he made a point of telling me that the *West Fargo Pioneer* would never make it and I would never make it selling for the *Pioneer.*

Hence the reason today as I talk to the people in our business who do the selling and keep the business going, I always mention these words, "Don't give up."

I have a quote here from Beverly Sills, an acquaintance of mine from the Metropolitan Opera in New York. I thought it was rather classic.

You may be disappointed if you fail,
But you are doomed if you don't try.

December 29, 2004
TURNING A NEW PAGE IN MY LIFE

As they say in opera, we have reached the finale. However, in this case, the finale has not been bad at all. We have found talking with our new owners, which is the Forum Communications Co., that they have been most congenial and have worked very well with our corporation. Of course, one of the small important things is that Bill Marcil, who is the owner of *The Forum*, informed me that I could have my desk – and all that stuff that's shelved behind my desk and on it – for as long as I wanted. Well, I couldn't ask for much more than that. Our transfer from Davon Press, Inc., has been most pleasant. *The Forum* people have visited with all of us, and our employees will remain, and the years that they have invested in the company will be honored. Our advantages with *The Forum* are many, and I'm most pleased to announce that we look forward to many good years. We have been informed that there will be no changes in our corporation. You will not notice any difference in the old *West Fargo Pioneer* than before, and you'll probably still have to put up with this corny column that I write each week. And, of course, the *Midweek* will be taken good care of along with all the other publications.

So... without further adieu, I might add again – this is my finale.

Made in the USA
Charleston, SC
09 October 2011